COLLEGE STUDENTS AND THEIR ENVIRONMENTS

Publication Number 2

AMERICAN SERIES IN STUDENT AFFAIRS
PRACTICE AND PROFESSIONAL IDENTITY

Edited by

NAIJIAN ZHANG, PH.D.

West Chester University
Department of Counselor Education
West Chester, Pennsylvania

COLLEGE STUDENTS AND THEIR ENVIRONMENTS

Understanding the Role Student Affairs Educators Play in Shaping Campus Environments

Edited by

CATHY AKENS, RAQUEL WRIGHT-MAIR, & JOSEPH MARTIN STEVENSON

Forewords by Naijian Zhang and Samuel D. Museus

(With 26 Other Contributors)

CHARLES C THOMAS • PUBLISHER, LTD.
Springfield • Illinois • U.S.A.

Published and Distributed Throughout the World by

CHARLES C THOMAS · PUBLISHER, LTD.
2600 South First Street
Springfield, Illinois 62704

© 2019 by CHARLES C THOMAS · PUBLISHER, LTD.

ISBN 978-0-398-09288-7 (paper)
ISBN 978-0-398-09289-4 (ebook)

Library of Congress Catalog Card Number: 2019019434 (print)
2019980714 (ebook)

With THOMAS BOOKS *careful attention is given to all details of manufacturing
and design. It is the Publisher's desire to present books that are satisfactory as to their
physical qualities and artistic possibilities and appropriate for their particular use.*
THOMAS BOOKS *will be true to those laws of quality that assure a good name
and good will.*

*Printed in the United States of America
MM-C-1*

Library of Congress Cataloging-in-Publication Data

Names: Akens, Cathy, editor. | Wright-Mair, Raquel, editor. | Stevenson,
Joseph Martin, editor.
Title: College students and their environments : understanding the role
student affairs educators play in shaping campus environments/ Edited
by Cathy Akens, Raquel Wright-Mair, & Joseph Martin Stevenson ;
Forewords by Naijian Zhang and Samuel D. Museus (With 26 Other
Contributors).
Description: Springfield, Illinois, USA : Charles C Thomas Publisher, Ltd.,
[2019] | Includes bibliographical references and index.
Identifiers: LCCN 2019019434 (print) LCCN 2019980714 (ebook) | ISBN
9780398092887 (paper) | ISBN 9780398092894 (ebk.)
Subjects: LCSH: College environment. | College students--Social conditions.
| Student affairs services--Administration. | Student
activities--Management.
Classification: LCC LB2324 .C65 2019 (print) | LCC LB2324 (ebook) | DDC
371.8--dc23
LC record available at https://lccn.loc.gov/2019019434
LC ebook record available at https://lccn.loc.gov/2019980714

CONTRIBUTORS

Samuel D. Museus is Professor of Education Studies at the University of California, San Diego. (UCSD) He is also Founding Director of the National Institute for Transformation and Equity (NITE). Prior to joining UCSD, he taught at Indiana University Bloomington, the University of Denver, the University of Hawaii at Manoa, and the University of Massachusetts Boston. Museus has produced over 250 publications and conference presentations focused on diversity and equity, campus environments, and college student outcomes. He has published in a wide range of journals, such as the *Harvard Educational Review, Journal of College Student Development, Journal of Higher Education, Research in Higher Education, Teachers College Record,* and *The Review of Higher Education.* He has produced 10 books, including Creating Campus Cultures: Fostering Success among Racially Diverse Student Populations, Asian American Students in Higher Education, and Racism and Racial Equity in Higher Education. Museus has previously received several national awards in recognition of the impact of his scholarship, including the Association for the Study of Higher Education (ASHE) Early Career Award in 2011, the NASPA George D. Kuh Outstanding Contribution to Research and Literature Award in 2014, and the Spencer Foundation's Midcareer Grant Award in 2018.

Florence M. Guido is professor emerita at the University of Northern Colorado. She is co-author of all three editions of *Student Development in College: Theory, Research, and Practice.* Currently, she also serves as a Senior Scholar for the American College Personnel Association. She has published over 25 peer reviewed journal articles and 10 book chapters on student development, organizational development, ethnic identity, and research paradigms. Flo has also presented at over 125 national, international, and regional peer-reviewed or invited conferences. Finally, her photography appears on four book covers in higher education and student affairs.

Courtney E. Matsumoto is the Program Administrator for the Advanced Manufacturing Sciences Institute at Metropolitan State

University of Denver where she is responsible for all student recruitment, engagement and retention activities. She holds a B.A. in Ethnic Studies and Sociology from Colorado State University and a M.A. in Higher Education and Student Affairs Leadership from the University of Northern Colorado. Courtney's professional endeavors have focused on providing access and support for underrepresented students in the science, technology, engineering and mathematics (STEM) fields.

Gabrielle McAllaster is a Masters student at the University of Northern Colorado, studying Higher Education and Student Affairs Leadership. She holds a B.A. in Psychology, minor in Sociology from the University of Northern Colorado. Gabrielle is passionate about student affairs through her love of learning, social justice, and creating inclusive environments for students at universities.

Blanca Rincón is an Assistant Professor of Higher Education in the Educational Psychology and Higher Education Department at the University of Nevada, Las Vegas. She received her Ph.D. in Education Policy Studies from the University of Illinois at Urbana-Champaign. Dr. Rincón's research agenda is concerned with equity issues in higher education, with a specific focus on access and success for underrepresented and underserved students in science, technology, engineering, and mathematics (STEM). Using both qualitative and quantitative methodologies, and with support from the National Science Foundation, she has explored various factors impacting access to and persistence in STEM for women, low-income, first-generation and students of color including issues of climate, financial aid, and intervention programs.

Tonisha B. Lane is an Assistant Professor of Higher Education and Student Affairs (HESA) in the Department of Leadership, Counseling, Adult, Career & Higher Education (LCACHE) at the University of South Florida. Dr. Lane's research agenda broadly examines diversity, equity, and inclusion in postsecondary education with the objective of advancing inclusive and transformative policies and practices. To this end, she investigates the experiences and outcomes of underrepresented groups in science, technology, engineering, and mathematics (STEM). Her research also focuses on the participation and achievement of Black students and professionals in higher education. She is the PI or co-PI on several grant-funded research projects including the national Black Doctoral Women Study (BDWS), the Women in Engineering Study (WIES), and the National Science Foundation Broadening Participation in Engineering (NSF-BPE) Bulls-Engineering Youth Experience for Promoting Relationships, Identity Development, & Empowerment (Bulls-EYE PRIDE). She has also been the recipient of several honors including 2017-2018 McKnight Fellow

(Florida Education Fund), 2018 ACPA Emerging Scholar, and a National Center for Institutional Diversity (NCID) Emerging Diversity Scholar.

Liliana Rodriguez is Vice Chancellor for Campus Life and Inclusive Excellence at the University of Denver. Dr. Rodriguez is committed to improving access to a quality education for students of all backgrounds. That mission was inspired by her own difficulties navigating university as a first-generation college student, from a very low-income background. She oversees the work of more than 130 full- and part-time staff in 22 departments, including academic advising, disability services, housing, and career services. As a social scientist and practitioner, her research investigates barriers to college access, retention, and success. She also explores how young adults develop their identity, especially how social identities are formed and influence the ways in which one engages in the world. Dr. Rodriguez earned a bachelor's degree in psychology from Williams College, and a master's degree and doctorate in psychology from the University of Massachusetts, Amherst.

Michele Tyson is a Clinical Assistant Professor of Higher Education at the University of Denver. She has previously worked in the field of higher education for 20 years, with significant experience in student affairs and enrollment management, including orientation and parent and family engagement, academic advising and student services, and outreach and admissions. Her professional and research interests include: issues of access and persistence for post-traditional students, adult education, organizational change, ethics in higher education, and the development of new professionals.

Lorenzo Baber is Assistant Professor and Division Head of Higher Education at Iowa State University. His research focuses on diversity and equity across three areas—community colleges, postsecondary STEM education, and campus experiences among students from underrepresented backgrounds. Prior to his faculty career, Dr. Baber worked for ten years as a student affairs practitioner in the areas of judicial affairs, multicultural affairs, and residence life. He holds both a B.A. degree (in English/Journalism) and M.Ed (Student Personnel Administration) from the University of North Carolina, Greensboro and a Ph.D. (Education Policy Studies/Higher Education) from Pennsylvania State University.

Raquel Wright-Mair is Assistant Professor of Higher Education at Rowan University. She conducts research that is grounded in social justice and focuses on issues of access, equity and inclusion in higher education. Dr. Wright-Mair's research agenda seeks to transform and advocate for the creation of more equitable and inclusive campus environments for underrepresented populations, specifically racially minoritized faculty. Through her research, she explores the experiences of racially minoritized populations on college campuses and examines ways in which institutions can create more supportive environments for these populations. Dr. Wright-Mair is also an affiliate faculty member at the National Institute for Transformation and Equity (NITE), where she conducts research focused on institutional transformation. In her role, she collaborates with institutions of higher education nationally to transform educational policies and practices to cultivate more inclusive campus environments for racially minoritized populations. Dr. Wright-Mair has produced several conference presentations and publications focused on diversity and equity initiatives and is active in several national education associations.

Cathy Akens is the Vice Chancellor for Student Affairs at University of North Carolina at Greensboro. In this role, she provides leadership for staff who oversee a wide array of programs and services that focus on impacting student success and learning through the co-curricular experience. Dr. Akens previously served as Associate Vice President for Student Affairs and Dean of Students, Assistant Vice President, and Director of Residential Life at Florida International University. She held other positions in residential life early in her career at Bowling Green State University. Dr. Akens has been engaged in professional service, scholarship and graduate teaching throughout her career. Her areas of interest include crisis management, student success, student development, and campus environments. She earned a bachelor's degree in communication from the University of Toledo and a master's degree in college and university administration from Michigan State University. Her doctorate in higher education is from Florida International University.

Zebulun Davenport is the Vice President for Student Affairs at West Chester University. He earned his Doctorate in Higher Education and Leadership from Nova Southeastern University, a Master of Education in College Student Personnel Administration, and a Bachelor of Science in Communications/Public Relations with a minor in Human Services from James Madison University. His contributions have advanced campus culture, organizational structure, and student success. Under his leadership, two divisions of student affairs have received Diverse Magazine's the distinction of "Most Promising Places to Work." His expertise includes the areas of student retention, outcomes assessment, strategic planning, and strategies for assisting first-generation college students. Davenport's publications include co-authoring two books entitled *First-Generation College Students—Understanding and Improving the Experience from Recruitment to Commencement;* and

Student Affairs Assessment, Evaluation, and Research: A Guidebook for Graduate Students and New Professionals, a chapter in an edited volume entitled *The Student Success Conundrum,* in B. Bontrager (Ed.), Strategic Enrollment Management: Transforming Higher Education; a chapter in an edited monograph entitled Creating Collaborative Conditions for Student Success in S. Whalen (Ed.), Proceedings of the 8th National Symposium on Student Retention 2012, and a chapter in the fourth edition of *The Handbook of Student Affairs Administration* in Jossey Bass 2016. He has presented at workshops for numerous public agencies; educational institutions; state, regional, and national conferences; as well as to thousands of college students and professionals throughout his career.

Lucy LePeau is an Associate Professor of Higher Education and Student Affairs at Indiana University. She serves as the Associate Director for the National Institute for Transformation and Equity (NITE). Prior to joining Indiana University, LePeau worked in roles such as the Assistant Dean of New Student Programs at the University of North Carolina at Charlotte, Project Consultant for the Association of American Colleges and Universities (AAC&U), and Campus Advocate in the Office of Student Conduct at the University of Maryland College Park. LePeau has produced over 50 publications and conference presentations focused on academic affairs and student affairs partnerships promoting diversity and equity initiatives, college student development, and improved student affairs teaching and practice. She has published in journals such as *The Review of Higher Education, The Journal of Higher Education, The Journal of Diversity in Higher Education, Innovative Higher Education,* and *The Journal of Student Affairs Research and Practice.* She was a recipient of the IU Trustees Teaching Award in 2018, Emerging Scholar and Annuit Coeptis awards from ACPA College Student Educators International in 2015, and the Melvene D. Hardee Dissertation of the Year from NASPA Student Affairs Administrators in Higher Education in 2013.

Delma Ramos is an Assistant Professor of Higher Education in the Teacher Education and Higher Education department at University of North Carolina at Greensboro. Her research focuses on college success, specifically examining the role of family, community, and culture in empowering students to navigate college. Her work engages historically marginalized populations and employs critical methodologies and theories to uncover systems of oppression that perpetuate inequity in education. Her work has been presented at annual national meetings of the Association for the Study of Higher Education, NASPA, and the American Educational Research Association and in journals including the ASHE Higher Education Report Series, JCOT, and JCSCORE.

FOREWORD

We shape our buildings, and afterwards, our buildings shape us.
Winston Churchill

This famous quote can be further interpreted as we student affairs educators shape our college environments, and our college environments shape us. *College Students and Their Environments* is a valuable book that implies the meaning of this quote. This book is purposely written for those who are training to become student affairs educators and those who are newer in the profession. This book not only provides the reader with a theoretical framework, but also some direction on how to create a college environment that is socially just and inclusive. *College Students and Their Environments* is also a valuable synthesis of the essential ideas that student affairs educators need to create an effective and conducive learning environment for college students. With the knowledge, skills, and ideas in this book student affairs educators in-training and new student affairs educators will be able to competently help college students gain unique educational experiences on American college and university campuses in the twenty-first century.

By reading *College Students and Their Environments,* you will better understand the relationship between college environments and student learning and development, and consequently how to create an inclusive learning environment for student success. Additionally, this book is a unique and valuable source for you to develop your professional competency and professional identity.

College Students and Their Environments is one of the essential volumes in the *American Series in Student Affairs Practice and Professional Identity.* The content of this book will assist student affairs educators in addressing their own professional competencies. As the book series does, this book purposely reflects the professional competency areas for student affairs educators set forth by ACPA/NASPA in 2015.

The best value that you as the reader may take from the text is the knowledge, skills, and wisdom offered by the editors and all the chapter authors. These editors and chapter authors have held positions across all levels in student affairs and academic affairs at colleges and universities across the nation. Particularly, the true scientists and practitioners are the book editors, Dr. Cathy Akens, Dr. Raquel Wright-Mair, and Dr. Joseph Martin Stevenson, who have experience in teaching, research, and in administrative positions at the most senior levels in higher education. All three editors are excellent scholars and classroom educators. Therefore, they are more than qualified not only to speak about how to create a college environment that is just and inclusive, but also to identify high qualified chapter authors to share their knowledge, skills, and wisdom on how to make college environments conducive and effective for all students. This team work has resulted in an invaluable product, *College Students and Their Environments* that is now presented to you—the future and new student affairs educators.

The book offers quite a few unique features on how to create a college environment that fosters student learning, growth, development, and supports student success. First, the book approaches the college environment issue from a philosophical foundation and shows the reader what has made student affairs work increasingly complex. By identifying some major shifts of student affairs work in history, the book demonstrates how student affairs service providers became student affairs educators who actively shape the environment instead of being shaped or reactionary.

Second, *College Students and Their Environments* attends to the theories that inform student affairs educators' understanding of campus environments and how campus environments shape college students' developmental processes. The book provides insights and implications on how environmental theories might inform practice and also recommends how to study campus environments. Furthermore, the book clarifies what student success is, explores the primary frameworks used to boost student success, and suggests what student affairs educators should consider when implementing student success initiatives.

Third, *College Students and Their Environments* addresses the intersection of professional competency areas through campus environment cultivation with social justice and inclusion for diverse student populations. To help student affairs educators understand and meet the needs of diverse student populations, the book identifies challenges and strategies and offers recommendations and action for practice. Specifically, the book informs student affairs educators how classroom experiences contribute to students' sense of inclusion on campus.

Finally, to address the professional competencies by ACPA/NASPA in 2015, the book emphasizes the importance of assessment of student needs and success. Particularly, the text provides useful and practical examples of how faculty can work with graduate students in training to conduct an assessment of student needs and success.

College Students and Their Environments is a valuable tool which not only examines the future direction of higher education and student affairs, but also provides the reader broad insights into how anticipated changes and emerging issues will impact the direction of those who work on college campuses. It is a book that also prepares emerging student affairs educators and new student affairs educators for the work they will do in shaping campus environments for years to come. This book is an indispensable volume of the *American Series in Student Affairs Practice and Professional Identity.*

American Series in Student Affairs Practice and Professional Identity is a unique book series that creates an integration of all ten professional competency areas for student affairs educators outlined by the College Student Educators International (ACPA) and the Student Affairs Administrators in Higher Education (NASPA) in 2015. The series reflects three major themes: professional competencies development, professional identity construction, and case illustrations for theory translation into application. All volumes in the series target graduate students in student affairs programs and new student affairs educators. The series blends contemporary theory with current research and empirical support and uses case illustrations to facilitate the readers' ability to translate what they have learned into application and decision making. Each volume focuses on one area of professional competency except the current volume which addresses the intersection of the professional competencies. The series helps graduate students in student affairs programs and new student affairs educators develop their professional competencies (ACPA/NASPA) by (1) constructing their personal and ethical foundations; (2) understanding the values, philosophy, and history of student affairs; (3) strengthening their ability in assessment, evaluation, and research; (4) gaining knowledge, skills, and dispositions relating to law, policy, and governance; (5) familiarizing with and learning how to effectively utilize organizational and human resources; (6) learning leadership knowledge and developing leadership skills; (7) understanding oppression, privilege, power, and then learning how to understand social justice and apply it in practice; (8) acquiring student development theories and learning how to use them to inform their practice; (9) familiarizing themselves with technologies and implementing digital means and resources into practice; and (10) gaining advising and supporting knowledge, skills and dispositions. As a result, the series helps graduate students in student affairs programs and new student affairs educators foster their professional identity and ultimately achieve their goal of the whole-person education.

Naijian Zhang, Ph.D.
West Chester University of Pennsylvania

FOREWORD

It is no secret that the U.S. population is becoming increasingly diverse. The students entering the nation's colleges and universities are rapidly diversifying as well. However, most of higher education's professional associations, graduate programs that prepare future college educators, and college campuses were not created to serve the increasing numbers of students from historically marginalized backgrounds, identities, and communities. This incongruence creates significant challenges for professionals entering higher education and student affairs. Specifically, most college educators are pressured—or forced—to conform to conditions that are not conducive to supporting diverse populations, while simultaneously asked to help these groups thrive.

Given the aforementioned realities, it is incumbent upon us, as student affairs educators, to collectively understand how to prepare the next generation of higher education and student affairs professionals to navigate these complexities. It is also appropriate to say that it is undeniably urgent that we generate such collective understanding, because doing so is necessary for us to ensure that all students have the opportunity to thrive in postsecondary education and achieve their full potential.

There are several indicators of hope—signs that we are more equipped today than we have ever been to prepare college educators to effectively work with these increasingly diverse student populations. For example, compared to any time in our nation's history, marginalized and minoritized communities are more represented among faculty, administrators, staff, and students on college campuses. In addition, higher education scholars have been conducting research on these populations for decades, and practitioners have been developing practical knowledge about how to effectively serve these students during this time as well. As a result, we collectively know more than ever before about how to construct environments (e.g., cultures and structures) that allow these populations to thrive in college.

The current volume is one manifestation of the aforementioned progress. Its diverse cadre of authors covers a wide range of topics relevant to campus environments and serving increasingly diverse college student populations. In the opening chapter, the authors chart the history of student affairs, underscoring the ways in which the role of student affairs professionals has evolved into that of critical educators who shape students' identities, experiences, and outcomes in profound ways. In doing so, the authors blur the lines between the classroom and larger campus, highlighting the need to think about campus environments broadly in conversations about effectively serving diverse students. The bulk of the book's chapters provide in-depth discussions of (a) the needs of today's diverse student populations, (b) ways in which educators can—and sometimes do—create environments that positively shape these students' experiences in and out of the classroom, and (c) strategies that educators working in graduate preparation programs can use to more effectively prepare student affairs professionals to achieve these goals.

Clearly, this volume makes an invaluable contribution to existing discourse in higher education. Rather than treating diversity and inclusion as add-on values or obligations—an approach that often results in their marginalization relative to more mainstream priorities (e.g., the quest for prestige and resources)—the chapters in this volume integrate an understanding of diverse student populations into discussions about constructing fundamental mainstream environments, spaces, and processes on college campuses. This integration of critical consciousness and cultural relevance throughout the design and delivery of education is exactly what we need if we are to see progress in the areas of diversity, inclusion, and equity in higher education. Indeed, the demographic makeup of the authors and their approach to conceptualizing educational environments and experiences are symbols of our current collective potential to re-envision a new system of higher education that is more diverse, more inclusive, more equitable, more relevant—more just.

But, if it is true that we are more representationally and intellectually equipped to create conditions that allow diverse populations to thrive within higher education, it is reasonable to ask the question, *why* has our postsecondary education system continued to perpetuate so many social inequities? What is missing from the efforts to create institutions and environments that effectively serve diverse populations? And, what are the barriers that will prevent college educators from applying the knowledge that is shared in the chapters in this volume?

Over the last decade, my research team has worked with thousands of people across over 100 campuses throughout the nation in order to support them in their efforts to advance inclusion and equity. We have gathered and analyzed data from over 1,000 interviewees and tens of thousands of survey participants—including administrators, faculty, staff, and graduate and undergraduate students—through research and assessment projects at colleges and universities across the country. Through these processes, we have gained some insight into these existing barriers and outlined a few of the most salient of them herein. The goal is to prompt readers to think about how they might more effectively advocate and implement some of the ideas and recommendations in the chapters that follow. It is important to note that the barriers that have been included in our work are not characteristic of all institutions, leaders, or educators, but rather represent formidable barriers that we have seen existing and unaddressed on many campuses across the nation.

The first barrier that appears to be pervasive is the common *absence of courageous leadership.* Despite the fact that we have increasing levels of knowledge about how to construct educational environments that are fair and designed for everyone, most institutional leaders refuse to invest sufficient resources necessary to transform education systems and make them more equitable. Most leaders reject the reality that they must divert some energy and resources from the goals that perpetuate systems of inequality—objectives such as the never-ending quest for prestige that consumes so much of the resources that run through our institutions—to those that advance it. College and university leaders must face the reality that they must choose the moral imperative of investing in equity, which requires sacrifices, or acknowledge that they will reinforce the status quo.

The second barrier that we have observed is related to college educators who are on the ground working with diverse student populations themselves. Although there are champions of diversity and equity on campuses across the country, these persons are often in the minority and marginalized within their institutions. At the same time, the majority working within our colleges and universities continues to go about business as usual and is characterized by a *refusal to engage in the deep personal transformation* necessary for them to adapt to the increasingly complex students and communities whom they are charged with serving. Most of us were trained in a system that was ill-equipped to teach us how to construct learning environments within which all students can thrive regardless of their backgrounds and identities. As a result, personal transformation is not only helpful but absolutely necessary for us to develop the capacity to effectively create such environments.

The third and final barrier that has become increasingly apparent for its ability to dissolve efforts to advance diversity, inclusion, and equity on college campuses is situated at the intersection of institutional leaders and college educators. Specifically, most college and university campuses *lack the campus cultures and structures needed to promote and sustain equity agendas.* Within higher education, everywhere you look, there are pervasive manifestations of cultures that inhibit equity agendas. Culturally, institutions unapologetically prioritize values of money and prestige over the moral values of diversity and equity on a daily basis and continuously in their decision-making processes. In addition, college and university campuses invest substantial amounts of energy in boosting their image as institutions that provide a "high-quality" and "internationally recognized" educational experience, leading to a culture in which dissent is feared and eradicated immediately when it emerges, rather than their becoming enthusiastically and productively engaged as an opportunity to improve their organization's capacity to fulfill its democratic and moral obligations.

Structurally, support and reward systems are designed in ways that allow educators who perpetuate the status quo to survive and thrive in higher education. Professional development opportunities, teaching evaluations, internal grants competitions, annual review systems, and promotion and tenure requirements are just a few examples of support and reward systems that drive behavior on college campuses but rarely require educators to ensure that an understanding of diverse communities or equity agenda is embedded within their professional development and work—and sometimes even punish educators for doing so. To overcome this barrier, institutional leaders and educators must work together to create structures that center and sustain equity agendas.

In sum, it is absolutely essential for institutional leaders and educators to make the sacrifices necessary to deconstruct systems, redistribute resources, challenge their pre-existing values and perspectives, and reconstruct environments so that they can effectively serve those who have historically been left out of the mainstream. Such commitments are also necessary to effectively enact the critical ideas that are outlined in the current collection of chapters. In 1967, Dr. Martin Luther King underscored our nation's inability to address the most significant social problems of the time despite its unprecedented scientific genius. He called for a radical revolution of values that shifted the nation's priorities from a thing-oriented society to a person-oriented one. And, he called on us to cultivate our moral genius so that we might live in a more just world. This call must be reinforced today, and responding to it is critical to breaking down the aforementioned barriers to advancing equity and creating institutions in which all students can thrive in higher education.

Samuel D. Museus, Ph.D.

ACKNOWLEDGMENTS

We applaud those who are working daily to create inclusive and engaging environments for all students coming to college. We are particularly grateful to our colleagues, the chapter authors, who contributed their research and passion to this book. We thank Coretta Roseboro Walker who provided technical, editorial, and logistical support throughout this process, and Patricia Corwin, whose editorial assistance was invaluable.

Working on this book together is an outcome of intentional teaching, learning, and mentorship. The editors reflect three generations of that process, with Joseph Stevenson having taught Cathy Akens in her doctoral program, and Cathy Akens having taught Raquel Wright-Mair in her master's program. Our continued connections, camaraderie, and professional engagement fueled us to explore a common passion we share—the notion that we as educators have a responsibility to learn about, understand, and create environments that best support success for all students.

Cathy Akens, Ed.D.
University of North Carolina at Greensboro

Raquel Wright-Mair, Ph.D.
Rowan University

Joseph Martin Stevenson, Ph.D.
Miles College and Union Institute University

CONTENTS

COLLEGE STUDENTS AND
THEIR ENVIRONMENTS

Chapter 1

THE ROLE OF STUDENT AFFAIRS EDUCATORS IN SHAPING COLLEGE ENVIRONMENTS: THE HISTORY, PHILOSOPHY, AND VALUES OF OUR PROFESSION

Florence M. Guido, Courtney E. Matsumoto, and Gabrielle A. McAllaster

The role of student affairs educators in shaping college and university environments began when, in the second half of the nineteenth century, U.S. faculty adopted the German research university model and student enrollments slowly increased because of an expanding U.S. higher education system (Thelin & Gasman, 2017). Around the same time, concern for larger numbers of women enrolled in higher education prompted the hiring of female administrators to oversee their well-being. Soon thereafter, in the 1890s, the first dean of women and the first dean of men made their appearance on campus at the University of Chicago and the University of Illinois, respectively (Schwartz & Stewart, 2017).

Since then, this important role for those in student affairs has journeyed from its beginnings as caretaker, disciplinarian, and campus policy enforcer to active educator in the academy more than a century later. In the decades that followed the advent of student affairs professionals' arrival as guardians of *in loco parentis* (i.e., in place of the parent) in the academy, they have shifted their mission, as students and the institutions they attended changed focus, too. In effect, student affairs professionals are shape shifters, always operating in a higher education environment, yet changing form over time to adapt to student, institutional, and societal needs.

This chapter lays the foundation for the detailed discussions that follow in this book on how student affairs educators shape college and university environments. First, the shifting philosophy and values of student affairs educators in shaping students' environments are traced to create an informed understanding of the past in order to minimize mishaps when shaping the unknown future of the profession. Next, the historical role of the student affairs profession sets the context and creates understanding of the eventual fluctuating status of the profession over time and its role in fashioning college and university environments. Third, a discussion of the shift from service providers to educators documents the convergence of circumstances that created this change. The transformation of roles for the student affairs educator from dichotomous in-class versus out-of-class silos to integration of the campus learning environment is highlighted. Fourth, student affairs educators as accepted partners in the academic enterprise is reviewed and critiqued. Finally, application of these concepts to practice, recommendations for the future, and reflective questions to consider are presented.

Philosophical Underpinnings of the Student Affairs Profession

The philosophical heritage of the student affairs profession is reflected in practice through educational documents produced from the first half of the twentieth century to the present. Several historians have marked the *Yale Report of 1828,* grounded in rationalism, as the first formal U.S. higher education philosophical statement (Brubacher & Rudy, 1976). Written by Yale faculty, it reinforced the notion of a traditional classical curriculum based primarily on "discipline of the mind" (Brubacher, 1982). Eventually, after the Civil War, this statement was rebuked as higher education and the diversity of its rapidly increasing students expanded and other significant changes were made to the curriculum offerings. Such changes included more practical courses of study (e.g., addition of agricultural and mechanical colleges), a pragmatic approach, and electives (begun by Charles W. Eliot, President of Harvard, in 1872), comprising one of the earliest signs of what would become a postmodern approach. One of the most recent student affairs documents, *Learning Reconsidered 2* (Keeling, 2006), discussed later in the chapter, reflects a postmodern philosophy putting the whole student and student learning ahead of teaching.

Dozens of educational philosophies have played out in U.S. higher education and student affairs since its inception. Many professionals need more than methods for problem solving in this environment, because "only by studying and applying underlying premises and deeply held assumptions can a practitioner of student affairs hope to bring insight to a novel problem, a 'different' student, a new situation" (Carpenter, 2011, p. 8). Selected pertinent philosophies are highlighted below, which offer explanations of how they have and can apply to student affairs professionals' role in shaping college environments.

Rationalism: Absolutes and Great Truths

Rationalism, one of the oldest philosophical traditions in the Western world, focuses on intellect and free will as that which separates us from other living organisms. Rationalists assume ideas are absolute and the writings of classical philosophers (e.g., Aristotle and Plato) contain the Truths and Ideas an educated person needs to know (Knock, 1988). More prevalent at the end of the nineteenth century than in the beginning of the twenty-first, college student affairs was singularly focused on and "shaped practices which are primarily concerned with creating and controlling a campus environment in order that students will develop intellectually" (Knock, 1988, p. 11). Thus, student affairs policies and practices, such as selective admissions and documentation of conduct wrongdoings, are congruent with rationalism. Any student service not supporting a student's intellectual development, such as student activities and career services, may be available but is not considered essential in the institution. The legal concept of *in loco parentis* fits well with a rationalist philosophical perspective. Although elements of rationalism are linked to the university today, most student affairs professionals are more likely to support the development of the whole student, making a focus only on this earlier perspective limited. Some Ivy League institutions lean heavily in this rationalistic direction in that these institutions' missions and practices focus almost exclusively on students' academic achievements.

Pragmatism: Learning by Doing

Much in concert with the notion of serving the whole student, pragmatism, unlike rationalism, frames reality as the "sum total of human experience" (Carpenter, Dean, & Haber-Curran, 2016, p. 10) and "rejects the idea of permanent, unchanging truth" (Knock, 1988, p. 11). Philosopher John Dewey, a quintessential pragmatist with a lasting influence on all levels of education (McDermott, 1981), was a champion of "learning by doing." He believed, like other pragmatists, that "experience is the real test of all things" (Butler, 1968, p. 377). As a result, pragmatic education puts the learner at the center, but what is experienced must be reflected on and reconstructed in order for learning to occur (Young, 2003). Cowley (1936/1994a) credited student affairs professionals with introducing pragmatism to faculty who favored rationalism and a strong singular focus on students' intellect. The seminal 1937 and 1949 *Student Personnel Point of View* documents both reflect a pragmatic philosophy of the field. In student affairs today, the legacy of pragmatism includes those student experiences that also provide students an opportunity to think about what their experience means. For example, service learning opportunities, where students can learn in the real world and are supervised by those who facilitate learning and do not treat students as knowledge receptacles, have roots in pragmatism. Any college environment created to allow students to learn what interests them, in or out of class, has similar philosophical origins.

Postmodernism: Experience Inseparable from Power

Popular in the twentieth century, postmodernism is a philosophical umbrella that can be applied to existentialism; phenomenology; structuralism, deconstruction, and reconstruction; poststructuralism; intersectionality; postcolonialism; and queer theory (Patton, Renn, Guido, & Quaye, 2016; Young, 2003), to name a few. In some ways, these philosophies differ dramatically from each other, but each unwaveringly questions modernism's assumptions about conventional forms of thinking and objectivity. Postmodernist thinkers, like pragmatists, keep the human context at the center and frame the individual human experience as incapable of separation from social power. In addition, postmodernists believe everything is subjective, which rationalists find abhorrent and wherein many minoritized groups feel they have a philosophical home. Postmodernism highlights "socially constructed education (over societal systems of education), lifelong learning (over time-bound classes), informal experiences (over formal ones), and multicultural education (over melting-pot education)" (Young, 2003, p. 95). Moreover, valuing learning over teaching, postmodernists generally place responsibility for learning on students, leaving faculty and student affairs professionals in a facilitator role.

In student affairs today, postmodernism, often devoid of deconstruction and reconstruction, is found within and between institutions. For example, the organizational structure of student affairs and the functional areas linked to a larger student affairs division can be connected to a business affairs division (e.g., residence life), or even at some institutions, tied to an academic affairs division (e.g., academic and career advisors within a major). From institution to institution, the variability is great. Fracturing of this kind within a large institution of higher education can make it difficult to serve students individually when the goal is to allow them freedom to chart their own learning and growth path. That said, it is necessary for student affairs professionals to integrate many perspectives in order to expand their own and students' worldviews. Environments most appropriate for minoritized students, including ways these may differ from dominant culture environments, need scrutiny, deconstruction, and thoughtful reconstruction if higher education is to succeed in welcoming all students to campus.

Intersectionality. Rooted in a critical worldview and postmodern by nature, *intersectionality* is a kind of deconstruction that allows individuals to examine their individual identity and its relationship to power. From this lens, "individuals experience the paradox of simultaneous marginalization and privilege" (Patton et.al, 2016, p. 30.) Although not a panacea, intersectionality allows a more complex way of examining the interplay of multiple identities and lived experience. Trailblazing student development theorists (e.g., Jones & Abes, 2013; Patton, 2011; Stewart, 2009) have offered ground-breaking theoretical viewpoints, not focusing on the center as in the past, but examining phenomenon at the margins or borderlands to demonstrate the "intersections of context, personal characteristics, and social identities" (Patton et al., 2016, p. 31). Student affairs professionals today who work closely with cultural centers on campus recognize the difficulty in meeting the needs of students who might identify with more than one culture and not feel welcome in either center. Add to it other identities, such as social class, ethnicity, sexuality and gender, and cognitive and intellectual development, and the complexity of an individual student's identity fans out exponentially. Student affairs professionals must keep this in mind when creating and sustaining environments and spaces for students (and faculty, too) who recognize the complications of intersecting, multiple identities.

Racial/Ethnic/Border/Liminal/Postcolonial Perspectives. Racial, ethnic, border, liminal, and postcolonial perspectives (e.g., black feminism, indigenous, Chicano, Asian, and Latino frameworks) emerged when "scholars recognized the powerful experiential differences between whites and African Americans, Anglos and Hispanic/Spanish speaking peoples, European Americans, and those (e.g., Native American peoples) who still experience the aftereffects of the colonial experience on their home soil" (Guido, Chávez, & Lincoln, 2010, p. 12). Far from the center of U.S. life, these perspectives highlight many minoritized individuals who shine a light on their lives in their respective cultures and through the critique of modernism, Eurocentric ideas, and Western thought. Though this snapshot of these related categories does not articulate much of the nuance within each perspective, each offers a story of oppression and superiority on the part of those who oppress. Other similarities include the important non-Eurocentric social, historical, and cultural experiences of minoritized groups in U.S. and other Western countries, including but not limited to indigenous peoples (e.g., Coulthard, 2014; Minthorn & Shotton, 2018; Smith, 2012; Smith, Tuck, & Yang, 2018), blacks (e.g., Fanon, 1967; hooks, 1992), and Chicanas (e.g., Anzaldúa, 1999, 2015; Pérez, 1999).

Many student affairs professionals, faculty, and students of color resonate soundly with these postmodern philosophical views of the world. It is incumbent on everyone in the academy to "consider multiple ways of being, languages, belief systems, and learning. Services, programs, and structures must be redesigned to be more inclusive of these student populations" (Guido et al., 2010, p. 13). Some examples that demonstrate an understanding of this philosophy in action include (a) offering web materials for students and prospective students in more than one language, (b) scheduling classes and meetings in line with a wide range of students' cultural values of time and "familia" responsibility, (c) creating a separate space for minoritized student groups to create community with each other on campus and safely reject the dominant culture (Sue & Sue, 2003), and (d) offering residential opportunities consistent with a variety of family structures (Guido et al., 2010).

Poststructuralism. *Poststructuralism* is a philosophy or paradigm that examines and critiques systems of oppression in order to generate new social phenomena void of marginalization. A poststructural paradigm is tied to the assumptions that reality is shaped by systems of oppression demanding deconstruction, constantly changing, and resistant to categorization (Lather, 2007). Grounded in the writings of Foucault (1978) and Derrida (1967/1978), poststructuralists view knowledge and truth as (a) social constructions of those who hold the most social power, (b) mirrors of the particular historical and cultural settings from which they were derived, and (c) constructions that do not embody objectivity or universality. Poststructuralism highlights how social institutions, such as educational institutions, use language and symbols to maintain power. Student affairs professionals interested in creating healthy learning environments are attuned to the language they use in public and private discourse and remove symbols on campus that maintain dominance of white culture. Students of color who tear down symbols of white supremacy on campus (e.g., removing the statue of Robert E. Lee on the campus of the University of North Carolina-Chapel Hill in 2018) are disrupting social power and shedding light on 150 years of racism in the South. In effect, this defiant act demonstrates a shift in power and represents tearing down the past to create a more equitable future.

Queer Theory. As a type of poststructuralist theory, *queer theory* "exposes the differential power structures that exist among socially constructed groups and identities [and] . . . illuminates the manner in which power structures unfold and reinforce ideas of normativity to maintain dominant and marginalized groups" (Patton et al., 2016, p. 33). Queer theorists affirm the ideas that gender and sexual identity are socially and continually constructed, and deconstruct categories assigned to sexuality and gender (Gamson, 2000). In queer theory, the process of sexual categorization is questioned and deconstructed. Specifically, queer theorists "question the binary opposition of homosexuality and heterosexuality, critique heteronormativity, and argue against any assumed sexual essentialism" (Broido & Manning, 2002, p. 441). Student affairs professionals can create an environment friendly to queer theory by examining admissions materials and college and university records, and questioning assumptions about gender and sexuality programming, to name a few ways in which to dispel the myth of distinct gender and sexual categories and to view sexuality and gender as more fluid and less concrete.

Values in Student Affairs: A Brief Review

The values held by those in student affairs are as varied as our diverse roots, diverse academic discipline base, and many wide-ranging, diverse functional areas in our practice. One student affairs scholar defined values as "beliefs that guide action toward desirable ends" (Young, 1993, p. 1). According to the *Oxford Dictionary of Philosophy* (Blackburn, 1996), values come into play when a person's belief is taken "into account in decision-making or . . . [the person is] inclined to advance it as a guiding consideration in influencing choice and guiding oneself and others" (p. 390). In a nutshell, values form the heart of our broader philosophical beliefs and aid us as student affairs professionals in making sense of ourselves, what we do, and how we behave.

Philosophical documents of the profession reflect its values. Some of the first values documented in the student affairs profession are revealed in the 1949 *Student Personnel Point of View* statement and center on individuation and community (Young, 1996). Individuation involves "respect for the growing person" (Young, 1996, p. 88), basically human dignity (Young & Elfrink, 1991), and is equivalent to educating the whole student, as emphasized in one of the profession's first two documents to profess about which it cares. Reflected in the earlier 1937 *Student Personnel Point of View* statement, education for democracy, education for everyone, and problem-based learning are values the profession borrowed from educational theorist and philosopher, John Dewey, who helped shift higher education from rationalism to pragmatism (Reason & Broido, 2011).

By the 1980s, several scholars implied or stated that student affairs was based on the values of self-awareness, independence, tolerance, respect and fairness toward others (Dalton & Healy, 1984), an ethic of caring (Canon & Brown, 1985), pluralism, freedom, and altruism (Sandeen, 1985), aesthetic appreciation and ethical reasoning (Kuh, Shedd, & Whitt, 1987), and honesty, fairness, integrity, predictability, courage, and confidentiality (Upcraft, 1988). During this decade, the profession had moved from a services orientation to more of a student developmental emphasis, and student affairs scholars focused mostly on moral and ethical development. In many ways, the student affairs profession in the 1980s saw itself as the moral voice of the academy, which, along with student affairs, was moving toward consumerism and professionalism and away from paternalism in any form.

Throughout the more than 150-year-old history of student affairs, principle and philosophical statements and documents, often initiated by our professional associations—predominately the American College Personnel Association (ACPA) and National Association of Student Personnel Administrators (NASPA)—reinforced a commitment to viewing students holistically, respecting individual differences, and appreciating what students bring to their own learning (Evans & Reason, 2001). Other values clearly articulated include intentional empirically grounded practice, responsibility to society, the educative role of the environment and context, and social justice advocacy (Reason & Broido, 2011). College and university environments can be shaped for optimal learning through buildings, groups of people, and characteristics of an organization (Strange & Banning, 2001). In recent years, with the evolution of the Student Development Movement and the Student Learning Movement, the profession has moved to placing value on the values we have held dear from the beginning (Evans & Reason, 2001; Reason & Broido, 2017): the whole development of students and their learning in college.

The Historical Role of the Student Affairs Profession

Although the student affairs profession is over a century old, few scholars (e.g., Caple, 1998; Carpenter, 1996; Dungy & Gordon, 2011; Fenske, 1989b; Hinton, Howard-Hamilton, & Rentz, 2016; Nuss, 1996; Reason & Broido, 2011; Schwartz & Stewart, 2017), who published their research primarily in book chapters, have focused solely on the history and/or philosophy of the student affairs profession. Oddly, the student affairs profession began by default (Fenske, 1989b), when scholars abdicated their responsibilities for students outside the classroom, and faculty turned to producing new knowledge (i.e., conducting research) over passing on new knowledge (i.e., teaching) and guiding the behavior and character of college youth. The first nonacademic personnel who were assigned to watch over and guide students are our first student affairs ancestors.

In the second half of the 1800s as events unfolded, the stage was set for our predecessors to commence with serving students. The passage of the Morrill Act of 1862, just after the Civil War, brought public higher education to women and men in much larger numbers than the small numbers of mostly elite young boys, sometimes as young as 11 or 12 years old, who were the few recipients of higher education before this time (Rudolph, 1962/1990). In the beginning of U.S. higher education where the institution and faculty served *in loco parentis,* these elite students became ministers and merchants in colonial America. In the second half of the nineteenth century, institutions of higher education created specifically for women—from Georgia Female Seminary in the South (Gordon, 1991) to the "seven sisters" in the Northeast (Solomon, 1985)—began to spread and create unique spaces for females to learn, unencumbered by the presence of males (Horowitz, 1984).

At the same time, in this deeply segregated society, historically black colleges were created, adding even more diversity in institutional types to the U.S. higher education landscape (Anderson, 1988; Roebuck & Murty, 1993). This last half of the 19th century brought a diversity of students and institutions, creating a need for nonacademic personnel to perform tasks that today would fall under the umbrella of student affairs. In the next section, a snapshot, from inception to the present, of the historical highlights of the broad movements of the profession are outlined and, in some cases, sprinkled with philosophy and values.

British Educational Model Influences in Early American Higher Education: 1636–1880

The beginnings of higher education in colonial America, founded in the name of religion and shaped by aristocratic tradition, were not popular institutions among the populace (Rudolph, 1962/1990). In this New World, "there was taking shape an environment that encouraged individual effort, that looked with jealously and hostility at privilege . . . order was giving way to the dynamics of mobility" (Rudolph, 1962/1990, p. 19). During this time, few went to college, but many, such as Benjamin Franklin, often prospered with little or no education. Those boys who did attend college lived among the faculty and president, who served *in loco parentis* to develop students' character, in living and learning structures built around a quadrangle borrowed from Oxford University's architectural design, referred to as the British model. At the time, a classical curriculum (i.e., Latin, Greek, and Mathematics) (Finkelstein, 1997), close living quarters with their caretakers for character development, and rote memorization as a primary learning tool forced students to look elsewhere for richer learning experiences.

Harvard College, the first institution of higher education in the British colonies, opened its doors in 1636 and was originally established to educate the "infidels," a goal never met (Wright, 1989; Wright & Tierney, 1991). Mimicking the British model in design and curriculum, the early campus structures took into consideration the relationship between student and elder (i.e., tutor, faculty, and president who oversaw students' moral character and learning) in what was thought to be the best environment for learning: classroom lectures and rote memory. Students became bored with this forced routine, so to extend their learning, when possible, created communities, many unknown to the institution, in the form of debate clubs and literary societies, precursors to today's Greek life (Schwartz & Bryan, 1983). Eventually, this context moved the philosophy of higher education away from *in loco parentis* and paternalism to the student personnel movement and the onset of the student affairs profession in the modern university.

German Model Influence: From Deans of Women and Men to Student Personnel Movement: 1890–1949

In the second half of the nineteenth century, conditions in the country changed rapidly after the Civil War, when the railroad finally traversed coast to coast and settlers moved west. One scholar cited almost a dozen conditions making ready for the birth of student affairs (Rhatigan, 2000), including

> the development of land grant institutions and the rise of public colleges and universities; expanding enrollments and the accompanying increase of heterogeneity of student populations; social, political, and intellectual ferment in the US; the rise of coeducation and the increase in numbers of women entering educational institutions; the introduction of the elective system in higher education; and an emphasis on vocationalism as a competitor to the liberal arts. In addition, the impact of science and the scientific method; the struggle between empiricism and humanism; impersonalism on the part of the faculty educated in German institutions; the industrialization and urbanization of the closing of the American "frontier"; the view of higher education as a social class phenomenon, with less student motivation for "academic" subjects; the establishment of a true university system; massive European immigration; and the changing roles of students in higher education. (pp. 6–7)

Some of these circumstances are external to higher education but several influences within it are key. Training scholars abroad during this time was necessary, and many attended university in Germany where the scientific method and empiricism superseded the British liberal arts and humanist model, as it does today. As faculty focus turned to research and teaching became secondary, deans of women, deans of men, and personnel workers stepped in to fill the faculty void and tend to students' personal development. From the start, our student affairs predecessors talked about the wholeness of the individual and the need to deal with students from this paradigm, still true today; however, "other voices felt this point of view was unrealistic, unnecessary, and unattainable" (Rhatigan, 2000, p. 9). The slow beginning of the student affairs field (i.e., over the last half of nineteenth century) ushered in a time of paternalism, where attention and control of college students who were believed to need supervision by deans of women and men was paramount.

In the last decade of the nineteenth century, deans of women and men began to serve in this capacity with little or no training or direction, but armed with their own education, moral compass, personal skills, and ability to lead. Most clung to *in loco parentis* as a philosophy of higher education, which coincidentally dominated from the colonial America era through World War II and the end of the student personnel movement. Ironically, the success of coeducation in U.S. higher education meant the demise of these two positions (i.e., deans of women and men) and the creation of the Dean of Students position, viewed more as a vocation than a job.

The philosophy of monitoring student behavior dominated the field until after World War II, at which time the returning soldiers cashed in on the GI Bill and older students enrolled in college as never before. These students, who registered in college in masses, had lived through the horrors of war and demanded emancipation from parental control or any entity in that role, such as higher education. The notion that college students were uniformly 18 to 22 years old fell by the wayside as older students enrolled in unprecedented numbers. Women who stayed behind during the war, most of whom went to work in factories or championed other war efforts, also came to college older (Solomon, 1985). Student affairs professionals saw their primary role as service providers emerge for all the students who enrolled in the late 1940s and early 1950s in unprecedented numbers.

Shift from Service Providers to Educators

The evolution of the student affairs profession from service providers to educators was a result of student activism and dynamics during the 1960s, reverberating the social justice philosophy of the profession. Before the shift, work within the profession focused on a reactionary rather than proactive stance about students. For service affairs professionals to understand the change in the profession's philosophies, responsibilities, and influences, the historical shift from service to education is addressed.

In 1936, the definition of service providers, or student personnel work, was debated and discussed. Personnel work had a broad definition in other fields, such as government or business, and student personnel workers were trying to collaborate, categorize, and connect their work, through "systematic discussion" (Cowley, 1936/1994a, p. 44). Through research and deliberation, one scholar defined student personnel work as that which "constitutes all activities undertaken or sponsored by an educational institution, aside from curricular instruction, in which the student's personal development is the primary consideration" (Cowley, 1936/1994a, p. 59). This particular definition shows the viewpoint of the profession as a "service" rather than that of serving in an educational role in the academy.

Today, the definition of student affairs work can be defined as the work of a professional who fosters student learning, growth, and development through facilitation and support of student success. In addition, these professionals provide services to assist the higher education enterprise offer students' support. Student affairs work has become increasingly complex because of our fast-growing diverse student populations, integration of policies influencing professional work, and implementation of theory to practice. Below is a brief history with a skeletal context of this switch from professionals' roles as a student service provider to a student affairs practitioner.

Student Personnel Services: Human Relations Administrators—Early 1950s

Arbuckle's (1953) work, *Student Personnel Services in Higher Education,* provides context for the service ideals that accelerated progression toward the reform of student affairs in the 1960s. The idea of service providers in higher education is highlighted, which provides basic techniques of, and approaches to the field, including various components of a well-rounded student affairs entity. Numerous factors, including high rates of student withdrawal, increasing demands of society for higher education, and the rapid advancement in the understanding of human growth and behavior, emphasized the need for student affairs professionals. Interestingly, all these factors remain today. Student affairs professionals at the time were not seen as educators, but rather as human relations administrators with "client-centered points of views" (Arbuckle, 1953, p. 36). The importance and main function of university administrators was to "create [a] climate for both students and faculty so that continuing growth may take place" (Arbuckle, 1953, p. 39). Nevertheless, program and administrative procedures, though centered on the particular needs of students, were created from a reactive rather than proactive environment.

Prior to student development theory, student affairs statements, such as the *Student Personnel Point of View* (American Council of Education [ACE] 1937/1994a, 1949/1994b), *Student Personnel Work in College* (Wrenn, 1951), *Student Personnel Work in Higher Education* (Mueller, 1961) all centered on educating the whole student, a departure from the earlier singular focus on students' intellectual prowess. The ACE (1937/1994a, 1949/1994b) documents defined the goals of student personnel work as well as effective student personnel programs, differentiating the profession from administrative duties. These documents emphasized the importance of students' needs in a college setting and which personnel services to provide, identifying 23 of them. Some of these services included offering student orientation to the college environment, achieving student success in course work, providing satisfactory living spaces, promoting balanced health, and interpreting and understanding emotions. Progress toward career goals, as well as developing the student individually, ethically, and socially, were all highlighted in these writings of this neophyte profession (ACE, 1937/1994a, 1949/1994b).

Although these documents represented needed progress toward defining goals of the profession, there were criticisms to which ACE (1937/1994a, 1949/1994b) yielded that furthered the divide between academics and student personnel services (Lloyd- Jones & Smith, 1954). The challenge for the profession was to share educating students in tandem with faculty, fostering the learning environment, stating high expectations for students, and working jointly across academics and student personnel services (Roberts, 1998). By the early 1950s, student affairs professionals realized that "the concepts of individual differences and the wholeness of personality are basic to curriculum development and to the provision of student personnel services" (Wrenn, 1951, pp. 4–5). By the next decade, imitating these ideas, prominent higher education professionals sought to bridge the gap of academics versus student personnel with a "theory of developmental tasks" (Mueller, 1961, p. 108). These included integrating and stabilizing the self, identifying roles a student might hold, and practicing and evaluating the activities and attitudes necessary for future roles.

These initial 1960s documents are important statements of the profession's commitment, which remains today, in developing the student in both informal and formal settings across campus, with the goal of developing and nurturing the whole student. Unfortunately, when these ideas were first proposed, they were not widely implemented across campuses. Student personnel services were caught between institutional instruction, public pressures, and their own ideas of what it meant to be working within the profession of student personnel services. These early professionals were not satisfied with only being service providers and wanted to make further impactful contributions to higher education. However, the shift from service provider to educator did not develop until the late 1960s and 1970s (Boland, Stamatakos, & Rogers, 1994).

Reform in Student Affairs: From Student Services Provider to Student Affairs Educator

Many trace the shift from service providers to educators as occurring during the free-speech protests in 1964 at the University of California, Berkeley, when the dean of students prohibited political activity and on-campus political organizations (Boland et al., 1994). What resulted were sit-ins, demonstrations, and protests, with national implications that lasted for nearly seven years. Often referred to as "the age of student activism," this time was ripe for the downfall of *in loco parentis,* the sexual revolution, and "years of civil disobedience" (Nuss, 1996, p. 33). Central student issues of the day included the Vietnam War, racial injustice, retaliation against rationalism, the need for student-centered values, and the challenging of university rules and authorities. Universities were under immense pressure from students and the general public to resolve these societal issues (Boland et al., 1994; Hinton et al., 2016; Nuss, 1996).

The previous approach of coordinating and managing services without an educational function was no longer adequate, and a call was made to reform, rethink, and reconceptualize the role of student affairs (Boland et al., 1994; Hinton et al., 2016; Nuss, 1996). Student affairs educators, with a tool-box of knowledge on student development, behavior, and mediation, were at the forefront in dealing with dynamic student activism, which took the form of retaliation against universities. As advocates and advisors for students navigating the academic environment, student affairs educators were conflicted by directions from university presidents to control student behavior. Student affairs educators acted as a buffer between and among state legislators, institutional boards, and students.

The 1960s were a time of increased federal involvement in higher education, ultimately leading to today's policies and regulations of student affairs professionals' work. Most of the legislation passed was aimed at creating equal opportunity and access for students. During 1963, Congress passed the Vocational Act, the Higher Education Facilities Act, and the Health Professions Act. Other examples of legislation influencing higher education during the decade were the Higher Education Act of 1965 and Title VI of the Civil Rights Act of 1964 (Nuss, 1996). The Higher Education Act increased federal monies for education in the form of grants, scholarships, and low-interest loans. Title IV of the Civil Rights Act of 1964 prohibited discrimination based on race, color, or national origin for organizations receiving federal funds or federal financial assistance.

Much of the legislation passed within this time period, such as Affirmative Action in 1961, allowed for a more diverse student population on college campuses. However, activism for support services, such as disability support, multicultural support services, and LBGTQ+ services, did not come from the academy. Rather, the activism of these groups was supported and pushed forward from outside the academy. Higher education implemented these services as a reaction and result of some social progress in society. Although higher education is frequently thought of as a means to cultivate progress in society, society held higher education accountable for adequate services for its ever diverse and increasing student population.

In the early 1960s, ACPA Presidents Hardee (1963/1994), Berdie (1966/1994) and Cowley (1964/1994b) moved the professional association from a student personnel to student development focus. Hardee called for reform in student personnel work in higher education and wanted ACPA members to have a strong voice at national, regional, and state levels in legislation impacting students, student affairs professionals, and college campuses. By 1965, there was discussion of the need for student affairs professionals to become more than procedural technicians and also serve in the role of proactive educators for the whole campus environment. In this light, Berdie raised the need for a redefinition of student personnel work, and in the late 1960s, Cowley appointed a committee, named the Committee on Professional Development—members of the Council of Student Personnel Associations in Higher Education (COSPA)—to define a new direction for the field. Accordingly, COSPA, consisting of various representatives in higher education, set a goal to redefine the field. Student personnel workers were cited as "student development specialists," as COSPA set guidelines for the field (Commission of Professional Preparation of COSPA, 1975/1994). Guidelines included ensuring student development specialists (a) receive needed professional development, (b) understand human development applied to students, (c) incorporate a proactive approach to policies that influenced diverse student populations, and (d) serve as facilitators for students. COSPA later defined professional competencies for professionals (Hinton et al., 2016). Today, ACPA and NASPA (2010) competencies are used in the field as a framework for student affairs professionals and define "essential knowledge, skills, and dispositions expected of all student affairs educators, regardless of functional area or specialization within the field" (p. 7).

About the same time (the late 1960s), there was a new emergence of published research, including theories of student development (e.g., Chickering, 1969; Kohlberg, 1969; Perry, 1968). Student development emerged as a separate movement within student affairs. With the diversification of student populations resulting in policies as described above, theories on marginalized students served as a focus (Hinton et al., 2016). Such theory assisted student affairs professionals in understanding how students grow and progress, as well as helped define the field as it sought legitimacy.

The 1970s began the emergence of student-centered educational programming, planned and implemented by student affairs educators (Brown, 1972). Programs aimed at understanding the impact of college on students became apparent (e.g., Pascarella & Terenzini, 1978) in the literature of this emerging field. The old approach of student affairs as service providers was deemed limited and outdated. Entering the field quickly, without question, opposition, or analysis (Boland et al., 1994), a new approach emerged that centered on student affairs professionals, commencing with proactive educational programs to promote student development (Miller & Prince, 1977). The emphasis on student development provided legitimacy, validity, and credibility to the field, which was often viewed as "less than" by those in academic administration, and clearly centered the student in higher education. As higher education expanded and became more specialized, professional titles and responsibilities shifted. A field that was once named student personnel became student affairs (Hinton et al., 2016; Nuss, 1996).

Development, Learning, and Professionalism: 1970 to the Present

Development and Learning. With changes in the academy, the field of student affairs produced documents that articulated the foundations of the field, such as *Student Development Services in Postsecondary Education* (COSPA 1975, 1994), *Student Development Tomorrow's Higher Education* (Brown, 1972), and *The Future of Student Affairs* (Miller & Prince, 1977). These documents enabled the newly established theories of student development to be applied to students within the academy. In 1979, the Council for the Advancement of Standards in Higher Education (CAS) was established with the mission to "codify and document effective practices in student services [in higher education]" (Schwartz & Stewart, 2017, p. 31). This led to the first professional standards of the field, which were published in 1986. A year later, the seven principles of good practice in undergraduate education were defined as (a) student-faculty contact, (b) cooperation among students, (c) active learning, (d) prompt feedback, (e) time on task, (f) high expectations, and (g) respect for diverse talents and ways of learning (Chickering & Gamson, 1987). Professional association documents and student development theories and principles allowed for transparency and goals for student affairs professionals to provide quality education to students.

Professionalism. Continuing into the 1970s, major policies and legislation were passed influencing the professionalism of student affairs and higher education. Legislation and public pressures required accountability by universities to serve students' needs and protect student rights. One piece of legislation, Title IX of the Educational Amendments Act, enacted during this era, required university restructuring (i.e., implementing Title IX offices) and is a good example of how the public demanded and shaped the role of the university. The university was not responsible for legitimizing these services to serve students; rather the university was legally demanded (rightfully) to do so by the public.

In the 1970s, with the end of *in loco parentis* as a result of the Dixon v. Alabama decision, students also acted with a new autonomy from the university. In 1972, Title IX of the Educational Amendments Act, referred to above, was passed to address sex discrimination. Although largely thought of as a means of gaining equal opportunities for women in athletic departments, many supporters were focused on equal access for women in higher education (e.g., in STEM fields). From this legislation, Women's Centers and Title IX offices and coordinators were created in the university setting (Schwartz & Stewart, 2017). In 1973, Section 504 of the Rehabilitation Act set the requirement for education entities to provide equal access for people with disabilities as well as provide adequate services and accommodations. As a result, disability support services offices were created on campuses.

This legislation was extended in 1990 under the Americans With Disabilities Act (ADA). ADA included a definition of disability that prohibited discrimination and extended workplace rights for students, staff, and faculty (Schwartz & Stewart, 2017). What is now known as the Federal Educational Records and Privacy Act, passed in 1974, gave students the right to decide who had access to their educational records, allowing them to withhold information from their parents. With passage of this act, "students now became consumers of their education and had the right to make certain demands of their educational institutions" (Schwartz & Stewart, 2017, p. 30). Pell grants were also created during this time, allowing lower socioeconomic status students access to the academy. Continued support for affirmative action was evident with the decision of the Regents of the University of California v. Bakke (Schwartz & Stewart, 2017). With a more diverse student body than before, universities were held responsible for creating offices that served underrepresented groups, such as women, students with disabilities, and racially minoritized and marginalized students of color, as a result of legislation.

Another path to professionalism in student affairs was created as research and literature increased, drawing on a broad stroke of literature originating in other disciplines. In this context, there were questions related to creating more graduate programs specifically for the field of student affairs. Fifty years ago, without the specialized graduate degree of student affairs available now, student affairs professionals often were at entry-level positions (Schwartz & Stewart, 2017). Today, the field of student affairs is elite, usually requiring a graduate-level degree to gain employment in most functional areas as well as attendance at professional development conferences and series, such as NASPA or ACPA, coming with a high price. As professionals redefine and shape the future of the profession, intentional thought and action surrounding minoritized and marginalized professionals who may not have access to the field needs reconsideration. In our efforts as student affairs educators to support diversity and inclusion for students and equal representation of diverse groups in the field, we must find ways with limited resources to best serve, educate, and build community for students.

From In-Class Versus Out-of-Class Support to Campus-Wide Learning Environment: From Silos to Integration

Student affairs professionals' roles, areas of expertise, and specialization expanded significantly over the last century as the profession matured. Despite the shift from service provider to educator, student affairs professionals within the co-curriculum are still not considered *equal* educational partners with faculty. Student services responsibilities remain solely in "nonacademic functional areas" (Magolda & Quaye, 2011, p. 388) or out-of-the classroom areas, whereas academic affairs covers responsibilities within the classroom focusing on curriculum and academic personnel matters (Birnbaum, 1988; Kezar, 2003).

Tracing back to as early as the mid-nineteenth century, resistance to the model of paternalism or *in loco parentis* at colleges and universities began to break down and extracurricular activities began to emerge (Fenske, 1989b). At this time, students began engaging in rich extracurricular activities, including participation in residence halls, athletic teams, debate teams, Greek-letter societies (i.e., fraternities and sororities), and various social organizations on campus (Fenske, 1989b; Nuss, 1996). The birth of the extra-curriculum naturally led to the birth of student services personnel. Past and neglected paternal functions were no longer the responsibility of faculty but rather assigned to non-instructional personnel. In this capacity, student services personnel were often limited by their function and took on unpopular tasks often "abandoned by trustees, administrators and faculty" (Fenske, 1989b, p. 6).

By the late nineteenth century, faculty's roles in student lives had transitioned from "total involvement to detachment" (Fenske, 1989b, p. 16), as presidents and governing boards gained more power in U.S. higher education. Faculty members' survival depended on reward systems heavily tied to individual research, scholarship, curriculum, and academic efforts. Faculty orientation towards research and scholarship was also exacerbated by academic specialization, and the creation of the elective system and academic departments (Fenske, 1989b).

By the end of the nineteenth century, many institutions came to believe students "should be free of administrative or faculty supervision of their academic and social affairs" (Fenske, 1989b, p. 20). Faculty remained unconcerned with what students did outside of class (Rudolph, 1976), because their only responsibility was "training . . . the student's mind" (Nuss, 1996, p. 26) and contributing to furthering knowledge. With this shift, faculty's work became private, known only to those in similar positions, whereas communication became siloed, and students' spiritual, emotional, and social development was completely turned over to nonfaculty.

The student personnel movement gained professional stature by 1918 (Brubacher & Rudy, 1958/1976), and distinct personnel functions had developed by 1925 (Nuss, 1996). However, the division between faculty and student personnel was set in stone. With the growth of large and complex organizations, specialized areas of expertise related to federal and state mandates, grants, and contracts, as well as governance issues heightened the division (Birnbaum, 1988). Additionally, limited resources and outside pressures often led to competition between the two areas (Birnbaum, 1988; Brubacher

& Rudy, 1997; Kezar, 2003; Westfall, 1999). Differing cultures and unclear faculty and student services personnel functions inflamed the split as did the lack of communication (Kezar, 2003), leading these two groups to communicate only "with people similar to themselves" (Birnbaum, 1988, p. 7).

The Student Development Movement

Students experience a disconnect between in-class and out-of-class personal lives and experiences (Westfall, 1999). With the emergence of a broad emphasis on students' development in the early twentieth century, the in-class versus out-of-class division intensified. Student personnel workers were hired as human development specialists offering vocational guidance, matching students' personality to specific occupations (Evans, Forney, Guido, Patton, & Renn, 2010; Nuss, 2003). Human development and noncognitive needs (e.g., personal, emotional, and identity development) typically resonated for students outside of the classroom (Evans, Forney, & Guido-DiBrito, 1998; Magolda & Quaye, 2011; Reason & Broido, 2011) so cognitive development could occur within the classroom (Magolda & Quaye, 2011).

Human development and the vocational focus of student affairs work endured throughout the 1920s until ACE's 1937 *Student Personnel Point of View* and the 1949 revised statement called on educators to focus on holistic learning, making both the personal and professional—or total—development of the student essential (Evans et al., 2010). Not until after significant diversification of the student body during the 1960s, due to the Vietnam War and the civil and women's rights movements, were student affairs leaders and professional associations finally able to assert the mission of student affairs wherein student development cannot thrive without the "support and influence of those in the academic domain" (Evans et al., 2010, p. 12).

Student development theories matured rapidly during the 1970s and 1980s, including the expansion of previous psychosocial and cognitive developmental theories, moral development, and epistemological development, as well as the emergence of typological, ecological learning styles and intellectual development of women (Evans et al., 2010; Strange, 2011). To this day, student development theories serve as the foundation for student affairs work and help legitimize student affairs as a profession. The student development movement also started the perception of student affairs professionals being seen as educators in students' holistic growth and development.

The Student Learning Movement

Although attention to holistic student development, both in and out of class, was emergent throughout the literature during the 1970s, the move toward collaborative student learning remained stagnant until the 1990s and

2000s. All this changed with the writing of three documents that were paramount to analyzing the role of student affairs professionals and their role in the student learning process. *The Student Learning Imperative* (ACPA, 1996), *Powerful Partnerships* (American Association for Higher Education [AAHE], ACPA, & NASPA, 1998), and *Learning Reconsidered* (Keeling, 2004) outlined a more holistic approach to understanding student learning and challenged the human-cognitive development dichotomy, in/out-of-class separation, and the academic-student affairs division of labor. These three key documents are discussed briefly in the following sections.

The *Student Learning Imperative* Document. The Student Learning Imperative (ACPA, 1996) outlined several basic assumptions about higher education, student affairs, and student development. Most important among these assumptions was the declaration that learning, personal development, and student development are inseparable (ACPA, 1996). *The Student Learning Imperative* also proclaimed the traditional way of organizing activities into academic affairs (learning, curriculum, classrooms, and cognitive development) and student affairs (co-curriculum, student activities, residential life, and affective or personal development) had little relevance to postcollege life, where individuals' job, family, and community are all interdependent. Moreover, *The Student Learning Imperative* stated in-class and out-of-class settings contributed to both learning and personal development and occurred through transactions between students and their environments. Student affairs professionals were to be seen as equal educators who are responsible for creating learning environments, along with faculty and other academic administrators (ACPA, 1996).

The *Powerful Partnerships* Report. The Powerful Partnerships report is one of the first documents to make the case that "only when everyone on campus" (AAHE, ACPA, & NASPA, 1998, p. 1)—especially those in academic affairs and student affairs staff—-share the responsibility for student learning will progress be made. *Powerful Partnerships* declared colleges and universities did not use collective wisdom to improve student learning processes and environments beyond individual faculty or staff members. To overcome this, the document outlined principles of cooperative practice to bring together academic and student affairs professionals to "make a difference in the quality of student learning" (AAHE, ACPA, & NASPA, 1998, p. 1). These principles stated that learning is a cumulative process involving the whole person and is strongly affected by the educational climate in which it takes place (AAHE, ACPA, & NASPA, 1998). Student learning also takes place informally with faculty, staff, and peers, beyond explicit teaching or the classroom (AAHE, ACPA, & NASPA, 1998).

The *Learning Reconsidered* Document. *Learning Reconsidered* provided a new definition of learning as a "comprehensive, holistic, transformative activity that integrates academic learning and student development, processes that have often been considered separate, and even independent of each other" (Keeling, 2004, p. 2). Learning was not something exclusively experienced in the classroom or by the acquisition of disciplinary content, but an integration of personal development with learning (Keeling, 2004). *Learning Reconsidered* also asserted that for students to have a powerful transformative education, they must be repeatedly exposed to multiple opportunities through the "formal academic curriculum, student life, collaborative co-curricular programming, community-based, and global experiences" (Keeling, 2004, p. 3).

Some scholars have made the argument that the academic and student affairs dichotomy, caused by fragmented organizational structures apparent throughout college life and curriculum, still plagues higher education today and often leaves student affairs professionals at odds with academic affairs (Keeling, 2004). Although learning involves "the constant search for meaning by acquisition of information, reflection, emotional engagement and active application in multiple contexts" (Keeling, 2004, p. 11), most institutions do not operate as integrated systems. Institutions must constantly assess and respond to change, understand the diversity of learners on their campuses, and reevaluate organizational structures and processes and their impact on students. Institutions can also engage in (a) mapping learning; (b) creating new organizational structures, positions, and roles; (c) identifying and implementing best practices; and (d) assessing and understanding student needs (Keeling, 2004). Furthermore, student affairs professionals can work with academics to provide transformative learning experiences to students, so they can take ownership of their own intentional learning and connect academic learning to student life (Keeling, 2004).

Student Affairs as Partners in the Academic Enterprise

The student development movement and the student learning movement helped define the work of student affairs professionals, making it clear student affairs professionals are not simply bystanders but equal contributors in the student learning process. However, the question remains, what does real collaboration look like (Kezar, Hirsch, & Burack, 2002)? By the mid-1990s, partnership thinking, collaboration, and teamwork were on the rise in the literature and as program topics at national conferences, and were beginning to appear in practice (Kezar et al., 2002; Martin & Samels, 2001). Simultaneously, complex questions arose about the nature of collaboration, including teamwork, leadership, accountability, and authority (Kezar et al., 2002; Martin & Samels, 2001). By the late 1990s, research outlining obstacles to creating successful partnerships between academic and student affairs expanded in the literature.

Since the early 2000s, many have written on the challenges of collaboration, including the historical tradition of division, the separation between formal and informal curriculum, and the perception of student affairs as serving only an ancillary function to the academic mission of institutions (Bourassa & Kruger, 2001), but few have articulated what can lead to successful collaborations (Kezar et al., 2002). Much of the current literature on successful partnerships remains exhortative without reference to empirical evidence, because little research has been done to identify specific aspects of effective academic and student affairs partnership programs (Whitt, 2011). However, for the purposes of this section, the documents *Learning Reconsidered 2* (Keeling, 2006), *Principles of Good Practice for Academic and Student Affairs Partnership Programs* (Whitt et al., 2008), along with other identified tools and strategies for creating sustainable and effective partnerships are explored.

The Learning Reconsidered 2 Document

Whereas *Learning Reconsidered* did a substantial job of fulfilling its purpose of re-examining "widely accepted ideas about conventional teaching and learning . . . [questioning] whether current organizational patterns in higher education support student learning in today's environment" (Keeling, 2004, p. 1) and maintaining that student affairs needs to be partners in broader campus curriculum, it did not address how notions of effective partnerships are procedurally implemented. Therefore, *Learning Reconsidered 2* (Keeling, 2006) is one of the first attempts to create dialogue and provide tools and materials to implement partnerships providing transformative student learning.

Rethinking how institutions define and understand learning is one of the initial steps in implementation of partnerships between student and academic affairs (Keeling, 2006). *Learning Reconsidered 2* was the first proclamation in the field to give concrete suggestions for success. Not only mapping the learning environment but also the process of recognizing, identifying, and documenting learning activities sites on campus help student affairs educators link their programs and activities to learning opportunities (Keeling, 2006). Thus, it is critical to ask questions, such as What is the mission of the campus? What are the campus' learning objectives or outcomes? How does the work of student affairs support those outcomes? Can help with the mapping process and academic-student affairs partnerships understand how learning is being disseminated on campus? (Keeling, 2006).

Another essential component of transformative learning is for program organizers to outline specific student learning outcomes. *Learning Reconsidered 2* (Keeling, 2006) presents several examples of student learning outcomes that can help guide creators of partnership programs. Some of these include (a) cognitive complexity, (b) knowledge acquisition, (c) integration and application, (d) civic engagement, and (e) interpersonal and intrapersonal competence. According to Keeling (2006), student affairs professionals can take two approaches when outlining outcomes. First, the outcome-to-practice approach is intentional and planned, because it identifies existing or new programs that might be needed to develop that outcome in targeted students. The second approach, practice to outcome, takes any existing program and maps it in learning-outcome clusters to see which ones it most likely advances.

Above all, it is important for student affairs professionals to remember that thorough implementation is a marathon, not a race, and that one of the key elements to implementation is to engage faculty members at the onset (Keeling, 2006). Although differentiation may persist between faculty and staff for historic, structural, and political reasons, "collaboration must be assumed, planned, and supported, and ideas, policies, and actions that emphasize or reinforce the division of campuses (and learning) into completely segregated cultures (the proverbial two sides of the house) must be challenged and resisted" (Keeling, 2006, pp. 70–71). Specific strategies, suggested by Keeling (2006), to creating successful partnerships include but are not limited to the following: (a) Start small—partners need to be realistic about the types of change they can actually make; (b) identify and support champions, but avoid overdependence—developing limited and well-planned collaboration that suits the needs of faculty life will help avoid burnout and strengthen commitment; (c) focus on real problems, not theoretical opportunities—faculty are more likely to respond to specific requests with specific outcomes; (d) initiate the conversation—student affairs professionals are well trained in processes of networking, relationship building, and empathy and should take the initiative to extend the olive branch; (e) expect and manage conflict—student affairs professionals should prepare for and embrace conflict and be ready to advocate for their contributions to student learning; and (f) evaluate the outcomes—assessment should be part of any partnership and should be a full commitment for both groups.

Principles of Good Practice for Academic and Student Affairs Partnership Programs

Academic and student affairs partnership programs have been championed to enhance undergraduate education, yet research documenting the characteristics of effective partnership remains sparse (Whitt et al., 2008). Initiated in 2001, the Boyer Partnership Assessment Project was an attempt to address those gaps in research (Whitt et. al., 2008). As a qualitative examination of academic and student affairs partnership programs at 18 diverse institutions, the inquiry led to the creation of seven principles of good practice for creating and sustaining effective partnerships. Each of the practices was consistent with and reflected the rich data gathered at each research site. Some of these areas are covered in more detail in the following sections.

Effective partnership programs must be reflected in the institutional mission. Reflecting an institution's mission of having a shared vision and common goals, for example, can foster commitment from planning through implementation (Westfall, 1999; Whitt et al., 2008). Good practice for partnership programs must implement assessment to ensure their mission, vision, and goals are met. Assessment should be used to guide, alter, and improve the program. Effective partnerships create learning opportunities in and out of class in both formal and informal settings. By embodying and fostering a learning-oriented ethos, institutions of higher education must "create seamless learning opportunities, environments, and experiences for students, and encourage pedagogical innovation and experimentation" (Whitt et al., 2008 p. 240).

Furthermore, effective partnerships build on and nurture existing relationships between and among academic and student affairs professionals, while at the same time, partnership programs must recognize, understand, and attend to institutional culture and the unique characteristics of students, faculty, staff, and administrators. Partnership programs should aim to thrive in both resource-rich and resource-limited contexts by using whatever resources are available to support student learning creatively and effectively. Good practice for partnership programs must rely on multiple forms of leadership to enhance student learning.

Creating Seamless Learning Environments

Regardless of the call to arms made in the student affairs seminal documents, institutions still operate as fragmented organizations that are not conducive to learning and educating students effectively (Whitt et al., 2008). Institutional growth, complex organizational structures, shifting demographics, historic traditions, technological advancements, globalization, and lack of funding continue to deepen the fragmentation of higher education (Whitt, 2011). However, institutions can take multiple steps to "deepen the quality of learning" (Keeling, 2004, p. 13) by providing students with seamless learning environments (Kuh, 1996). In seamless learning environments, students learn both in and out of class and through academic and nonacademic, curricular and co-curricular, or on- and off-campus experiences and opportunities. Creating seamless learning environments is an endeavor of the whole institution. All members must be committed to working together to create programs focused on learning environments, both in and out of the classroom and should be championed by current faculty and staff (Kuh, 1996). Logically, seamless learning environments are easier to implement at smaller institutions with specific educational missions.

It is fair to argue that creating seamless learning environments between academic and student affairs constitutes an "all-purpose response to a wide variety of campus issues" (Whitt 2011, p. 484), including challenges regarding access, enrollment, retention, and graduation. Moreover, seamless learning environments with productive partnerships have positive impacts on educational climate, quality, and most importantly, student success (Kuh, Kinzie, Schuh, Whitt, & Associates, 2005; Whitt, 2011; Whitt et al., 2008). Partnership programs also help students acclimate to their institutions, especially first-year students transitioning from high school to college (Elkins Nesheim et al., 2007). Students' sense of identity and community are significantly impacted by partnership programs. Participation fosters student engagement both in and out of the classroom and increases awareness of campus activities and events, while at the same time, students spend more time in partnership program study, use academic resources, and connect with faculty and staff. Interactions with faculty and peers outside of class allow students to see each other and faculty as "real people" (Elkins Nesheim et al., 2007, p. 442). Partnership programs also provide students an opportunity to become involved in their community both locally and nationally through community service, service learning, community activism, and civic opportunities (Elkins Nesheim et al., 2007).

Learning environments are also influenced by several models of the human environment (Strange, 1991). The physical model includes the bricks and mortar, facilities, and aesthetic setting, encompassing architectural design, space, amenities, distance, noise, temperature, and even air quality (Stern, 1986; Strange, 1991; Strange, 2011). The aggregate model includes the significant impact on learning of an environment's norms, social customs, and ethnic identification set by the people inhabiting a space (Strange, 1991). All these features interact and highly influence students' attitudes, behaviors, performance, and ultimately, learning (Strange, 2011). By not analyzing physical aspects of a learning environment in conjunction with the non-physical, students may not be able to make connections between curricular and co-curricular experiences and may not be able to integrate cognitive and affective knowledge. Additionally, if physical spaces are not favorable to learning, students' ability to think critically, ask questions, and ultimately, take ownership of their learning is stifled (Elkins Nesheim et al., 2007).

Blending the Distinct Cultures of Student Affairs and Academic Affairs

One of the most critical steps in collaboration is seeing student affairs professionals as "full partners" (Keeling, 2004, p. 25) in the academic enterprise and creating areas of intentional collaboration. With academic affairs and student affairs working in true partnership, the alignment of university goals across campus is attainable. As societal issues arise, resources are cut, and as student demographic and institutional change occurs, it is critical for student affairs professionals to be treated as equals to their faculty counterparts in their contributions to student learning (Magolda & Quaye, 2011; Stage, Watson, & Terrell, 1999).

Partnership planners may have difficulty creating seamless learning environments because of the distinct cultural differences between student affairs and academic affairs. Student affairs was founded on collaborative group work to solve problems, whereas faculty "engage in solitary, autonomous work" (Bourassa & Kruger, 2001, pp. 13–14). The individualistic nature of the academy may not lend itself to working in groups, shared goals, multidisciplinary teaching, or cross-divisional work (Kezar et al., 2002, p. 2). Other cultural barriers to partnerships can include lack of faculty and staff time, faculty disciplinary ties, faculty resistance, and lack of cooperative spirit and the ability to work together (Kezar, 2001).

Nevertheless, overcoming cultural differences is possible by ensuring teams have representatives from multiple levels within the organization to foster extensive collaboration (Martin & Samels, 2001). Incorporating all levels of communication in the early stages of partnership planning is also integral in building successful partnerships, leading to group trust among one another and eventually valuing others' opinions, rather than colliding and becoming ineffectual (Martin & Samels, 2001). The team, the goals of the team, and the eventual success of the team outweigh cultural differences within these two environments. Other strategies to overcome cultural differences include cross-institutional dialogue, staff development, common vision development, common language development, communication strategies, redefining the mission, and generating enthusiasm (Kezar, 2001; Kuh, 1996; Whitt, 2011).

Overcoming Structural Barriers

A national study on trends related to academic and student affairs collaboration revealed that structural and organizational obstacles often have more impact on creating effective partnerships than cultural-oriented obstacles (Kezar, 2001). Thus, the importance for institutional environments to remain dynamic and respond quickly to change (Strange, 2011) cannot be overstated. Although all institutions are both dynamic and static (i.e., environments tend to resist change), academic and student affairs professionals can remain committed to student growth and development by encouraging each other to challenge the status quo and remain creative in their endeavors (Strange, 2011). Other strategies to take into consideration for remaining dynamic include combining fiscal resources, changing promotion and tenure requirements, reassigning duties, restructuring, planning, setting expectations, establishing accountability, modifying the reward system, and implementing systematic change (Kezar, 2001; Kuh, 1996; Whitt, 2011).

Providing Multifaceted Leadership

Good practice for partnership programs demands and cultivates multiple manifestations of leadership (Whitt et al., 2008). In effectively shaping higher education environments, higher education and student affairs leaders must reflect many qualities. As equal partners sharing leadership responsibilities, academic and student affairs leaders must also possess strong organizational leadership skills. These two groups of university leaders must identify supportive individuals or departments in collaborative efforts, as well as recognize areas of resistance (Westfall, 1999) and how to overcome them. All of these leaders must pay attention to detail and have strong communication, while managing multiple efforts, people, and commitments (Westfall, 1999). Leaders must manage time effectively by understanding how long a project may take and learn quickly to ensure the success of a program (Westfall, 1999). Most importantly, multifaceted leadership means academic and student affairs leaders recognize how they create the tone and environment for effective partnerships in the academy (Lemonedes, 2018).

Creatively Controlling the Budget

One of the greatest sources of failures in partnerships is lack of financial support (Martin & Samels, 2001). Partnership planners must be creative when thinking about sources of funding and how to obtain them. A few ways to accomplish this is by joining budget task forces or cultivating partnership with institutional advancement (Martin & Samels, 2001). Additionally, partnership planners should consider leveraging the budget whenever possible, especially in times of turnover. It is also important for planners to understand the financial risks and resources of participation (Westfall, 1999).

Conducting the Assessment and Evaluation

Although, academic and student affairs partnerships are relatively new, many programs conduct outcome assessments (Kezar, 2001). Data from assessment can help support, guide, and give direction to future collaboration. When done correctly, assessment is

> a process through which departments, divisions, or entire institutions determine the highest and best use of their unique resources to achieve their goals. Strategic planning supports the organization's mission, must be consistent with its vision, and responds to its current and anticipated educational, administrative, political, competitive, and fiscal challenges and opportunities. (Keeling, 2006, p. 53)

Assessment can help institutions determine readiness for students' transformative learning, address challenges and strengths, identify wasted resources, and create future action steps (Keeling, 2006). One of the most useful assessment tools in student affairs is the CAS (2003) Self-Assessment Guides. Using the processes and tools outlined in these self-assessment guides helps institutions identify what they are doing well, what needs improvement, and how both of these assessments can affect the many campus environments as well as how student affairs can shape them to the benefit of all on campus.

Challenges and Opportunities

The world is changing faster than higher education can accommodate. Several challenges await student affairs professionals in the future as vastly different learning environments take hold. For starters, as the digital age and technology continue to penetrate every aspect of our lives, one of the greatest challenges in student affairs work is how to create an effective online learning and growth environment for students. Today, students use various forms of technology, including the internet, online media, social networking sites, social news services, social media communication, microblogging, and blogging, to integrate their online and real-world experiences (Rokkum & Junco, 2017). Yet, there seems to be a lag between the most state-of-the-art technology and how institutions are learning about it and using it. For example, Did you know that QR code technology is currently making a comeback (Pierce, 2017)? Were you even aware QR technology left? If you are one of those individuals who did not realize QR technology was a thing of the past, herein lies the problem.

This disconnect can be attributed to the opposite cultures of social media acceptance and pushback (Rokkum & Junco, 2017). Those engaging in pushback, or the adult normative perspective, may view social media as a "negative influence" on development and student engagement (Rokkum & Junco, 2017, p. 346). Because of this, student affairs professionals may inadvertently be removing an effective tool to support students (Rokkum & Junco, 2017). However, becoming current on technology and understanding how students are using social media both in and out of the classroom and throughout their lives is an opportunity for student affairs professionals to shape these learning environments for learning. Not only do sites, such as Facebook, LinkedIn, Twitter, and Instagram, encourage and engage students in conversations, debates, and lectures in the classroom, it helps students collaborate, communicate, and build a sense of community beyond the classroom (Rokkum & Junco, 2017). Understanding how these types of social media platforms influence student learning and engagement is extremely important as institutions move to the flipped classroom or the classroom of the future, replacing age-old discussion boards and technologies (Rokkum & Junco, 2017).

A significant opportunity for student affairs professionals is creating environments most conducive to student development and learning for students of color and other minoritized and/or marginalized groups due to systemic and institutional oppression. Developing multicultural competence is an absolute necessity in creating multiculturally sensitive, inclusive campuses and transformative learning environments (Pope & Mueller, 2017). Unfortunately, "few practitioners have received adequate training in multicultural issues and even fewer have had their work performance evaluated using multicultural competence as a criteria" (Pope & Mueller, 2017, p. 392). Although lack of multicultural training and the incorporating of multiculturalism as a core competency remain significant challenges for student affairs and higher education, these challenges also present a great opportunity for student affairs educators to improve their practice.

Student affairs educators can develop multicultural competence on both a personal and professional level (Pope & Mueller, 2017). They must make a personal commitment to incorporate multicultural competence into their daily lives, while simultaneously establishing multiculturalism as a guiding principle and expectation at an individual, unit, and organizational level. In order to achieve multicultural competence, practitioners need to heighten their awareness around identities and how they intersect, educate themselves and others (students, colleagues, and friends) on social justice topics, and apply their competence to practice in seeking to create inclusive environments for a diverse population of faculty, staff, and students on college campuses. Creating these inclusive spaces is an ongoing practice to which student affairs professionals must be dedicated. Once multicultural competence is obtained on a personal level, multicultural change is possible. Multicultural competence and change lead to greater diversity at institutions, ultimately having a positive influence on college satisfaction, student development, learning, and transformative learning environments (Pope & Mueller, 2017).

Opportunities for student affairs and higher education professionals in the future are too numerous to discuss in this limited space. In the past, high-

er education helped shape society, and now society increasingly shapes higher education. Potentially, one of student affairs' most enduring opportunities
could be to model for and show students how to have difficult dialogues with
others who disagree (Watt, 2015). Deconstructing the most difficult societal
topics up for discussion today, including race, social class, sexuality, gender,
ethnicity, ability, religion, and on and on, in a respectful way, demands
courage and skill in managing conflict within, between, and among student
groups. Opportunities that create better understanding are in step with a
postmodern, postcolonial philosophy and a democratic society.

Another opportunity for student affairs to shape the university environment for student success includes an openness and support for a wide range
of student activism on campus (Evans & Reason, 2001). As U.S. society
becomes politically more violent, hostile, volatile, and fractured, teaching
this centuries-old behavior, necessary for a democratic society, is more necessary than ever. Often seen as threatening by many bureaucratic, rationalist organizations, such as higher education, facilitating students' learning as
they protest or enact other forms of dissent can teach students peaceful approaches to dealing with conflict and effecting social change. Shaping this
environment requires that student affairs professionals are skilled and adept
in such areas as conflict resolution, change strategies, multicultural competence, and collaborative leadership (ACPA & NASPA, 2010) to name a few.
Opportunities for student affairs professionals to influence the environments
college students live in, interact with, and even avoid are limitless.

Recommendations for Practice

Dedication to student development, the student learning process, and
enhancing the "educational potential of campus environments" (Reason &
Broido, 2011, p. 88) are the underpinnings of student affairs work. With this
in mind, the recommendations for practice offered below focus on macro or
organizational dynamics for change, and summarize what student affairs
professionals can do on a micro or individual level to improve development,
learning, and campus environments when working with students.

Educators in student affairs professional training programs must work to
better incorporate academic affairs in postsecondary education theory and
college culture courses. Prior to entering college campuses, learning about
the ideas of shared governance, faculty culture, and history; how research,
teaching, and service influence faculty responsibilities; and the tenure process would give new student affairs educators a better understanding of their
counterparts. Additionally, providing multicultural training opportunities
and having classes focused on modernization and technology and its influence on college campuses would be extremely helpful in overcoming the

challenges referenced previously. Managers of graduate assistantships have the responsibility of providing opportunities to graduate students that combine theory, classroom learning, and practice. This is another area where new student affairs professionals can learn how to create meaningful partnerships with academic affairs during their respective apprenticeships in graduate programs. Ultimately, all student affairs educators must become scholarly practitioners (Hatfield & Wise, 2015) in order to be equal partners with faculty for effective partnerships and generate new knowledge about students and their college environments as a way to give back to the profession. Graduate programs in student affairs may have a duty to instill in their students the value of becoming a scholarly practitioner in order to protect our future.

Adding these components to student affairs professional training programs allows for the natural next step of hiring student affairs educators in academic units. Not only would student affairs educators have the background knowledge of the lives and demands on the faculty with whom they work, but they would also have the training to bring students to the center of their work and the ability to offer a welcoming environment, regardless of students' backgrounds. Additionally, student affairs educators can take on multiple roles or wear different hats within the unit and help out in times of need, which would facilitate student affairs becoming "full partners" in the academic enterprise (Keeling, 2004, p. 25) and help harness opportunities for intentional collaboration. For example, student affairs professionals can work hand in hand with faculty in the academic advising arena, event coordination, recruitment and outreach efforts, and partnership program planning. Consequently, having student affairs professionals' presence in academic units could be an answer to the blending of the two distinct cultures and the creating of seamless learning environments.

To ensure successful environments, both academic and student affairs professionals must also build and cultivate relationships with a wide variety of partners outside of their individual unit or area. Student affairs professionals can foster relationships with others by stepping outside their comfort zone, joining committees in areas where they may not possess expertise, or simply having a conversation with a faculty neighbor. One of the smallest gestures that can lead to the largest outcomes in promoting collegial relationships is for student affairs professionals to present their work to academic departments during departmental meetings. One hour of dedicated time can help faculty better understand what it is that student affairs professionals do, help clarify roles and responsibilities, and promote communication between faculty and student affairs professionals. For example, student affairs professionals who assist departments in the creation of articulation agreements can present to academic units to inform them of policies, resources, and other pertinent information in agreement creation. The next time faculty have questions, they have a contact person who can assist them. Similarly, financial aid counselors can present beneficial information to faculty about students' financial aid eligibility and how this may impact their class registration and enrollment. Institutions still operate as fragmented organizations (Keeling, 2004; Whitt, 2011; Whitt et al., 2008), and faculty are often siloed and do not understand what another side of the organization may be doing, as discussed earlier. But with little effort, it can become apparent that all parties are contributing equally to creating transformative learning environments for students (Keeling, 2006).

Senior university leaders can also contribute to the success of shared partnerships and environments by strategically creating cross-functional teams with shared vision and goals. Key players purposefully placed on teams can lead to more inclusive policies and practices that best serve all students. In successful cross-functional teams, membership should be reflective of all levels of the institution, including students, new and mid-level professionals, classified administrative staff, directors, faculty, and senate representatives, to name a few. Selecting well-positioned leaders of cross-functional teams is important to the creation of long-lasting sustainable partnerships. Student affairs educators and faculty must have regular access and contact with each other and senior leaders to keep them abreast of the team's progress, providing motivation and multifaceted leadership (Lemonedes, 2018). Cross-functional teams must have shared vision and goals that are outlined with senior university leaders. Conversely, senior leaders must be open to listening to the vision offered by the teams' members and leaders. Official documents, strategic plans, and short- and long-term goals can easily be available to members and leaders of cross-functional teams to ensure longevity.

Conclusion

Indeed, the university environment has always shaped the philosophy, values, and even the history of student affairs and college students. In the twenty-first century, student affairs educators and college students are now shaping the values, philosophy, and history of higher education environments in deeply meaningful ways. In over 350 years, higher education as well as student affairs has moved from a rationalist view of the academic enterprise to a postmodern perspective. Indeed, student affairs professionals are permanent shape shifters in higher education both focusing on a student's holistic development and offering services necessary for student success. Instead of adding a role when another drops off, the profession mostly adds continuous layers or allows student needs to emerge and then responds. Limited resources, mostly time and money, tend to make the profession more reactive than proactive but must not be used as excuses for not moving forward.

The history, philosophy, and values of student affairs have shaped the higher education environment and will continue to do so, whether students attend class in person or on-line. Because we are living in a postmodern, poststructuralist world, it behooves us as student affairs educators to think creatively and quickly about how to create environments welcoming to all students, particularly minoritized and marginalized students whose voices have often been unwelcome in academe. Although student affairs has traditionally served as the keeper of the moral code for college-age students in a rationalist academy, thankfully those doors have mostly closed, and we must now find the doors that allow us to create space and meaning for those voices silenced in the past as our institutions and students face an uncertain future in a postmodern world.

Reflection Questions

1. What philosophies and values will be honored and represented in student affairs practice in the next 25 years? How can student affairs professionals and the profession plan now for what *might be* in the future?
2. What educational and social science philosophy(ies) related to the student affairs profession and college students resonate with you? How does it (they) play out in higher education and student affairs practice?
3. How has the history and philosophy of student affairs informed how we think about college environments and their influence on our diverse students?
4. What values do you hold dear and how do they resonate or not with the values of the student affairs profession?
5. Discuss five of the prominent documents in the last 80 years of the student affairs profession. If we stand on the shoulders of those who come before us, what philosophy and values from the past do you hope will resonate for the profession in the future? What is not there now that needs inclusion?

References

ACPA: College Student Educators International & NASPA: Student Affairs Administrators in Higher Education. (2010). *ACPA/NASPA Professional competency areas for student affairs practitioners.* Washington, DC: Authors.

American Association for Higher Education (AAHE), American College Personnel Association (ACPA), & National Association of Student Personnel Administrators (NASPA). (1998). *Powerful partnerships: A shared responsibility for learning.* Washington, DC: Authors.

American College Personnel Association (ACPA). (1996). *The student learning imperative: Implications for student affairs.* Washington, DC: Author.

American Council on Education (ACE). (1994a). The student personnel point of view. In A. L. Rentz (Ed.), *Student affairs: A profession's heritage* (2nd ed., pp. 66–77). Lanham, MD: University Press of America. (Original work published 1937).

American Council on Education (ACE). (1994b). The student personnel point of view. In A. L. Rentz (Ed.), *Student affairs: A profession's heritage* (2nd ed., pp. 108–123). Lanham, MD: University Press of America. (Original work published 1949).

Anderson, J. D. (1988). *Education of Blacks in the South, 1860–1935.* Chapel Hill, NC: University of North Carolina Press.

Anzaldúa, G. E. (1999). *Borderlands, la frontera: The new Mestiza* (2nd ed.). San Francisco: Aunt Lute Press.

Anzaldúa, G. E. (2015). *Light in the dark, luz en lo oscuro: Rewriting identity, spirituality, reality.* Durham, NC: Duke University Press.

Arbuckle, D. (1953). *Student personnel services in higher education.* New York: McGraw-Hill.

Berdie, R. (1994). Student personnel work: Definition and redefinition. ACPA presidential address. In A. Rentz (Ed.), *Student affairs: A profession's heritage* (2nd ed., pp. 210–218). Washington, DC: American College Personnel Association. (Original work published 1966)

Birnbaum, R. (1988). *How colleges work: The cybernetics of academic organization and leadership.* San Francisco: Jossey-Bass.

Blackburn, S. (1996). *Oxford dictionary of philosophy.* Oxford, England, United Kingdom: Oxford University Press.

Boland, P. A., Stamatakos, L. C., & Rogers, R. R. (1994). *Reform in student affairs: A critique of student development.* Greensboro, NC: ERIC Counseling and Student Services Clearinghouse, School of Education, University of North Carolina at Greensboro.

Bourassa, D. M., & Kruger, K. (2001). The national dialogue on academic and student affairs collaboration. *New Directions for Higher Education, 116,* 9–38. doi:10.1002

Broido, E. M., & Manning, K. (2002). Philosophical foundations and current theoretical perspectives in qualitative research. *Journal of College Student Development, 43*(4), 434–445.

Brown, R. D. (1972). *Student development in tomorrow's higher education: A return to the academy.* Alexandria, VA: American College Personnel Association.

Brubacher, J. S. (1982). *On the philosophy of higher education.* San Francisco: Jossey-Bass.

Brubacher, J. S., & Rudy, W. (1976). *Higher education in transition: A history of American colleges and universities, 1636–1976.* New York: Harper & Row. (Original work published 1958).

Brubacher, J. S., & Rudy, W. (1997). *Higher education in transition: A history of American colleges and universities* (4th ed.). New Brunswick, NJ: Transaction.

Butler, J. D. (1968). *Four philosophies and their practice in education and religion* (3rd ed.). New York: Harper & Row.

Canon, H. J., & Brown, R. D. (Eds.). (1985). Applied ethics in student services. *New Directions for Student Services, 30.* San Francisco: Jossey-Bass.

Caple, R. B. (1998). *To mark the beginning: A social history of college student affairs.* Washington, DC: American College Personnel Association.

Carpenter, D. S. (1996). The philosophical heritage of student affairs. In A. Rentz & Associates (Eds.), *Student affairs functions in higher education* (2nd ed., pp. 3–27). Springfield, IL: Charles C Thomas.

Carpenter, S. (2011). The philosophical heritage of student affairs. In N. Zhang & Associates (Eds.), *Rentz's student affairs practice in higher education* (4th ed., pp. 3–29). Springfield, IL: Charles C Thomas.

Carpenter, S., Dean, S., & Haber-Curran, P. (2016). The philosophical heritage of student affairs. In N. Zhang & Associates (Eds.), *Rentz's student affairs practice in higher education* (5th ed., pp. 3–29). Springfield, IL: Charles C Thomas.

Chickering, A. W. (1969). *Education and identity.* San Francisco: Jossey-Bass.

Chickering, A. W., & Gamson, Z. F. (1987, June). Seven principles for good practice in undergraduate education. *AAHE Bulletin,* 1–6.

Commission of Professional Preparation of COSPA. (1994). Student development services in post-secondary education. In A. L. Rentz (Ed.), *Student affairs: A profession's heritage* (2nd ed., pp. 428–437). Alexandria, VA: ACPA Media. (Original work published 1975).

Coulthard, G. S. (2014). *Red skin, white masks: Rejecting the colonial politics of recognition.* Minneapolis, MN: University of Minnesota Press.

Council for the Advancement of Standards in Higher Education (CAS). (2003). Washington, DC.

Council of Student Personnel Associations in Higher Education (COSPA). (1975). Washington, DC.

Council of Student Personnel Associations in Higher Education (COSPA). (1994). Washington, DC.

Cowley, W. (1994a). The nature of student personnel work. In A. L. Rentz (Ed.), *Student affairs: A profession's heritage* (2nd ed., pp. 43–66). Lanham, MD: American College Personnel Association. (Original work published 1936)

Cowley, W. (1994b). Reflections of a troublesome but hopeful Rip van Winkle. In A. L. Rentz (Ed.), *Student affairs: A profession's heritage* (2nd ed., pp. 190–197). Lanham, MD:cAmerican College Personnel Association. (Original work published 1964).

Dalton, J., & Healy, M. (1984). Using values education activities to confront student conduct issues. *NASPA Journal, 22,* 19–25.

Derrida, J. (1978). *Writing and difference* (A. Bass, Trans.). Chicago, IL: University of Chicago Press. (Original work published 1967).

Dungy, G., & Gordon, S. A. (2011). The development of student affairs. In J. H. Schuh, S. R. Jones, S. R. Harper, & Associates (Eds.), *Student services: A handbook for the profession* (5th ed., pp. 61–79). San Francisco: Jossey-Bass.

Elkins Nesheim, B., Guentzel, M. J., Kellogg, A. H., McDonald, W. M., Wells, C. A., & Whitt, E. J. (2007). Outcomes for students of student affairs–academic affairs partnership programs. *Journal of College Student Development, 48*(4), 435–454. doi:10.1353

Evans, N. J., Forney, D. E., & Guido-DiBrito, F. (1998). *Student development in college: Theory, research, and practice.* San Francisco: Jossey-Bass.

Evans, N. J., Forney, D. E., Guido, F. M., Patton, L. D., & Renn, K. A. (2010). *Student development in college: Theory, research, and practice* (2nd ed.). San Francisco: Jossey-Bass.

Evans, N. J., & Reason, R. D. (2001). Guiding principles: A review and analysis of student affairs philosophical statements. *Journal of College Student Development, 42*(4), 359–377.

Fanon, F. (1967). *Black skin, white masks.* New York: Grove Press.

Fenske, R. H. (1989a). Evolution of the student services profession. In U. Delworth & G. Hanson & Associates (Eds.), *Student services: A handbook for the profession* (2nd ed., pp. 25–56). San Francisco: Jossey-Bass.

Fenske, R. H. (1989b). Historical foundations of student services. In U. Delworth & G. Hanson & Associates (Eds.), *Student services: A handbook for the profession* (2nd ed., pp. 5–24). San Francisco: Jossey-Bass.

Finkelstein, M. (1997). From tutor to specialized scholar: Academic professionalization in eighteenth and nineteenth century America. In L. F. Goodchild & H. S. Wechsler (Eds.), *The history of higher education* (2nd ed., pp. 80–93). ASHE Reader Series. Needham Heights, MA: Simon & Schuster Custom Publishing.

Foucault, M. (1978). *The history of sexuality: Vol. I. An introduction* (R. Hurley, Trans.). New York: Vintage Books.

Gamson, J. (2000). Sexualities, queer theory, and qualitative research. In N. K. Denzin & Y. S. Lincoln (Eds.), *Handbook of qualitative research* (2nd ed., pp. 347–365). Thousand Oaks, CA: Sage.

Gordon, L. G. (1991). *Gender and higher education in the progressive era.* New Haven, CT: Yale University Press.

Guido, F., Chávez, A. F., & Lincoln, Y. S. (2010). Underlying paradigms in student affairs research and practice. *Journal of Student Affairs Research and Practice, 47*(1), 1–22. Retrieved from http://journals.naspa.org/jsarp/vol47/iss1/art1/

Hardee, M. D. (1994). Perception and perfection: ACPA presidential address. In A. Rentz (Ed.), *Student affairs: A profession's heritage* (2nd ed., pp. 180–189). Washington, DC: American College Personnel Association. (Original work published 1963).

Hatfield, L. J., & Wise, V. L. (2015). *A guide to becoming a scholarly practitioner in student affairs.* Sterling, VA: Stylus.

Hinton, K., & Howard-Hamilton, M., & Rentz, A. (2016). A historical perspective of higher education and student affairs. In N. Zhang & Associates (Eds.), *Rentz's student affairs practice in higher education* (5th ed., pp. 28–61). Springfield, IL: Charles C Thomas.

hooks, b. (1992). *Black looks: Race and representation.* Boston: South End Press.

Horowitz, H. L. (1984). *Alma mater: Design and experience in the women's colleges from their nineteenth-century beginnings to the 1930s.* New York: Knopf.

Jones, S. R., & Abes, E. (2013). *Identity development of college students: Advancing frameworks for multiple dimensions of identity.* San Francisco: Jossey-Bass.

Keeling, R. P. (Ed.). (2004). *Learning reconsidered: A campus-wide focus on the student experience.* Washington, DC: American College Personnel Association & National Association of Student Personnel Administrators.

Keeling, R. P. (Ed.). (2006). *Learning reconsidered 2: A practical guide to implementing a campus-wide focus on the student experience.* Washington, DC: American College Personnel Association (ACPA), Association of College and University Housing Officers–International (ACUHO-I), Association of College Unions–International (ACUI), National Academic Advising Association (NACADA), National Association for Campus Activities (NACA), National Association of Student Personnel Administrators (NASPA), and National Intramural-Recreational Sports Association (NIRSA).

Kezar, A. (2001). Documenting the landscape: Results of a national study on academic and student affairs collaborations. *New Directions for Higher Education, 116,* 39–51.

Kezar, A. (2003). Enhancing innovative partnerships: Creating a change model for academic and student affairs collaboration. *Innovative Higher Education, 28*(2), 137–156.

Kezar, A., Hirsch, D. J., & Burack, C. (Eds.). (2002). Understanding the role of academic and student affairs collaboration in creating a successful learning environment. *New Directions for Higher Education, 116,* 1–8.

Knock, G. H. (1988). The philosophical heritage of student affairs. In A. L. Rentz & G. L. Saddlemire (Eds.), *Student affairs functions in higher education* (2nd ed., pp. 3–20). Springfield, IL: Charles C Thomas.

Kohlberg, L. (1969). Stage and sequence: The cognitive-developmental approach to socialization. In D. A. Goslin (Ed.), *Handbook of socialization theory and research* (pp. 82–173). Skokie, IL: Rand McNally.

Kuh, G. D. (1996). Guiding principles for creating seamless learning environments for undergraduates. *Journal of College Student Development, 37*(2), 135–148.

Kuh, G. D., Kinzie, J. I., Schuh, J. H., Whitt, E. J., & Associates. (2005). *Student success in college: Creating conditions that matter.* San Francisco: Jossey-Bass.

Kuh, G., Shedd, J., & Whitt, E. (1987). Student affairs and liberal education: Unrecognized (and unappreciated) common law partners. *Journal of College Student Development, 28,* 252–260.

Lather, P. (2007). *Getting lost: Feminists efforts toward a double(d) science.* Albany, NY: State University of New York Press.

Lemonedes, G. (2018). *Academic and student affairs educators make meaning of their collaboration on campus* (Doctoral dissertation). Retrieved from ProQuest Dissertations and Theses database. (Accession No. 2099234321)

Lloyd-Jones, E. M., & Smith, M. R. (1954). *Student personnel work as deeper teaching.* New York: Harper Collins.

Magolda, P. M., & Quaye, S. J. (2011). Teaching in the co-curriculum. In J. H. Schuh, S. R. Jones, S. R. Harper, & Associates (Eds.), *Student services: A handbook for the profession* (5th ed., pp. 385–398). San Francisco: Jossey-Bass.

Martin, J., & Samels, J. E. (2001). Lessons learned: Eight best practices for new partnerships. *New Directions for Higher Education, 116,* 89–100. doi:10.1002.

McDermott, J. J. (Ed.). (1981). *The philosophy of John Dewey: Vol. 1—The structure of experience & Vol. 2—The lived experience.* Chicago: University of Chicago Press.

Miller, T. K., & Prince, J. S. (1977). *The future of student affairs: A guide to student development for tomorrow's higher education.* San Francisco: Jossey-Bass.

Minthorn, R. S., & Shotton, H. J. (Eds.). (2018). *Reclaiming indigenous research in higher education.* New Brunswick, NJ: Rutgers University Press.

Mueller, K. H. (1961). *Student personnel work in higher education.* Boston: Houghton-Mifflin.

Nuss, E. (1996). The development of student affairs. In S. R. Komives & D. Woodard (Eds.), *Student services: A handbook for the profession* (3rd ed., pp. 22–42). San Francisco: Jossey-Bass.

Nuss, E. M (2003). The development of student affairs. In S. K. Komives, D. B. Woodard, Jr., & Associates (Eds.), *Student services: A handbook for the profession* (4th ed., pp. 65–88). San Francisco: Jossey-Bass.

Pascarella, E. T., & Terenzini, P. (1978). The relation of student's precollege characteristics and freshman year experience to voluntary attrition. *Research in Higher Education, 9*(4), 347–366. Retrieved from http://www.jstor.org.unco.idm.oclc.org/stable/40195235

Patton, L. D. (2011). Perspectives on identity, disclosure, and the campus environment among African American gay and bisexual men at one historically black college. *Journal of College Student Development, 52,* 77–98.

Patton, L. D., Renn, K. A., Guido, F. M., & Quaye, S. J. (2016). *Student development in college: Theory, research, and practice* (3rd ed.). San Francisco: Jossey-Bass.

Pérez, E. (1999). *The decolonial imagery: Writing Chicanas into history.* Bloomington, IN: Indiana University Press.

Perry, W. G., Jr. (1968). *Forms of intellectual and ethical development in the college years: A scheme.* New York: Holt, Rinehart, & Winston.

Pierce, D. (2017). The curious comeback of the dreaded QR code. *WIRED Magazine.* Retrieved from https://www.wired.com/story/the-curious-comeback-of-the-dreaded-qr-code/

Pope, R. L., & Mueller, J. A. (2017). Multicultural competence and change on campus. In J. H. Schuh, S. R. Jones, & V. Torres (Eds.), *Student services: A handbook for the profession* (6th ed., pp. 392–407). San Francisco: Jossey-Bass.

Reason, R. D., & Broido, E. M. (2011). Philosophies and values. In J. H. Schuh, S. R. Jones, S. R. Harper, & Associates (Eds.), *Student services: A handbook for the profession* (5th ed., pp. 80–95). San Francisco: Jossey-Bass.

Reason, R. D., & Broido, E. M. (2017). Philosophies and values. In J. H. Schuh, S. R. Jones, & V. Torres (Eds.), *Student services: A handbook for the profession* (6th ed., pp. 39–55). San Francisco: Jossey-Bass.

Roberts, D. C. (July 1998). Student learning was always supposed to be the core of our work—What happened? *About Campus, 3*(3), 18–22.

Rokkum, J., & Junco, R. (2017). Left behind: How the profession of student affairs is underprepared to meet students where they (digitally) are. In J. H. Schuh, S.

R. Jones, & V. Torres (Eds.), *Student services: A handbook for the profession* (6th ed., pp. 344–358). San Francisco: Jossey-Bass.

Rudolph, F. (1976). The American college student: From theologian to technocrat in 300 years. *National Association of Student Personnel Administrators Journal, 14,* 13–39.

Rudolph, F. (1990). *The American college and university: A history.* Athens: University of Georgia Press. (Original work published 1962).

Sandeen, A. (1985). The legacy of values education in college student personnel work. In J. Dalton (Ed.), *Promoting values development in college students* (Monograph Series, Vol. 4, pp. 1–16). Washington, DC: NASPA.

Schwartz, R. A., & Bryan, W. A. (1983). Introduction and overview. In W. A. Bryan & R. A. Schwartz (Eds.), *The eighties: Challenge for fraternities and sororities* (pp. 1–5). Carbondale, IL: ACPA Media.

Schwartz, R., & Stewart, D. L. (2017). The history of student affairs. In J. H. Schuh, S. R. Jones, & V. Torres (Eds.), *Student services: A handbook for the profession* (6th ed., pp. 20–38). San Francisco: Jossey-Bass.

Smith, L. T. (2012). *Decolonizing methodologies* (2nd ed.). London, England, United Kingdom: Zed Books.

Smith, L. T., Tuck, E., & Yang, K. W. (Eds.). (2018). *Indigenous and decolonizing studies in education: Mapping the long view.* New York: Routledge.

Solomon, B. M. (1985). *In the company of educated women: A history of women and higher education in America.* New Haven, CT: Yale University Press.

Stage, F. K., Watson, L. W., & Terrell, M. (1999). *Enhancing student learning: Setting the campus context.* Lanham, MD: University Press of America.

Stern, R. A. (1986). *Pride of place: Building the American dream.* New York: Houghton Mifflin.

Stewart, D. L. (2009). Perceptions of multiple identities among Black college students. *Journal of College Student Development, 50,* 253–270.

Strange, C. (1991). Managing college environments: Theory and practice. In T. K. Miller, R. B. Winston, Jr., & Associates (Eds.), *Administration and leadership in student affairs: Actualizing student development in higher education* (2nd ed., pp. 159–199). Muncie, IN: Accelerated Development.

Strange, C. (2011). Student development: The evolution and status of an essential idea. In M. E. Wilson (Ed.), *College student development theory* (2nd ed., ASHE Reader Series, pp. 17–33). Boston: Pearson.

Strange, C., & Banning, J. H. (2001). *Educating by design: Creating campus learning environments that work.* San Francisco: Jossey-Bass.

Sue, D. W., & Sue, D. (2003). *Counseling the culturally different: Theory and practice* (4th ed.). New York: Wiley.

Thelin, J. R., & Gasman, M. (2017). Historical overview of American higher education. In J. H. Schuh, S. R. Jones, & V. Torres (Eds.), *Student services: A handbook for the profession* (6th ed., pp. 3–19). San Francisco: Jossey-Bass.

Upcraft, M. (1988). Managing right. In M. Upcraft & M. Barr (Eds.), Managing student affairs effectively (pp. 65–78). *New Directions for Student Services, 41.* San Francisco: Jossey-Bass.

Watt, S. K. (Ed.). (2015). *Designing transformative multicultural initiatives: Theoretical foundations, practical applications and facilitator considerations.* Sterling, VA: Stylus.

Westfall, S. B. (1999). Partnership to connect in- and out-of-class experiences. *New Directions for Student Services, 87,* 51–61. doi:10.1002

Whitt, E. J. (2011). Academic and student affairs partnerships. In J. H Schuh, S. R. Jones, S. R. Harper, & Associates (Eds.), *Student services: A handbook for the profession* (5th ed., pp. 482–496). San Francisco: Jossey-Bass

Whitt, E. J., Elkins Nesheim, B., Guentzel, M. J., Kellogg, A. H., McDonald, W. M., & Wells, C. A. (2008). Principles of good practice for academic and student affairs partnership programs. *Journal of College Student Development, 49*(3), 235–249. doi:10.1353.

Wrenn, C. G. (1951). *Student personnel work in college with emphasis on counseling and group sessions.* New York: Ronald Press.

Wright, B. (1989). "For the children of the infidels"?: American Indian education in the colonial colleges. *American Indian Culture and Research Journal, 12*(3), 1–14.

Wright, B., & Tierney, W. G. (1991, March). American Indians in higher education: A history of cultural conflict. *Change, 23*(2), 11–18. doi:10/1080/00091383.1991.9937673

Young, R. B. (1993). Editor's notes. In R. B. Young (Ed.), Identifying and implementing the essential values of the profession. *New Directions for Student Services, 61,* 1–3. San Francisco: Jossey-Bass.

Young, R. B. (1996). Guiding values and philosophy. In S. R. Komives, D. B. Woodard, Jr., & Associates (Eds.), *Student services: A handbook for the profession* (3rd ed., pp. 83–105). San Francisco: Jossey-Bass.

Young, R. B. (2003). Philosophies and values guiding the student affairs profession. In S. R. Komives, D. B. Woodard, Jr., & Associates (Eds.), *Student services: A handbook for the profession* (4th ed., pp. 89–106). San Francisco: Jossey-Bass.

Young, R. B., & Elfrink, V. L. (1991). Essential values of the profession. *Journal of College Student Development, 32,* 47–55.

Chapter 2

THEORETICAL FRAMEWORKS ON ENVIRONMENTS

Tonisha B. Lane and Blanca E. Rincón

The university's mariachi band was practicing on the quad in preparation for the big night. Before the graduation ceremony, with the familiar sound of the violins and trumpets in the background, Juanita and her family posed for pictures in front of the murals depicting the Chicano[1] Movement. Juanita was excited that her 4 years at California State University[2] would culminate with her parents joining her in walking across the stage during the Latinx Graduation, a student-organized graduation ceremony. In many ways, receiving her titulo (degree) as an ingeniera (engineer) was a family affair. It only seemed fitting then that her family, both near and far, could join in celebrating this accomplishment without having to worry about ticket allotments or language barriers. Juanita was proud that she could honor her family's sacrifices and support by becoming the first in her family to finish college. She was also joined by members of her sorority, her family away from home.

The interaction between students and the campus environments in which they are situated is depicted in the vignette above, where we learn about Juanita who is graduating from the California State University, a Hispanic serving institution (HSI). The following questions speak to such interaction: How do Latinx[3] students' ethnic identity development differ by institutional

---

1. Chicano is the term used to refer to a person of Mexican American descent. The origins of the term are attributed to the Chicano Movement of the 1960s, thus the term also connotes a leftist political leaning.
2. The institutions profiled in this chapter are simply examples used to describe and illuminate aspects of the environmental theories addressed in the chapter. To further your learning, we encourage you to apply the theories to your own institutional context.
3. Latinx is a gender inclusive term used to refer to a person of Latin American descent.

type? How does attending a HSI support Latinx students' sense of belonging on campus? Campus environments consist of the physical, psychological, and socially constructed spaces that shape the behaviors and experiences of those who lead, work, and study in colleges and universities. Conversely, each campus environment is molded by members of its community. The study of campus environments is important for student affairs educators because it provides the context in which students experience college and where student development can be promoted or thwarted. Environmental or ecological-based theories differ from other student development theories in that they do not explain student development outcomes (e.g., social identity, cognitive, and self-authorship outcomes). Rather, they attend to the processes that lead to developmental outcomes, that is, how and why a particular developmental outcome occurs.

Unlike other important factors leading to student learning and success, campus environments can be altered. As student affairs educators, we are tasked with constructing and cultivating learning environments that lead to optimal development for all students who enroll at our colleges and universities. Because many colleges and universities were not originally designed with students who hold marginalized identities in mind, we must deconstruct and reconstruct spaces with low-income; first-generation; women; students of color; undocumented; and LGBTQ+ (lesbian, gay, bisexual, transgender and queer [or questioning], and others) students in mind. As such, throughout the chapter, the examples we provide center on promoting campus spaces with marginalized students in mind. In this chapter, we attend to the theories that inform our understanding of campus environments and how campus environments shape college students' developmental processes. Then, we discuss as implications, how environmental theories might inform our practice as student affairs educators. We conclude by discussing the opportunities for future research and extensions of ecological approaches to the study of higher education and student affairs, offering recommendations for practitioners.

Campus Environments

Several theories and frameworks inform our understanding of campus environments. This review begins with an overview of theoretical perspectives by discussing the attributes of campus environments.

Attributes of the Campus Environment

In a comprehensive review of the literature, Strange and Banning (2015) identified four interconnected attributes of the campus environment: (a) physical, (b) human aggregate, (c) social construction, and (d) organizational. Together, these four components provide a framework for understanding how campus environments shape student experiences, their level of involvement, sense of safety, and feelings of belonging on campus.

The Physical Dimension. The *physical* dimension refers to both the natural and human-constructed aspects of the campus environment that shape student behaviors. For example, the natural component may consist of a park that sits at the center of campus, like the one you will find at the University of California Irvine. The open space and greenery may define the physical space as one that functions as a gathering place among friends, a place to engage in outdoor activities, or a good place to read under the shade of the trees. Human-built components include the design of buildings, such as the University of Nevada-Las Vegas' Hospitality Hall, which was designed to reflect a hotel you might find on the Las Vegas strip. The intentionality behind this building's construction, which includes a test kitchen and a student-run cafe, provides experiential learning spaces that prepare students to master elements of the hospitality industry.

The Human Aggregate Dimension. The second dimension, the *human aggregate,* depicts how the dominant characteristics of the student body on campus collectively shape the campus environment. These characteristics include students' personality traits, interests, and demographics. For example, Marquette University, a private Catholic Jesuit university, may attract students who are drawn to the servant leadership model found at many Jesuit institutions. As such, students may develop service-based student organizations, get involved in alternative spring breaks, and expect service-learning pedagogies in the classroom. The demand for service-based experiences, then, may reinforce the university's focus of service to others.

The Socially Constructed Dimension. The *socially constructed* dimension of the campus environment focuses on the ways students perceive and make meaning of their environments, that is, where students' perception of their campus environment constitutes their lived reality and dictates their behaviors within the institutional context. Many scholars have aimed to describe the phenomenon of social climate, but few have been as impactful to our understanding of the experiences of racially and ethnically minoritized groups as Hurtado, Milem, Clayton-Pedersen, and Allen's (1998) campus racial climate framework. The campus racial climate framework builds on previous environmental theories to show the interconnectedness between human aggregates, represented by *structural diversity,* an institution's physical and organizational dimensions; a university's *historical legacy of inclusion;* and the social construction, that is, *psychological* and *behavioral* responses of actors within an institutional context. These four dimensions exist within a larger sociohistorical and political context. Together, these external and internal factors shape the racial context of the student experience.

Returning to the vignette at the beginning of this chapter, we might infer that the social and political climate of California, where California State University is situated, coupled with a racially and ethnically diverse student body and culturally relevant curricular and co-curricular offerings (e.g., Latinx graduation and Chicana and Chicano studies) may cultivate a campus environment that fosters meaningful and productive cross-racial/ethnic peer interactions. It might also be safe to infer that students like Juanita feel a sense of belonging on a campus where they see themselves and their communities reflected in positive ways (e.g., murals and mariachi music).

The Organizational Dimension. Finally, the *organizational* dimension is depicted by institutional structures and processes in place to support institutional goals. Paul Quinn College's (n.d.) vision of transforming "ability into action and potential into achievement by encouraging all students to embrace ideals of disciplined work, servant leadership, and initiatives in preparation for lives of financial freedom, community engagement, and outstanding character" (para. 3) is supported by its urban college model. In pursuit of this goal are university leadership-led efforts to turn the football field into an organic farm. The creation of this farm met the purpose of providing jobs for students, many of whom are Pell eligible, and healthy food options to the neighboring community surrounding the college, a federally designated food desert.

Organizational processes can also be understood through a cultural lens, that is, members' collective understanding of the university's values and beliefs. Tierney (1988) defined *organizational culture* as the "values, processes, and goals held by those most intimately involved in the organization's workings [and is] reflected in what is done, how it is done, and who is involved in doing it" (p. 3). He identified six essential concepts for understanding organizational cultures in academic settings: environment, mission, socialization, information, strategy, and leadership. Similarly, Gonzáles (2002) identified three elements of the campus culture: the social, physical, and epistemological world. The *social world* consists of the demographic makeup of students, staff, and faculty on campus, and their proximity to political power. For example, one might question a university's commitment to diversity if the student body reflects gender, sexual, racial/ethnic, and religious diversity, yet the staff and faculty do not. The *physical world* includes architectural design, symbols, and artifacts. In the opening vignette, we see how the mural of the Chicano Movement might serve as a source of inspiration and strength for Juanita, one that depicts her and her family's experience of resistance in the face of oppression. Such representation can be powerful for students attending historically white colleges and universities. Conversely, the university's mascot, which perpetuates racist depictions of indigenous communities as violent, may send a strong message to indigenous students that they are not valued by the institution and do not belong. The *epistemo-*

logical world refers to various ways of knowing and how these knowledges are situated within the university. For example, whether women's and gender studies courses are offered, taught by tenure-track faculty, or a general requirement for graduation sends a strong message about their value.

Campus Environments and Student Development

In this section, the authors explore person-environment frameworks that inform our work in higher education and student affairs. To begin, they present Bronfenbrenner's ecological model of human development as a lens through which to view campus environments in relation to student development. Then, more specifically, they discuss the impact of institutional types on student behavior and development.

Bronfenbrenner's Ecological Model of Human Development. Scholars have studied the role of campus environments in shaping students' developmental outcomes. Informed by human ecology—the study of how humans adapt to or alter their environment for the purpose of survival— Bronfenbrenner's (1979) ecological model of human development posits that student development results from the reciprocal interaction between the person and environment.

Like other developmental theories, the ecological model of human development still focuses on the individual; however, central to Bronfenbrenner's model is the environment in which an individual is embedded. As such, the campus environment provides the context in which college student development can be cultivated or thwarted. Since the initial model, several iterations have followed. We present the most current iteration, the ecobiological model of human development, in Figure 2.1 (Bronfenbrenner & Morris, 2006). We revisit the vignette at the beginning of the chapter to discuss the convergence between Juanita's STEM (science, technology, engineering, and math) and ethnic identity development through Bronfenbrenner's ecological model of human development.

Four interconnected and interactive components comprise this model: process, person, context, and time. Bronfenbrenner's (1979) model describes the process by which an individual's resources, demand, and dispositions (e.g., Juanita's math or science proclivities and access to same-ethnicity peers), represented by person, responds to the context within a given time interval. *Time* is understood at various levels, including *microtime, mesotime* which speaks to the duration of developmental activity, and *macrotime* which includes general trends in society at large (e.g., current efforts to get more women and students of color into STEM majors). The *context* is represented by four levels, each embedded within the others and surrounding the person: micro, meso, exo, and macro. The *microsystems* include persons (e.g.,

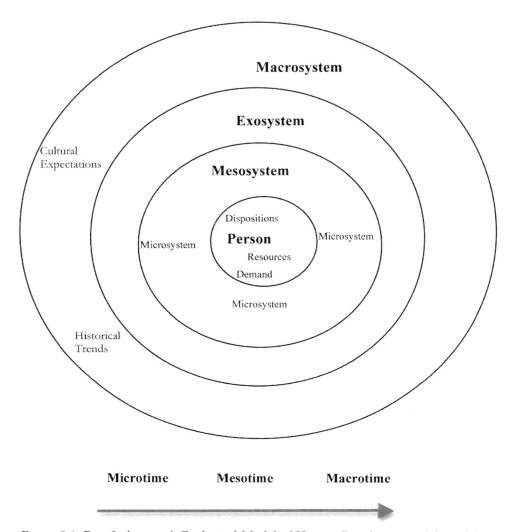

Figure 2.1. Bronfenbrenner's Ecological Model of Human Development. Adapted from *Making Human Beings Human: Bioecological Perspectives on Human Development* by U. Bronfenbrenner, 2005, Thousand Oaks, CA, Sage Publications.

Juanita's sorority sisters, engineering peers, and family members) and symbols that are closest to the individual. The *mesosystem* represents the interactions between microsystems (e.g., the interaction between Juanita's sorority responsibilities and engineering responsibilities). These interactions can be synergistic or dissonant, resulting in disparate impacts. For example, if Juanita's sorority sisters are also pursuing engineering majors, then the roles and responsibilities based on these identities will be complementary; however, if these consist of two separate peer groups, this may result in a fragmentation between Juanita's identity as a member of her sorority and as an engineer. Outside of the micro- and mesosystems are the *exo-* and *macrosystems,* which represent external forces immediately removed (e.g., family) and further removed (e.g., societal constructions of what it means to be an engineer or Latinx) from the individual, respectively. These external factors are less malleable than other aspects of the model. Taken together, the various components of the model shed light into why different students' developmental processes, in this case, Juanita's ethnic and STEM identity, may manifest in vastly different ways.

Institutional Types. Institutional type, size, and mission can have different impacts on student behavior and development. For example, research shows that black women in STEM fare better at historically black colleges and universities (HBCUs) (Perna et al., 2009). Environmental factors, such as faculty interaction, smaller classrooms, and access to mentors and role models, all seem to benefit the persistence of black women. HSIs promote a positive academic self-concept among Hispanic students (Cuellar, 2014). In addition to other objectives advanced by stakeholders and student needs, institutional missions may be shaped by geographic location (e.g., urban vs. rural). For example, for-profit colleges and universities (FPCUs) tend to be located in urban metropolitan areas where significant numbers of people of color reside (Pusser & Turner, 2004). For students disinterested in relocating to attend college, these for-profit institutions create a viable option for them (Boykin, 2017). The changing higher education landscape necessitates that student affairs educators have an awareness of the diverse institutional types and how they can be leveraged to support positive student outcomes. The following institutional types are presented below: community colleges, minority serving institutions (MSIs), and for-profit colleges and universities (FPCUs).

COMMUNITY COLLEGES. Community colleges have multiple foci, including the offering of (a) associate degrees or the first two years of coursework of a baccalaureate degree, (b) vocational training, (c) developmental education, and (d) lifelong learning opportunities (Hirt, 2006). Because of these various foci, community colleges also have broad access policies (Iloh & Toldson, 2013). Hence, they admit students with a different set of admissions requirements than do traditional colleges and universities, and they have a vested interest in supporting students, regardless of their readiness for college. Their relative affordability and flexibility of instruction and degree offerings (e.g., associates and certificates) lend themselves to a diverse student population across race, age, generational status, and employment status. College involvement tends to be a problem at community colleges because many students attend part-time and have other responsibilities (e.g., work and parenting) that prevent them from getting engaged in the campus environment (Hagedorn, 2014). Some student affairs educators mitigate these challenges by offering day-time and online opportunities (Hagedorn, 2014), but this phenomenon continues to be an issue. Yet, community colleges that have managed to offer services, such as daycare, are seeing upward trends, especially among women, in student engagement (Stavredes & Herder, 2014).

There is also some research that suggests community colleges could do more to be inclusive of LGBTQ+ students. Pitcher, Camacho, Renn, and Woodford (2018) highlighted that gay-straight alliances can be found in some community colleges, but there are far fewer resources available than at other types of institutions. Part of the reason is due to limited funding; however, researchers have also suggested the climate impacts progress in this area. In a mixed-methods study on the experiences of LGBTQ students in community colleges, Garvey, Taylor, and Rankin (2015) illuminated how in-classroom experiences influence student experiences with the overall campus climate. Specifically, these classroom environments tend to be unwelcoming to LGBTQ communities and are less likely to have representation in the course content. The authors concluded that institutional leaders should conduct campus climate studies, make more resources available for faculty (especially part-time faculty) to incorporate course materials related to these populations, and institute spaces for LGBTQ students.

MINORITY-SERVING INSTITUTIONS. Minority serving institutions (MSIs) encompass HBCUs, tribal colleges and universities (TCUs), HSIs, and Asian American/Native American/Pacific islander-serving institutions (AANAPISIs). It is important to note that HBCUs and TCUs were created for the purpose of meeting the needs of racially and ethnically diverse students, whereas the HSI and AANAPISI designation emerged out of the populations these institutions enrolled. In addition to racial-ethnic representation, HSIs and AANAPISIs must have at least 50 percent low-income students (U.S. Department of Education, 2017). We provide an overview of MSIs in Table 2.1.

Many of these institutions focus on undergraduate teaching, community engagement, and culturally relevant practices. Institutions, such as HBCUs and TCUs, also intentionally recruit faculty who represent the student populations who attend their institutions (Conrad & Gasman, 2015). Students who attend MSIs often report a greater sense of belonging, and cultural pride, and an emphasis on collectivism (Conrad & Gasman, 2015). Conrad and Gasman (2015) found that the artifacts, symbols, and traditions practiced at many MSIs also reflect the students who attend them, which strengthens their connectedness to these institutions. Finally, interactions among students and faculty, staff, and administrators—inside and outside the classroom environment—play an instrumental role in how students experience these environments. In particular, they perceive them as "inclusive and welcoming" (Conrad & Gasman, 2015, p. 24).

Table 2.1
OVERVIEW OF MINORITY-SERVING INSTITUTIONS (MSIS)

Institutional Type	Established/ Designation Rendered	Designation	Example	Number of Institution	Other
Asian American/ Native American/ Pacific Islander Serving Institutions AANAPISIs)	2009 (federal government designation created)	Asian Americans and Pacific Islanders comprise at least 25 % of undergraduate enrollment and 50% low-income students	University of California, Los Angeles	172	Comprise 3% of all U.S. institutions and enrolls more than 41% of AAPI and boasts 78% retention rate
Hispanic Serving Institutions (HSIs)	1980 (federal government designation created)	Latinx students comprise at least 25% of total undergraduate enrollment and 50% of low-income students	University of Houston	492	Enrolls 21.9% of all U.S. college students and 60.8% of all Hispanic students
Historically Black Colleges and Universities (HBCUS)	1837 (Cheney University first HBCU founded)	Established prior to 1964 to educate Black Americans	Jackson State University	102 (including public and private institutions) 121 institutions existed in the 1930s	Accounts for 9% of Black student enrollment and 22% of bachelor's degree attainment
Tribal Colleges nd Universities (TCUs)	1968 (Navajo Nation created, now called Diné College as first TCU)	Indigenous and/or Alaskan Native students comprise at least 25% of undergraduate enrollment	Diné College	38 (37 TCUs in the U.S. and 1 in Canada)	86% of TCU students complete their degrees compared to 10% at PWIs

Source: U.S. Department of Education, National Center for Education Statistics, Integrated Postsecondary Education Data System (IPEDS), 2017.

Because HSIs and AANAPISIs were not established as MSIs in the same way HBCUs and TCUs were, some of these institutions have been slower to intentionally enact practices that will support their growing populations. To this end, Garcia and Okhidoi (2015) recommended that HSIs improve their environments to better serve Latinx students. Some examples include requiring ethnic studies courses as part of the general education requirements for graduation, establishing an ethnic studies department, and institutionalizing equal opportunity programs that have been known to advance positive outcomes among Latinx students (e.g., TRiO Student Support Services).

FOR-PROFIT COLLEGES AND UNIVERSITIES. FPCUs are impacted by exosystem and macrosystem factors undergirded by market-driven decision making. FPCUs are treated as marginal higher education institutions, in part due to their missions, values, and student outcomes (Zamani-Gallaher, 2004). Yet, as Boykin (2017) pointed out, these institutions are growing in popularity and appear to be a mainstay within the U.S. higher education landscape. One reason may be that FPCUs create opportunities to earn credentials for individuals not adequately served within the current system of higher education. Currently, individuals without some type of postsecondary credential will be less likely to secure gainful employment and livable wages (Boykin, 2017). FPCUs mostly train students for vocational purposes in fields that are increasingly in demand (e.g., information technology, nursing, business, and education) (Ruch, 2001). Such emphases have resulted in certain types of students making up a majority of their student population including women, people of color, married individuals with children, and part-time and full-time professionals (Iloh & Toldson, 2013). Many have expressed concerns about the high debt and low employment for-profit graduates encounter upon degree completion (Deming, Goldin, & Katz, 2012). Yet, two-year degree earners at FPCUs tend to have higher wages than community college associate degree recipients. Although their programs and institutional mission provide much flexibility, some have questioned how these institutions may further marginalize minoritized groups due to the less-than-ideal outcomes of their graduates (Iloh & Toldson, 2013).

Holistic student learning and development seems to be limited at FPCUs, where much attention is placed on academic success. As part of market-driven strategies, FPCUs invest heavily in programs and services, such as intrusive advising models, early warning systems, and mandatory tutoring and counseling (Cohen, Brawer, & Kisker, 2013). According to Cohen et al. (2013), "From a profit-making perspective, money spent helping students reach their educational training goals is far less than the loss of students' tuition revenues if they drop out" (p. 478). However, students at FPCUs may miss out on important opportunities for socialization and holistic development. As Cohen et al. (2013) noted, "Because for-profits have a paucity of amenities—rarely a campus, no libraries or recreational facilities—students spend little time milling about between classes or in extracurricular activities" (p. 476). For instance, contrary to ideals of public higher education, Persell and Wenglinsky (2004) found that FPCUs are less politically involved in terms of voting and other political engagement. They are also less likely to be involved with other forms of civic engagement (e.g., community service).

In sum, although the aforementioned institutional types have different levels of support for students, they are all involved with making college more accessible for marginalized groups. Some institutions have established institutional practices ensuring the successful outcomes of students, whereas others may need to think more creatively about student learning and development.

Implications

Physical Space

The physical environment plays an important role in helping students find community as well as feelings of safety and inclusion. Having physical spaces, such as centers, institutions, common areas, and thematic residence halls, are critical for encouraging students to gather with individuals who have similar or different backgrounds and interests. Concerning the latter, research has shown these spaces may be vital for promoting cross-racial relationships (Park, 2014). When considering the physical components (e.g., terrain and landscape), campus designers should provide adequate green space for students to gather or engage in individual activities, such as studying or relaxing. These spaces can be stimulating for both active engagement and reconnecting to nature. Students who possess personal characteristics that find value in taking advantage of the outdoors can benefit from these arrangements.

On the other hand, these spaces should also be assessed to ensure they are accessible. Far too often, spaces designed to be aesthetically appealing may present danger for students who may be wheelchair bound or have other limited forms of mobility. Additionally, adequate parking spaces for persons with disabilities should be available and in close proximity to buildings. Restroom facilities should also be examined to ensure that they have enough space for wheelchairs to enter and exit. Further, centering students with disabilities within a Bronfenbrenner's ecological systems model can be helpful in understanding all the ways college campuses may or may not be equipped to support these students.

Online learning environments may or may not be attached to a traditional college or university that encompasses a face-to-face component. Whereas some institutions operate solely online, traditional colleges and universities are increasingly offering online degrees. Yet, the question remains: How can student affairs educators help students foster a sense of community and access the resources and services they need in order to be productive students and citizens? In these spaces, student affairs educators may be able to work with faculty and other administrators to think more creatively about how to keep these students engaged. Group work in courses and co-curricular experiences, such as internships and service-learning experiences in students' local communities, may represent ways to help online learners feel part of the campus community.

Student Development

Because one's development is influenced by the environment, some contexts lend themselves to more substantial growth and development of particular student populations. For instance, Conrad and Gasman (2015) illuminated how MSIs create opportunities for students to engage in collaboration to solve problems that impact their communities. By doing so, students are able to advance the democratic and liberal principles upon which modern higher education was founded, "while maintaining and replenishing their identities by engaging in culturally relevant learning" (Conrad & Gasman, 2015, p. 262). Their study also highlighted how students are empowered to be both teachers and learners in these settings, demonstrated through their leadership and ownership of programs, such as supplemental instruction and peer-led team learning. Although similar programs exist at PWIs, the environmental elements that undergird these practices in MSIs may result in greater efficacy. Unlike some traditional institutions, Conrad and Gasman found that among the 12 MSIs in their study, students were valued contributors to knowledge production and transmission.

Additionally, Conrad and Gasman (2015) posited that collectivism and a belief in the intellectual capacities of *all* students took precedence in these environments. Developmental outcomes, such as racial identity congruence and intellectual growth, may be more plausible because these settings are more welcoming and inclusive of the backgrounds, knowledge, and identities that students bring to college. Further, Conrad and Gasman argued that more educational institutions should apply the practices enacted at MSIs.

Bronfenbrenner (2005) pointed out developmentally instigative characteristics can induce or inhibit experiences in the college environment. To this end, student affairs educators should work to create engaging environments on their college campuses to encourage students to get involved and establish a community. Involvement in challenging and supportive opportunities can also be instrumental in student persistence (Astin, 1999; Sanford,

1966). Yet, when planning such opportunities, much of what is available on college campuses caters to white, middle-class, able-bodied, heterosexual, cisgender, and legacy students.

Ecological theories can help student affairs educators consider who may be left out of these experiences. For example, programs that encourage sex positivity may unknowingly leave out students who are LGBTQ+. Additionally, there are many campus spaces that subscribe to the gender binary, including bathrooms, residence halls, and single-sex lounges (Nicolazzo & Marine, 2015). Such failures to establish environments that include all students may lead to difficulties finding a community, getting involved, and feeling safe and included on campus (Strange & Banning, 2001). Hence, the scholarly essay, "Where's My Queer BBQ?: Supporting Queer Students at Historically Women's Colleges" by Dews (2018), shows how one student navigated her queer and gender identity at a women's college. In this essay, Dews noted that although there were many aspects of her college-going experience that were affirming to her identity as a woman, there was substantial room for improvement to help her feel more integrated in the institution as a queer student.

Ecological models also aid in understanding the processes students may undergo while in college. Student affairs educators are an important socializing agent in preparing students to be part of a democratic society (during and) once they leave college. Although many students may live in homogenous communities prior to coming to college (Tatum, 1997), the work of college professionals should encompass intentional efforts to encourage more open-mindedness concerning diversity and build interest in establishing cross-racial relationships. For example, Park (2014) found that student clubs and organizations create subcultures that may be insightful into understanding why monoracial relationships and friendships persist on college campuses. Whereas students of color tend to have more cross-racial friendships, white students largely do not. Using the *National Longitudinal Study of Freshman*, Park found that Greek, religious, and ethnic student organizations negatively predicted the likelihood of cross-racial relationships. As such, Park suggested that student affairs educators encourage their student leaders to consider why their organizations are more likely to recruit certain kinds of members. Her findings also highlighted the opportunity to facilitate collaborative programming for groups that tend to have lower levels of cross-racial participation. Such collaborations could yield more cross-racial participation in student groups and higher possibilities of individuals interacting across racial identities.

Policy

Bronfenbrenner's (2005) ecological model shows that although students may not be involved or present in the exosystem, the policies and practices established at this level impact their daily lives directly or indirectly. This notion is especially apparent at community colleges where change happens much more quickly than at other institutional types (Cohen et al., 2013). Such changes can have draconian effects on students who typically attend community colleges (e.g., adult learners, parents with children in the household, and working professionals). A failure to stay abreast of the changing policies and practices can result in financial consequences, a lower GPA, or even attrition. Professionals working in these environments should consider how technology can be used to aid students in accessing information in a timely manner. On the other hand, community college professionals should also be cognizant that the significant number of adult learners attending college for the first time and/or for the purposes of retooling may be less familiar with computer technology (Stavredes & Herder, 2014). Making admissions applications available in paper form and responding to phone call inquiries are ways to alleviate student stressors and ease transitions into college life.

Students of color and LGBTQ+ students seeking out spaces where students similar to themselves gather should be normalized and validated on college campuses. In the seminal text, *Why Are All the Black Kids Sitting Together in the Cafeteria,* Tatum (1997) showed that although the gathering of black students and other students of color is perceived as self-segregation by dominant groups, students of color are seeking spaces that provide a critical mass where they do not have to feel isolated and alienated. Other researchers, such as Nicolazzo, Pitcher, Renn, and Woodford (2017), pointed out that trans* students are also interested in identifying spaces where they can gather and form kinships with other trans* individuals. Student affairs educators should also be mindful that when white, heterosexual, and cisgender individuals congregate, this is not perceived as an abnormal decision in the same way that it is for minoritized groups. Recognizing such biases is an important step to creating more inclusive environments on our college campuses through enacting supportive policies. Pitcher et al. (2018) suggested institutionalizing campus spaces for these groups, enacting nondiscrimination policies, and conveying rationales for inclusive policies (e.g., gender-inclusive housing to facilitate student success). Finally, with all the campus climate data being collected, institutions can use these sources of data to justify policies for creating inclusive campus spaces and policies.

Practice

Although relatively little is known about the work of student affairs educators in FPCUs—keeping in mind the basic needs of any college student, regardless of the environment—academic advising, financial aid, and career services are central to the institutional success and outcomes of students in those settings. If these services are not readily available and easily accessible for students, they will be less satisfied with their college experience. Student affairs educators at these institutions can conduct environmental scans of their institutional resources, both online and physical environments, to determine where the gaps may be. Because for-profit institutions tend to engage in market-driven practices and policy making (Boykin, 2017), the approach of using evidence from assessments of the environment and applying an ecological lens may be helpful in showing the utility of any proposed changes.

Previous research shows that student satisfaction plays an integral role in a student's persistence (Astin, 1999; Tinto, 2010). For students of color, racial climate is linked to their satisfaction with their college environment (Hurtado, Alvarez, Guillermo-Wann, Cuellar, & Arellano, 2012). In institutions with fewer students of color, these groups are more likely to report an unwelcoming racial climate (Rankin & Reason, 2005). Though some educational leaders purport that recruiting more diverse students can negatively impact efforts to admit academically competitive students, Oseguera and Rhee (2009) found that an increase in compositional diversity does not result in lower degree-completion rates. In fact, Museus, Nichols, and Lambert (2008) showed that diverse campus environments have positive rates of degree attainment. These researchers uncovered that even indirect interactions with racially diverse peers was important. However, this finding was based on a single dimension measuring this outcome, indicating that more research is needed in this area.

Ecological models can inform how institutions recruit and retain diverse students, faculty, and staff. Research has shown the educational benefits of interacting with diverse peers. In the Grutter v. Gratz case, evidence showed that having experiences with diverse peers may help better prepare students to interact with a global society (Hurtado et al., 2012). Outcomes, such as "understanding multiple perspectives, negotiating conflict, openness to having one's views challenged, and tolerance of different worldviews" (Hurtado et al., 2012, p. 53), can be acquired/transmitted through these interactions. Consequently, students should be exposed to diversity in curricular and co-curricular spaces so they have multiple and frequent opportunities to inform their development in embracing a more pluralistic society. Ensuring a critical mass of students of color (SOCs) on a college campus is a requisite for such opportunities. In the exosystem, student affairs educators should advocate for more racial-ethnic diversity within the institution so that SOCs are not dealing with solo-status (Hurtado et al., 2012) or stereotype threat (Steele, 1997). Student affairs educators should be involved with recruiting and retaining faculty and senior administrators of color. Once these individuals are on campus, student affairs educators can be instrumental in helping SOCs connect with faculty of color to serve as role models and mentors.

Ecological Niches

In this section, we discuss ecological niches to highlight some of the microsystems that exist on college campuses. These niches have been influential in student belongingness as well as persistence and retention. First, learning communities vary in size, type, and objectives. Tinto (2003) posited that learning communities have three common characteristics: (a) "shared knowledge" (p. 2) based on an area of study, (b) "shared knowing [that allows students] to get to know each other quickly and fairly intimately" (p. 2), and (c) "shared responsibility" (p. 2) for the learning of the group. Institutions who have high numbers of commuter students may use learning communities to help these students feel a greater sense of belonging to the campus and peers. There is some research to support the finding that students who participate in these communities have more satisfaction with their educational experiences, better GPAs, and higher retention rates (Stassen, 2003; Zhao & Kuk, 2004). Second, living learning communities (LLCs) apply some of the same services and programs as learning communities, but they have an extra component of a residential or housing option. At large public research universities, LLCs make the campus more digestible and help students create subcultures/niches within the larger campus environment. Not only do students benefit from more peer-to-peer interaction, especially with individuals in their field of study, but students in LLCs also have more opportunities to interact with faculty and staff whose classrooms and offices may also exist in these spaces.

Third, STEM intervention programs (SIPs) have emerged as another mechanism for recruiting and retaining students of color in STEM. Many have existed since the 1970s, but they are starting to see a resurgence in visibility as national efforts seek to broaden participation in STEM. SIPs use wrap-around services and case management approaches to establish environments that will be supportive to the transitions and persistence of students of color in these disciplines (Lane, 2016). Lane (2016) advanced a model that elucidates four components that contribute to the retention of underserved students in SIPs, including (a) proactive caring, (b) holistic support, (c) community building, and (d) STEM identity development catalysts.

Proactive caring comprises enactment of proactive advising and notions of an ethic of care. Such philosophies undergird the practices of student affairs educators who work in these programs and motivate the ways they establish trust, hold students accountable, and encourage students to persist in STEM despite seemingly insurmountable barriers. Holistic support builds upon the work of Museus's (2014) Culturally Engaging Campus Environments (CECE) model in showing the multifaceted ways these professional support students' academic, psychosocial, and professional development in addition to providing transitional and pragmatic support. Community building occurs at three levels: cohort relationships, peer-to-peer mentoring, and student-to-staff relationships. These levels of relationships create an overall familial atmosphere where reciprocity and care for the well-being of others are central to the success of the individual and community. Lastly, STEM identity development catalysts are instigative practices that influence strong science identity development. Although the staff recognize they are not best equipped to prepare STEM professionals, because many of them do not hold these degrees, they do have the capacity to create environmental conditions that can ignite students' aspirational capital (Yosso, 2005). Such practices include validating students' belongingness through building their confidence, providing opportunities to engage in undergraduate research, and facilitating informal and formal ways to celebrate students' accomplishments.

Research

Much of our research focuses on individual student behaviors and outcomes without considering how institutional actors and practices (in college environments) influence these outcomes and behaviors (Hurtado et al., 2012). These inquiries do little to move the needle on why some students persist whereas others depart. A greater emphasis in our research on the environment could lend itself to potentially more feasible and amendable ways to increase student retention. Focusing solely on student inputs can be fruitless because an individual's behavior and subsequent development is a function of the person in the environment (Bronfenbrenner, 2005; Lewin, 2014). Additionally, we cannot change students' background characteristics and identities, but educational leaders can reimagine the ways we design institutional contexts to support a myriad of students, thus leading to greater rates of persistence and retention. Lane and Brown (2004) argued that few researchers investigate institutional culture because it is a difficult element to define. Culture can also be interpreted and understood in very different ways, depending on the actors (Lane & Brown, 2004). Researchers may also overlook the unique organizational characteristics that differentiate certain types of institutions from the perceived traditional institutional context.

A research agenda on college environments should consider some of the following lines of inquiry, such as What is the role of diversity programming on our college campuses? What are the attempts to scaffold intellectual development concerning equity and inclusion? and How do artifacts vary based on institutional types and college contexts? According to Hurtado et al. (2012), "Research in higher education provides evidence that diverse learning environments are related to the development of these crucial cross-cultural competencies for civic life" (p. 53). Students who interact with diverse peers frequently are more likely to get involved politically to improve social conditions, support others through challenges and engage in efforts to promote environmental sustainability as well as other forms of community activism (Gurin, Dey, Hurtado, & Gurin, 2002). Diversity programming can be instrumental in creating these kinds of opportunities, in addition to admitting a diverse student class overall. According to the literature, the diversity programming should encompass a variety of program types, opportunities for low (e.g., cultural events) and high-risk (e.g., intergroup dialogue) engagement, and levels of intellectual complexity (e.g., recognizing privilege vs. understanding how to dismantle systemic oppression). Yet, few data exist on the outcomes of such programs. In particular there is limited, longitudinal data that follows students after they leave college environments.

Another aspect of college environments are the artifacts that inhabit them. Artifacts are used to articulate the culture of an institutional setting (Lane & Brown, 2004). Symbols, such as campus mascots, institutional logos, presidential statements, and architectural building designs, communicate certain norms and values. On the other hand, FPCUs may use images in commercial advertisements to convey similar types of messages. Questions from studying artifacts may include, How do artifacts convey certain messages and to whom?

FPCU environments remain among the most understudied college context. One exception is Illoh's (2016) ethnographic account of one for-profit institution, which revealed that students were concerned about the lack of transparency (about institutional accreditation), functional Wi-Fi, and quality instruction. Students also felt that far too much attention was spent on students at risk of institutional departure. Another environmental tension emerged from the mixed-age classroom settings. Some students embraced these dynamics, citing that it represented the workplace contexts they would enter, but others felt institutions should intervene to limit these practices. Although this study made a significant contribution to an environment that is relatively invisible in the empirical research, we still know relatively little about the co-curricular experiences of students in these environments. These findings are helpful for student affairs educators who may enter FPCUs, however more research is needed to understand and identify support mechanisms for students within these institutions.

Recommendations for Practitioners

- Conduct a climate audit and use findings to improve the environment for marginalized student populations.
- Include student representatives (e.g., students with disabilities and LGBTQ+ students) and respect their voices on committees designed to establish new—or reimagine existing—centers, institutes, and thematic residence halls.
- Develop academic and student affairs collaborations that support creating community for online learners.
- Identify promising practices at MSIs that may be applicable to local institutional contexts and helpful in supporting student success among students of color.
- Recruit and retain faculty, staff, and administrators of color to serve as mentors and role models for students of color, in addition to providing a subject-matter expertise in cultivating a more welcoming campus environment.

Conclusion

Understanding campus environments and the theories that inform our study of them are instrumental to the work of student affairs educators. The curricular and co-curricular aspects of the college experience are situated within various campus environments that have disparate impacts on the holistic development and learning of an increasingly diverse student body. As such, it is our responsibility to examine, deconstruct, and reconstruct campus spaces that aid in supporting all students on campus.

Reflection Questions

1. Thinking about your own college experience, which environments were more or less welcoming on your college campus and/or conducive to your development? Why do you think that is? If you could change it, how would you do so?
2. Throughout the chapter, we provide examples of colleges and universities that help us better understand, describe, and illuminate aspects of environmental theories and student development: Consider what other institutions you might include in this chapter? Why would you include them? Consider policies and practices at these institutions.
3. Has your institution conducted a campus climate study? Do you know what was learned from this study? How was this information shared? Have there been any efforts to address the concerns outlined in the study?

4. What should student affairs educators consider in creating accessible environments for students with disabilities?
5. What are some of the environmental needs of students at (a) community colleges, (b) for-profit colleges and universities, (c) MSIs, and (d) online colleges and universities? How could student affairs professionals be instrumental in addressing those needs?

References

Astin, A. W. (1984). Student involvement: A developmental theory for higher education. *Journal of College Student Development, 25*(4), 297–308.

Astin, A. W. (1999). Student involvement: A developmental theory for higher education. *Journal of College Student Development, 40*(5), 518–529.

Boykin, T. F. (2017). For profit, for success, for black men: A review of literature on urban for-profit colleges and universities. *Urban Education, 52*(9), 1140–1162.

Bronfenbrenner, U. (1979). Contexts of child rearing: Problems and prospects. *American Psychologist, 34*(10), 844–850.

Bronfenbrenner, U. (2005). *Making human beings human: Bioecological perspectives on human development.* Thousand Oaks, CA: Sage.

Bronfenbrenner, U., & Morris, P. A. (2006). The bioecological model of human development. In R. M. Lerner & W. Damon (Eds.), *Handbook of child psychology: Theoretical models of human development* (pp. 793–828). Hoboken, NJ: John Wiley & Sons.

Cohen, A. M., Brawer, F. B., & Kisker, C. B. (2013). *The American community college* (6th ed.). San Francisco: Jossey-Bass.

Conrad, C., & Gasman, M. (2015). *Educating a diverse nation: Lessons from a minority serving institution.* Cambridge, MA: Harvard University Press.

Cuellar, M. (2014). The impact Hispanic-serving institutions (HSIs), emerging HSIs, and non-HSIs on Latina/o academic self-concept. *The Review of Higher Education, 37*(4), 99–530.

Deming, D. J., Goldin, C., & Katz, L. F. (2012). The for-profit postsecondary school sector: Nimble critters or agile predators? *Journal of Economic Perspectives, 26*(1), 139–164.

Dews, S. D. (2018). Where's my queer BBQ?: Supporting queer students at historically women's colleges. *The Vermont Connection, 39*(1), Article 4. Retrieved from https://scholarworks.uvm.edu/tvc/vol39/iss1/4

Garcia, G. A., & Okhidoi, O. (2015). Culturally relevant practices that "serve" students at a Hispanic serving institution. *Innovative Higher Education, 40,* 345–357.

Garvey, J. C., Taylor, J. L., & Rankin, S. (2015). An examination of campus climate for LGBTQ community college students. *Community College Journal of Research and Practice, 39*(6), 527–541.

González, K. P. (2002). Campus culture and the experiences of Chicano students in a predominantly white university. *Urban Education, 37*(2), 193–218.

Gurin, P., Dey, E., Hurtado, S., & Gurin, G. (2002). Diversity and higher education: Theory and impact on educational outcomes. *Harvard Educational Review, 72*(3), 330–367.

Hagedorn, L. S. (2014). Engaging returning adult learners in community colleges. In S. J. Quaye & S. R. Harper (Eds.), *Student engagement in higher education: Theoretical perspectives and practical approaches for diverse populations* (pp. 307–321). New York: Routledge.

Hirt, J. B. (2006). *Where you work matters: Student affairs administration at different types of institutions.* Lanham, MD: University Press of America.

Hurtado, S., Alvarez, C. L., Guillermo-Wann, C., Cuellar, M., & Arellano, L. (2012). A model for diverse learning environments. In M. B. Paulsen & L. W. Perna (Eds.), *Higher education: Handbook of theory and research* (Vol. 27, Ch.2, pp. 41–122). Dordrecht, Netherlands: Springer.

Hurtado, S., Milem, J. F., Clayton-Pedersen, A. R., & Allen, W. R. (1998). Enhancing campus climates for racial/ethnic diversity: Educational policy and practice. *The Review of Higher Education, 21*(3), 279–302.

Iloh, C. (2016). Exploring the for-profit experience: An ethnography of a for-profit college. *American Educational Research Journal, 53*(3), 427–455.

Iloh, C., & Toldson, I. A. (2013). Black students in 21st century higher education: A closer look at for-profit and community colleges (Editor's commentary). *The Journal of Negro Education, 82*(3), 205–212.

Lane, J. E., & Brown, C. (2004). The importance of acknowledging context in institutional research. *New Directions for Institutional Research, 124,* 93–103.

Lane, T. B. (2016). Beyond academic and social integration: Understanding the impact of a STEM enrichment program on the retention and degree attainment of underrepresented students. *CBE-Life Sciences Education, 15*(3), ar. 39. doi:10.1187/cbe.16-01-0070

Lewin, K. (2014). Psychological ecology. In J. J. Gieseking, W. Mangold, C. Katz, S. Low, & S. Saegert (Eds.), *The people, place, and space reader* (Section 1). New York: Routledge.

Museus, S. D. (2014). The culturally engaging campus environments (CECE) model: A new theory of success among racially diverse college student populations. In M. B. Paulsen & L. W. Perna (Eds.), *Higher education: Handbook of theory and research* (Vol. 29, pp. 189–227). Dordrecht, Netherlands: Springer. doi:10.1007/978-94-017-8005-6_5

Museus, S. D., Nichols, A. H., & Lambert, A. (2008). Racial differences in the effects of campus racial climate on degree completion: A structural model. *The Review of Higher Education, 32*(1), 107–134.

Nicolazzo, Z., & Marine, S. B. (2015). "It will change if people keep talking": Trans* students in college and university housing. *Journal of College & University Student Housing, 42*(1), 160–177.

Nicolazzo, Z., Pitcher, E. N., Renn, K. A., & Woodford, M. (2017). An exploration of trans* kinship as a strategy for student success. *International Journal of Qualitative Studies in Education, 30*(3), 305–319.

Oseguera, L., & Rhee, B. S. (2009). The influence of institutional retention climates on student persistence to degree completion: A multilevel approach. *Research in Higher Education, 50*(6), 546–569.

Park, J. J. (2014). Clubs and the campus racial climate: Student organizations and interracial friendship in college. *Journal of College Student Development, 55*(7), 641–660.

Paul Quinn College. (n.d.). About Paul Quinn. Retrieved from http://www.pqc.edu/about-paul-quinn/

Perna, L., Lundy-Wagner, V., Drezner, N. D., Gasman, M., Yoon, S., Bose, E., & Gary, S. (2009). The contribution of HBCUs to the preparation of African American women for STEM careers: A case study. *Research in Higher Education, 50*(1), 1–23.

Persell, C. H., & Wenglinsky, H. (2004). For-profit post-secondary education and civic engagement. *Higher Education, 47*(3), 337–359.

Pitcher, E. N., Camacho, T. P., Renn, K. A., & Woodford, M. R. (2018). Affirming policies, programs, and supportive services: Using an organizational perspective to understand LGBTQ+ college student success. *Journal of Diversity in Higher Education, 11*(2), 117–132.

Pusser, B., & Turner, S. E. (2004). Nonprofit and for-profit governance in higher education. In R. G. Ehrenberg (Ed.), *Governing academia* (pp. 235–527), Ithaca, NY: Cornell University Press.

Rankin, S. R., & Reason, R. D. (2005). Differing perceptions: How students of color and White students perceive campus climate for underrepresented groups. *Journal of College Student Development, 46*(1), 43–61.

Ruch, R. S. (2001). *Higher ed, Inc.: The rise of the for-profit university.* Baltimore: Johns Hopkins University Press.

Sanford, N. (1966). *Self and society: Social change and individual development.* New York: Atherton Press.

Stassen, M. L. (2003). Student outcomes: The impact of varying living-learning community models. *Research in Higher Education, 44*(5), 581–613.

Stavredes, T. M., & Herder, T. M. (2014). Engaging students in an online environment. In C. C. Strange & J. H. Banning (Eds.), *Designing for learning: Creating campus environments for student success* (2015). San Francisco: Jossey-Bass.

Strange, C. C., & Banning, J. H. (2001). *Educating by design: Creating campus learning environments that work.* San Francisco: Jossey-Bass.

Strange, C. C., & Banning, J. H. (2015). *Designing for learning: Creating campus learning environments for student success* (2nd ed.). San Francisco: Jossey-Bass.

Steele, C. M. (1997). A threat in the air: How stereotypes shape intellectual identity and performance. *American Psychologist, 52*(6), 613–629.

Tatum, D. (1997). *Why are all the Black kids sitting together in the cafeteria?* New York: Basic Books.

Tierney, W. G. (1988). Organizational culture in higher education: Defining the essentials. *The Journal of Higher Education, 59*(1), 2–21.

Tinto, V. (2003). Learning better together: The impact of learning communities on student success. *Higher Education Monograph Series, 1*(8), 1–8.

Tinto, V. (2010). From theory to action: Exploring the institutional conditions for student retention. In M. B. Paulsen & L. W. Perna (Eds.), *Higher education: Handbook of theory and research* (Vol. 25, pp. 51–89). Dordrecht, Netherlands: Springer.

U.S. Department of Education. (2017). Asian American and Native American Pacific Islander-serving institutions program: Laws, regulations, and guidance. Retrieved from https://www2.ed.gov/programs/aanapi/aanapi-statute.pdf

Yosso, T. J. (2005). Whose culture has capital? A critical race theory discussion of community cultural wealth. *Race Ethnicity and Education, 8*(1), 69–91.

Zamani-Gallaher, E. M. (2004). Proprietary schools: Beyond the issue of profit. *New Directions for Institutional Research, 124,* 63–79.

Zhao, C. M., & Kuh, G. D. (2004). Adding value: Learning communities and student engagement. *Research in Higher Education, 45*(2), 115–138.

Chapter 3

CAMPUS ENVIRONMENTS
AND STUDENT SUCCESS

Liliana Rodriguez

Preparing today's student for success in tomorrow's workforce has many challenges. The world is changing quickly, and individuals need to have a greater global perspective in the workplace. The very definition of work is changing, and it is now estimated that as much as 85 percent of the jobs our students will hold in the future have yet to be invented (Dell Technologies, 2017). How do you prepare a student for a career that does not yet exist? To complicate matters, the experience and needs of students are far more complex today than they were decades ago when the college-going population was much more homogenous and economically secure.

It is necessary for higher education to continue to evolve to meet the needs of an ever-changing world. Providing college students with opportunities to find a sense of meaning and purpose in life will help serve as a protective factor, building resilience for the challenges they face now and in the future (Dezutter et al., 2014; Trevsian, Bass, Powell, & Eckerd, 2017). Self-actualizing and reconciling one's identity is not easy to do without the appropriate guidance and support navigating available resources. While the needs of students we serve have changed dramatically in recent years, colleges and universities have been slow to meet these needs with new services, support programs, and restructuring. Even more directly, students are not being taught how to define success for themselves or what student success means beyond the institutional metrics used.

Defining student success in higher education, then, is the first step toward actualizing it. And given the variety of contexts in which students are educated in the United States, the variety of economic and cultural backgrounds students come from, and the varying identities they carry, student success is neither easy to define nor to achieve. This chapter seeks to explore (a) the ways student success has been defined in the literature, (b) the primary frameworks used to understand how to boost student success, and (c) important aspects of the environment or educational ecosystem to consider when implementing student success initiatives.

Defining Student Success

Kuh, Kinzie, Buckley, Bridges, and Hayek (2006) defined student success as encompassing "academic achievement, engagement in educationally purposeful activities, persistence, acquisition of desired knowledge, skills and competencies, satisfaction, attainment of educational objectives, and post college performance" (p. 1). Despite a growing body of work that has expanded the understanding of student success, most research focuses on fairly simplistic metrics, such as retention (persistence and degree attainment), academic achievement, and student engagement and satisfaction levels in students.

Retention (Persistence and Degree Attainment)

Student success is most commonly defined by enrollment, retention, and completion rates. The prevailing view of student retention has focused on efforts that take on an institutional perspective, asking what an institution can do to retain their students, as opposed to asking how an institution can help students persist in higher education. Typical retention efforts often focus on pre-orientation experiences, designated advisors for specific populations, or early warning indicators. For instance, institutions have begun to pay close attention to mid-semester grades, hoping to reach out to students before they fail a course. Some universities have specialized programs, such as pre-orientation experiences for first-generation students, or academic advisors designated for higher-risk populations, such as athletes or transfer students (Burkum, Habley, McClanahan, & Valiga, 2010). According to Tinto (2016), institutions must understand the student perspective if they truly seek to improve retention or degree attainment: "The latter, rarely asked, requires institutions to understand how student experiences shape their motivation [and] . . . what they can do to enhance that motivation" (para. 3). On average, 60 percent of students who attend a four-year college or university graduate "on time"—usually defined as within a six-year time frame (McFarland et al., 2017). Although it is difficult to identify the root cause of every student's reason for leaving a college or university, in many cases, it is the result of a number of circumstances and conditions.

Academic Achievement

How well students perform academically is also an important and commonly used measure of student success. Grade point averages, standardized testing, and honors or other scholarly designations are common too. Unlike grades and persistence rates, academic struggles are not tracked as well. One empirical study on Pell Grant recipients found that at least 20 percent of students were on academic probation by the end of their first year (Scott-Clayton & Schudde, 2016). Pascarella and Terenzini (2005) stated that "even given their limitations . . . college grades may well be the single best predictors of student persistence, degree completion, and graduate school enrollment" (p. 396). The relationship between first-year GPA and likelihood to persist has been well established. For instance, Ishitani and DesJardins (2002) found that students were less likely to drop out if they had higher GPAs. Tracking grades and probationary status are important factors to consider when implementing persistence and retention initiatives. In fact, as universities struggle to find cost-effective methods of intervening, the concept of electronic "nudges" has become quite popular. A nudge is an email or text message to a student requesting that they seek specific support if they appear to be struggling (e.g., "Writing tutors are available tonight") or reminding them of an important deadline (e.g., "Financial aid paperwork is due next week). The idea behind the success of nudges is to provide a non-intrusive way of reminding students that the university cares and that there are numerous resources available to support them, in hopes of influencing their behavior toward more successful habits.

Student Engagement and Satisfaction

Over the last few decades, a vast amount of literature has focused on the types of engagement within and outside the classroom that can increase student success. *Student engagement* represents the time and effort students devote to activities that are linked to the positive outcomes of college and what institutions do to induce students to participate in these activities (Kuh, 2009). The quality of student involvement is more important than the quantity of involvement for positive academic outcomes (e.g., Shernoff, 2010). The bulk of research suggests that students from all backgrounds benefit from engaging on campus, although certain types of experiences may be more beneficial for some students over others (Pascarella & Terenzini, 2005). Engagement in educationally purposeful activities, for example, was related to a much higher increase in first-year GPA for Latinx students compared to white students; this engagement was also associated with higher second-year retention for black students compared to their white peers (Kuh, Cruce, Shoup, Kinzie, & Gonyea, 2008).

A meta-analysis of the effects of high-impact practices on low-income students and other underrepresented groups showed the importance of these practices on first-generation students (Finley & McNair, 2013). Examples of high-impact practices include (a) research with a faculty member, (b) service projects in the community, or (c) holding a leadership role in an organization related to their identity. First-generation students who participated in one or two high-impact practices reported levels of engagement and perceived gains that were, on average, 11 percent higher on the standardized scale than those of first-generation students who did not engage on campus. When first-generation students participated in three or four high-impact practices during their time in school, their levels of engagement and their perceived gains were, on average, 24 percent higher than those of first-generation students who did not engage (Finley & McNair, 2013).

Toward a Holistic Approach to Student Success

Higher education is a time of transition and growth for students. It is a natural aspect of their development as they enter emerging adulthood, a phase defined by the process of grappling with one's identity and seeking a sense of purpose. In a diverse and developed nation like the United States, these goals become significantly more challenging for students, given the variety of choices offered and changes to social expectations and constructs (Arnett, 2000).

Nevertheless, the purpose of a general or liberal arts education has historically been defined in terms of the content of courses within the curriculum and not necessarily the growth of the whole person. Yet, the goals of education—usually assigned to academic affairs, and the goals of holistic development—traditionally assigned to student affairs, are inherently compatible and interconnected (Astin, 1991; Meacham & Gaff, 2006). Pascarella and Terenzini (2005) reached a similar conclusion in their exhaustive study on the effects of the college experience: "The evidence strongly suggests that . . . learning is holistic rather than segmented, and that multiple forces operate in multiple settings to shape student learning in ways that cross the 'cognitive-affective' divide" (p. 269). An intentional partnership between academic affairs and student affairs is essential to providing a transformative education. Faculty and staff educators need to "work together to complete conceptual mapping of the student learning, collaboratively identifying activities inside and outside the classroom that focus upon and contribute to specifically defined learning objectives" (Keeling, 2004, p. 24).

The move toward holistic student development is also much more consistent with the majority of university mission statements and institutional goals, ones that often include learning goals far outside of academic and intellectual growth (Astin, 1991), such as interpersonal skill development (Cohen, 2006), emotional and multiple intelligences (Gardner, 1999), and spiritual intelligence (Zohar & Marshall, 2000). The notion that emotional learning matters is quite ancient and global in its reach. The words "know thyself" were carved on the wall of the oracle of Apollo at Delphi 2,500 years ago and served as an organizing idea for Greek society (as cited in Snell, 1982), as well as serving as the foundational concepts of several African, North American, and South American indigenous philosophies.

What then do we mean when we seek to educate the whole student? The primary constructs for holistic student development seek to help students grow in the following core areas, suggested by Cuseo (2007):

- *Intellectual* development: developing skills for acquiring and communicating knowledge . . . [and critical thinking];
- *Emotional* development: developing skills for understanding, controlling, and expressing emotions;
- *Social* development: enhancing the quality and depth of interpersonal relationships, leadership skills, [mentoring networks,] and civic engagement;
- *Ethical* development: formulating a clear value system that guides life choices and demonstrates personal character;
- *Physical* development: acquiring and applying knowledge about the human body to prevent disease, maintain wellness, and promote peak mental [and physical performance];
- *Spiritual* development: appreciating the search for personal meaning [and] the purpose of human existence, [and providing meaning for life or "calling"]. (p. 2)

An additional core area essential for holistic student development is identity development: formulating a cohesive and integrated identity that appreciates one's personal idiosyncrasies as well as the complexities of the social identities one carries.

The need to move toward a more holistic view of student success is underscored by research that consistently demonstrates that the majority (75 to 85%) of students who withdraw from college are in good academic standing at the time of their departure (Tinto, 1993). After years of cross-institutional research seeking to improve the first-year experience and retention, one major conclusion drawn is that a strict concentration on academic matters alone does not have a significant impact on student retention without equal concentration devoted to all the non-academic elements of the student experience (Smith, 2003).

Four Internal Influences of Student Success

Student success, therefore, should be defined as a holistic concept that embraces the many dimensions involved in developing the whole person, as well as the many goals of higher education in the twenty-first century. The concepts reviewed below are regarded as foundational predictors of student success: Without a strong sense of belonging, self-efficacy, or life purpose, it is harder to navigate the challenges higher education presents. The best practices should seek to increase the following in students' self-perception:

Sense of Belonging. Widely agreed to be important, the concept of belonging has been well established in the literature (Baumeister & Leary, 1995; Hurtado & Carter, 1997; Jacoby & Garland, 2004. In most psychological studies, belonging is conceptualized as an individual's connectedness to an institution and its social and environmental contexts (Baumeister & Leary, 1995); an individual feels some level of belonging in response to social interactions, relationships made, levels of engagement within the institution, and other environmental features. As a result, sense of belonging is highly contextualized. Hurtado and Carter (1997) suggested that sense of belonging is both a cognitive and affective experience. In other words, students who feel connected to a peer group or mentor at the institution are more likely to find satisfaction with their experience and thus remain enrolled and engaged. Sense of belonging is credited as one of the more critical factors of student retention and future engagement with the institution as alumni.

Applying the study of belonging to the college context is complicated because students arrive with a multitude of identities and histories. There are individual and cultural variations in how people perceive their environment and how they express and satisfy the need to belong. For instance, we all define friendships and relationships differently, we all have different expectations for our classrooms and relationships with faculty, and we have varying expectations of student support services and extra-curricular offerings. Hurtado, Milem, Clayton-Pedersen, and Allen (1998) noted that college campuses "are complex social systems defined by the relationships between the people, bureaucratic procedures, structural arrangements, institutional goals and values, traditions, and larger socio-historical environments" (p. 10).

A growing body of research has documented the circumstances that engender students' sense of belonging. Some scholars have pointed to the importance of a positive campus climate and strong faculty mentors in sustaining a sense of belonging on campus (Hoffman, Richmond, Morrow, & Salomone, 2002). A number of studies have shown that sense of belonging is related to other variables, such as social class and student engagement

(Astin, 1993). Arguably, it is interpersonal relationships, both on and off campus, that play the biggest role in determining whether a student feels they belong to the community. This view is consistent with a social networks perspective that college students' relationships with faculty and staff and peers as well as family, friends, and mentors contribute to student satisfaction, persistence, and a sense of belonging (Astin, 1978, 1993; Kuh et al., 1991; Kuh et al., 2005; Pascarella & Terenzini, 1991, 2005; Tinto, 1987, 1993).

Self-Efficacy. Bandura (1977) is well known for his social learning theory and his ideas about modeling as an important means by which children learn. Over time, Bandura further added to his work, incorporating the idea that human behavior is influenced by personal, behavioral, and environmental influencers that require internal regulation, ultimately renaming his theory, social cognitive theory (Bandura, 1986). This led to the concept of *self-efficacy* being added to his slate of teachings, defined as the beliefs a student carries about their own ability to master new skills and tasks, often in a specific academic domain (Pajares, Miller, & Levin, 1994). For example, a learner judges their self-efficacy from their actual performance results, the feedback they receive from others or comparisons they make against others, and their physiological reactions to those experiences. It is well supported that self-efficacy impacts choice, effort, persistence, resilience, and achievement (Bandura, 1997; Schunk, 1995). Compared with students who doubt their abilities, those who feel confident and efficacious in academic settings work harder, persist longer when they encounter difficulties, and achieve at a higher level (Schunk & Pajares, 2002). The concept, *growth mindset,* a more contemporary view of learning that draws from Bandura's work on self-efficacy, suggested that through effort and perseverance, one can become better at any task (Dweck, 2007). This is contrary to the belief that we are born with fixed talents and intelligence.

Sense of Purpose (or Meaning-Making). The majority of research examining one's sense of purpose is based on the works of Frankl (1959), who proposed that the world is full of a variety of people and backgrounds to encounter and meanings to make sense of and pursue. Nash and Murray (2010) argued that life purpose is particularly critical in young adulthood because young adults often begin to question—and are questioned about—their purpose in life. They struggle with questions of purpose precisely because they have not yet fully resolved the questions regarding meaning. Therefore, what makes an individual's educational experience worthwhile and justifiable is the meaning they attribute to it.

Much of the research on purpose in life has focused on college students. These studies have found that purpose in life is related to core aspects of identity development and physical and psychological well-being, and may be predictive of a personality style that facilitates student success (Dezutter et al., 2014). Molasso's work (2006) demonstrated that active engagement with peers or educators within the campus community and participation in activities where that type of engagement is facilitated are positively related to a student's development of purpose, whereas more isolating activities, such as TV and social media, are negatively related to their search for meaning and personal fulfillment. Zika and Chamberlain (1992) found that students are less likely to be depressed, hopeless, or anxious if they have identified a life purpose. Similarly, they are better able to cope with life crises or stressors (Reker, Peacock, & Wong, 1987; Trevisan et al., 2017).

Context Is Everything: Considering Environmental Factors as Inclusive Praxis

The reason that context should be of particular interest to educators is that it contributes to the inequities found in student success and their ability to feel a sense of belonging, efficacy, and purpose. The vast majority of students do not lack the intelligence or resilience to succeed in college, but they often lack an environment or ecosystem that is sensitive to the factors in their life impeding their success. As Maslow (1954) found, humans cannot move toward growth and self-actualization without first having the majority of their needs met. In Palardy's (2013) study examining educational environments, context was the greatest contributor to the achievement gap among Black and Latinx children, who typically attend schools that either do not regard context as important or are financially unable to make the needed improvements. What then are the environmental factors impeding student success that higher education practitioners need to consider in this era?

Housing and Food Insecurity

There has been much more attention paid to housing and food insecurity as income inequality increases and families struggle to make ends meet. *Housing insecurity* is defined as having difficulty paying rent, being forced to move frequently, or living in dangerous or overcrowded conditions in order to afford housing. *Food insecurity* is defined as having limited access to nutritious food and experiencing hunger on a regular basis. A national report found pervasive levels of food and housing insecurity on community colleges (55%) and university campuses (47%) (Dubick, Mathews, & Cady, 2016). Just over 48 percent of students faced food insecurity in the previous month, according to the report's findings, with 22 percent reporting "very low levels of food security that qualify them as hungry" (p. 7) more often than not. The report showed that of those experiencing food insecurity, 68 percent also experienced housing insecurity, with 15 percent experiencing homelessness. Insecurities were more common with students of color (especially Black students), first-generation students, and community college students. Students experiencing housing and food insecurity suffered significant educational setbacks, causing them to skip classes, withdraw from courses, or not be able to purchase required supplies. Unfortunately, interventions, such as campus meal plans, Pell Grants, student loans, and the Supplemental Nutrition Assistance Program (SNAP) have not been enough to ease student hunger (Dubick et al., 2016).

Financial Stress

Even with the recent focus on the debt and financial stressors college graduates face, much less has been written about the impact of financial stress on currently enrolled students (Trombitas, 2012). The cost of college in the United States is easily four times more when compared to every other developed nation, and graduates now carry over 1 trillion dollars of debt (Delisle, 2014). Add to that the increase in the cost of living and it is reasonable to expect that college students are spending more time working in order to afford college (Scott-Clayton, 2012). Indeed, about 75 percent of students are working during the academic year, with 15 percent working full time. Most students are spending more time working (20 hours on average) than on engaging in the offerings of their respective college or university (*National Survey of Student Engagement* [NSSE], 2011). These numbers are troubling when one considers that working more than 10 hours a week is associated with a decline in academic success (Bound, Lovenheim, & Turner, 2010; Stinebrickner & Stinebrickner, 2003). In fact, when students work 20 hours per week during the academic year, they report that the burden of working so many hours had a negative impact on their academic progress and performance (46% vs. 24%) and that they reduced their academic course load due to stress (49% vs. 24%) when compared to those who worked fewer hours (NSSE, 2011).

One of the easiest ways to assuage much of this stress is to provide better funding for education. The amount of aid a student receives directly impacts student retention and timely graduation. Financial aid indirectly lowers the risk of attrition by reducing the need to work and enhancing overall performance in college (Fike & Fike, 2008; Singell, 2004). Moreover, a student who is well resourced financially will spend more time studying and in meaningful engagement while in college than on working to afford their education. A recent study has demonstrated that the average student spends twice as much time working to afford their tuition than they do studying

(Hongkong & Shanghai Banking Corporation Holdings Limited, 2017). According to that study, faced with mounting debts and other school expenses, 85 percent of current students report spending an average of 4.2 hours each day at work—compared with 2.8 hours studying at home, 2.3 hours in lectures and 1.5 hours at the library.

Campus Climate, Stereotype Threat, and Safety

Given the importance of sense of belonging to a student's success, it makes sense that *campus climate*—the attitudes, behaviors, and standards of the campus community concerning the level of respect for all individuals and groups—is a major factor to consider. More often than not, individuals from historically marginalized or underrepresented communities are asked to assimilate into the majority culture of any setting, be it school, workplace, or neighborhood. It becomes the responsibility of the individual and not the institution to change and adapt to difference. Studies on campus climate are trying to change that and place the responsibility on the institution to move toward inclusivity rather than on the individual to move toward assimilation.

And in fact, there is little support for the oppositional identity theory (Fordham & Ogbu, 1986)—the idea that racial minorities resist educational success out of fear of "acting white" (Downey, 2008). It is access to financial, social, and cultural capital that has been shown to be critical in explaining differences in student success (Massey, Charles, Lundy, & Fischer, 2003). *Stereotype threat*—the fear that one is at risk of conforming to stereotypes about one's social group—has been shown to undermine academic achievement, standardized testing, and a variety of other outcomes (Steele, 1988, 1998). The stereotype threat model has been validated in many laboratory and field experiments (Aronson, Fried, & Good, 2002; Cohen, 2006; Cohen, Garcia, Apfel, & Master, 2006; Major & O'Brien, 2005; Walton & Cohen, 2007), as well as in a meta-analytic study of laboratory and field experiments (Walton & Spencer, 2009). In other words, if stereotypes are spoken often and prejudicial language or behavior is present on campus, students will be more likely to experience stereotype threat and potentially have their success undermined.

It is stressful to live in an environment in which one does not feel welcome or safe. In a national study, 90 percent of over 13,000 students felt safe and comfortable on campuses (NSSE, 2016). Although campuses are generally safe and welcoming, perceptions vary by student identity. Trans students and genderqueer students felt less safe and welcomed compared to their cisgender peers. Black students felt significantly less safe (14% disagreement). One in four black students felt less valued by their college, whereas Native students were the least likely to feel like part of the campus community (two out of five disagreed). These NSSE (2016) findings demonstrate the importance of institutional attention to safety and inclusion concerns. A campus cannot be inclusive until community members from historically underrepresented backgrounds feel safe, valued, and included.

Before students can succeed academically, they must feel safe, both physically and mentally. Although universities use a variety of measures to ensure students' physical safety (e.g., campus safety officers, prevention education, video cameras, and alarm systems), it is impossible to guarantee safety. Today, 90 percent of schools have planned their response to school shootings, and 70 percent of schools have drilled students on the plan (Musu-Gillette, Zhang, Wang, Zhang, & Oudekerk, 2017). Community violence, such as school shootings, suicides, or other experiences, may cause trauma and anxiety. The more traumatic experiences a student is exposed to, the more likely the student will have difficulty with socio-emotional interactions and academic tasks, and in turn, will perform poorly. Even without experiencing violence directly, the reports of school shootings and random acts of group violence across this nation have added to a perception that we lack safety in society. This is truer for people of color than other groups.

Mental Health and Well-Being

Emerging adulthood is an important phase in development. It is also a tough one. Individuating from family can be difficult. Having to make important choices about values and purpose, managing formative relationships, and supporting oneself financially, all while being a full-time student, present significant stressors. According to the American College Health Association (2015), 54 percent of students reported feeling overwhelming anxiety. The Association for University and College Counseling Center Directors (Gallagher, 2016) found that 47 percent of students seeking counseling suffered from anxiety, and 40 percent reported suffering from depression, whereas 9 percent reported seriously considering suicide in that last year. Moreover, a quarter of students harm themselves through cutting or other forms of self-mutilation, and a quarter of women are sexually assaulted while on campus. In other words, there is a lot going on in terms of mental health concerns on colleges across the country. Colleges and universities are currently grappling with the question of how to respond effectively to the sudden and dramatic increase in mental health needs and demands. In order to adequately meet rising demands with limited resources, counseling centers must strive to align their policy and funding decisions with institutional priorities (e.g., supporting survivors of sexual assault or managing suicidality) in order to provide the most effective care.

Students from historically marginalized communities experience a variety of difficult situations that likely lead to higher levels of distress. Being victims of micro-aggressions and racism, Islamophobia, and so many other negative environmental challenges can cause intensive feelings of isolation and loneliness. Difficulties posed by these circumstances may be worsened when students lack a supportive network and face barriers to seeking help. Therefore, ensuring that counseling centers and health educators provide an inclusive environment and understand how to approach care with a diverse population of students is critical. One longitudinal study found that the retention rate for students who received psychological counseling was 85 percent, compared with 74 percent for the general student body (Turner & Berry, 2000). Students experiencing high levels of distress are less academically successful: They use fewer resources, have more test anxiety, and lower academic self-efficacy (Brackney & Karabenick, 1995). Given that less than 50 percent of young adults that need mental health treatment actually receive it (Merikangas et al., 2010), it is important to have highly visible programming that normalizes help-seeking behaviors to have positive effects on student success.

Drug Use

As youth enter adulthood, substance use appears common for many of them. In a report by Lipari and Jean-Francois (2016), more than one-third of full-time college students engaged in binge drinking in the past month; about one in five used an illicit drug in the past month. Almost one in four of the nation's college students (22.9%, some 1.8 million) meet the medical criteria for substance abuse or dependence. And the drug abuse problem among college students goes far beyond alcohol. According to Schulenberg et al. (2017), since the early 1990s, the proportion of students using marijuana daily has more than doubled. Use of drugs like cocaine and heroin is up 52 percent. Student abuse of prescription opioids, stimulants, and tranquillizers has exploded. From 1993 to 2005, the proportion of students who abuse prescription painkillers, such as Percocet, Vicodin, and OxyContin, shot up 343 percent; stimulants, such as Ritalin and Adderall, 93 percent; tranquilizers, such as Xanax and Valium, 450 percent; and sedatives, such as Nembutal and Seconal, 225 percent (Schulenberg et al., 2017).

There are group differences in rates of substance use in college and even before entering college. For instance, according to the Substance Abuse and Mental Health Services Administration (2014), the age of illicit drug use after 12 years of age is as follows: 3.1 percent among Asians, 8.8 percent among Hispanics, 9.5 percent among whites, 10.5 percent among blacks, 12.3 percent among American Indians or Alaska Natives, and 14.0 percent among Native Hawaiians or other Pacific Islanders. Among full-time college students, the rate of current illicit drug use was 9.4 percent for Asians, 19.7 percent for blacks, 21.5 percent for Hispanics, and 25.1 percent for whites. According to this same source, white males use more and more often than any other group on most campuses. This is important information for educators to consider when targeting public health education. Substance use constitutes one of the most serious public health issues for young people in the United States, because overdoses are now the leading cause of death for young adults (Scholl, Seth, Kariisa, Wilson, & Baldwin, 2018), creating negative economic and health consequences for the nation as a whole.

Universal Design, Transitions, and Access

Students with disabilities are attending college in larger numbers. Studies suggest that as many as 10% of college students have some type of disability, apparent or not (Newman, Wagner, Cameto, & Knokey, 2009). College students with disabilities have lower retention rates, take longer to complete degrees, and have lower degree completion rates than do their peers without disabilities (Murray, Goldstein, Nourse, & Edgar, 2000; Wessel, Jones, Markle, & Westfall, 2009). Not surprisingly, students with disabilities face a number of significant challenges adjusting to college and have unique transition needs. Moreover, they do not necessarily receive the services needed to ensure success. Of all disabled students on a campus (mobility-impaired, vision-impaired, hearing-impaired, depressed, etc.), statistics show that those with learning differences and attention-deficit disorder are most likely to receive services. Nationally, 51.1 percent of students with learning differences receive services (accommodations) on campus, compared with 19 percent of mobility-impaired students and 22 percent of visually or hearing-impaired students (Livingston & Wirt, 2003).

Along with serving a greater number of students with disabilities, many colleges and universities are also experiencing an influx of "first-generation" college students (Chen, 2005). Many first-generation students are less academically prepared, given the under-resourced neighborhoods and schools they often live in. Moreover, first-generation college students often face unique familial, cultural, and social transitions that may make the transition to, and completion of, postsecondary school challenging (Ishitani, 2003; Strayhorn, 2006). A study by Lombardi, Murray, and Gerdes (2012) found that first-generation students with learning disabilities have unique stressors. As such, it is important for disability service providers and other student support personnel to be aware of these needs so that services can be tailored or intensified for this population.

In fact, equity and access is the basis of Universal Design, a framework asking educators to consider all users from the very beginning, and achieving accessibility for the widest possible range of learners by meeting the needs and desires (Burgstahler, 2012). The concept of universal design originated in the field of architecture, questioning the appropriateness of placing the burden of adaptations to the physical space on the individuals with needs rather than on the institution to meet those needs. Adaptations to buildings, such as ramped entrances and automatic doors, are examples of universal design in architecture. For educators, the interpretation of this concept is similar to a student-centered approach that appreciates the need to educate the whole individual. Universal design asks educators to provide students with multiple means of representation, expression, and engagement. However possible, students should have access to content or materials in multiple formats and multiple ways to show what they know, and educators should use multiple methods of motivating learners (Eison, 2010).

Recommendations

Creating the conditions that foster student success in college has never been more important. High school graduates need some form of postsecondary education (McCabe & McCabe, 2000) to prepare them to live well in an increasingly complex and global world, with many challenges and opportunities to be had. Earning a baccalaureate degree is a point of access for social mobility (Bowen & Bok, 1998; Pascarella & Terenzini, 2005). Yet, if current trends continue, the United States may face a 14 million shortfall of college-educated working adults by 2020 (Carnevale & Desrochers, 2003). Research has suggested that we, as institutions, have not done a great job of prioritizing student success. In a national study of retention programs at four-year college campuses conducted by the College Board (2009), it was discovered that campus resources for initiatives aimed at increasing student persistence were "minimal and inadequate" (p. 10) and that the majority of educators in charge of those initiatives were given "little or no authority" (p. 10); the study concluded that "overall, there is little evidence that institutions of any type are consistently making a strong effort to manage and organize student retention efforts" (p. 10).

There is a need to become much more holistic and intentional in our support of students and consider all the environmental challenges they face in the contemporary world. Moreover, academic affairs and student affairs organizations need to work much more collaboratively to better meet student needs. A more holistic student success model requires sensitivity to three main areas of the student experience: (a) the context students navigate each day in order to learn and be capable of focusing on learning—on and off campus; (b) the psychology of the individual student, namely their perceptions of belonging, efficacy, and purpose; and (c) the kind of training that will be required of faculty and staff in order to sustain this model—including trauma-informed practices, cultural competency, and assessment. Building this type of ecosystem will not only improve the student experience socially and academically, but also increase their engagement with institutions long after they have earned their diplomas. That is the power of a transformative education and the relationships required to deliver one.

The need is clear for an integrated student success model that can inspire students to feel empowered to define success for themselves through meaningful relationships and high-impact educational experiences. The Double Helix model proposed by Haefner and Ford (2010) is one such model. In it, the authors argued that colleges and universities should consider the learning happening outside the classroom as important as the in-classroom experience. They call this approach a "co-major" and suggest a formal and intentional integration of the co-curricular into the academic experience.

Every single campus has its own culture and serves different types of students. So, it is important for colleges and universities to have a firm sense of *their* culture, the barriers experienced by *their* students, and the specific learning outcomes desired by the campus. What works in one community will not necessarily work in others. In building a student success eco-system, educators should ask themselves the following:

- What theoretical frameworks are guiding your initiatives? Do your goals match your initiatives? How is that being assessed?
- What is the campus climate of the institution and how are students experiencing the current environment?
- How are environmental stressors and barriers being tracked? How can the support system be proactive in meeting the most common needs?
- Are there pathways for students to share their story report needs or concerns? Are those systems accessible?
- What are the training needs of faculty and staff and how will they be implemented in a developmental and personalized way?
- Who thrives on your campus? What behaviors, choices, and attitudes are successful students making that can be shared with others?

Universities and colleges, by the nature of their role to educate and develop informed citizens, are well positioned to develop best practices in these areas. Institutions of higher education offer a unique opportunity to address the most significant social, health, and cultural challenges facing society; this is a challenge worthy of investment.

Reflection Questions

1. In considering your own college experience, what environmental or contextual factors most influenced your experience? Were those factors negative or positive influences? Explain.
2. What have you found to have the greatest impact on your sense of belonging, efficacy, and/or purpose in a college or university setting?
3. Can you identify any other barriers that impact student success? If so, define and describe them.
4. What types of ecosystems have you created to enhance your success?
5. Design a transformative collaboration between academic and student affairs to enhance student success. Describe the elements of your co-curricular idea and why it would enhance student outcomes.

References

American College Health Association (2015). *2015–2016 Annual report.* Retrieved from https://www.acha.org/documents/About/ACHA_AnnualReport_2015 -2016.pdf

Arnett, J. J. (2000). Emerging adulthood: A theory of development from the late teens through the twenties. *American Psychologist, 55,* 469–480.

Aronson, J., Fried, C. B., & Good, C. (2002). Reducing the effects of stereotype threat on African American college students by shaping theories of intelligence. *Journal of Experimental Social Psychology, 38,* 3–125.

Astin, A., (1978). *The American freshman: National norms for fall 1977.* Los Angeles: California University, Lab for Research on Higher Education.

Astin, A. W. (1991). *Assessment for excellence: The philosophy and practice of assessment and evaluation in higher education.* New York: Macmillan.

Astin, A., W. (1993). *The American freshman: National norms for fall 1993.* Los Angeles: California University, Lab for Research on Higher Education.

Bandura, A. (1977). Self-efficacy: Toward a unifying theory of behavioral change. *Psychological Review, 84*(2), 191–215.

Bandura, A. (1986). *Social foundations of thought and action: A social cognitive theory.* Englewood Cliffs, NJ: Prentice-Hall.

Bandura, A. (1997). *Self-efficacy: The exercise of control.* New York: W. H. Freeman.

Baumeister, R. F., & Leary, M. R. (1995). The need to belong: Desire for interpersonal attachments as a fundamental human motivation. *Psychological Bulletin, 117,* 497–529.

Bound, J., Lovenheim, M., & Turner, S. (2010). Why have college completion rates declined? An analysis of changing student preparation and collegiate resources. *American Economic Journal: Applied Economics, 2,* 129–157.

Bowen, W., & Bok, D. (1998). *The shape of the river: Long-term consequences of considering race in college and university admissions.* Princeton, N.J.: Princeton University Press.

Brackney, B. E., & Karabenick, S. A. (1995). Psychopathology and academic performance: The role of motivation and learning strategies. *Journal of Counseling*

Psychology, 42(4), 456–465.

Burgstahler, S. (2012). *Universal design of instruction (UDI): Definitions, principles, guidelines, and examples.* Retrieved from http://www.washington.edu/doit/Brochures / Academics/ instruction.html

Burkum, K., Habley, W., McClanahan, R., & Valiga, M. (2010, May/June). *Retention: Diverse institutions—diverse retention practices?* Paper presented at the 2010 AIR Forum, Chicago, IL.

Carnevale, A., & Desrochers, D. (2003). Preparing students for the knowledge economy: What school counselors need to know. *Professional School Counseling, 6*(4), 228–236.

Chen, X. (2005). *First generation students in postsecondary education: A look at their college transcripts* (NCES 2005-171). Washington, DC: U.S. Government Printing Office.

Cohen, J. (2006). Social, emotional, ethical and academic education: Creating a climate for learning, participation in democracy and well-being. *Harvard Educational Review, 76*(2, summer), 201–237. Retrieved from www.hepg.org /her/abstract/8

Cohen, G., Garcia, J., Apfel, N., & Master, A. (2006). Reducing the racial achievement gap: A social-psychological intervention. *Science, 313*(5791), 1307–1310. doi:10.1126/science.1128317

College Board (2009). *How colleges organize themselves to increase student persistence: Four-year institutions.* Retrieved from professionals.collegeboard.com/profdownload /college-retention.pdf

Cuseo, J. (2007). Student success: Definition, outcomes, principles and practices. In *Esource for College Transitions* (Electronic newsletter), The big picture [column]. National Resource Center for the First-Year Experience & Students in Transition, University of South Carolina.

Delisle, J. (2014). *Dumbing down America: The war on our nation's brightest young minds (and what we can do to fight back).* Waco, TX: Prufrock Press.

Dell Technologies. (2017). *The next era of human-machine partnerships: Emerging technologies' impact on society and work in 2030* [online]. Palo Alto, CA: Author. Retrieved from https://www.delltechnologies.com/content/dam/delltechnologies/assets/perspectives/2030/pdf/SR1940_IFTFforDellTechnologies_Human-Machine_070517_readerhigh-res.pdf

Dezutter, J., Waterman, A. S., Schwartz, S. J., Luyckx, K., Beyers, W., Meca, A., .& Caraway, S. J. (2014). Meaning in life in emerging adulthood: A person-oriented approach. *Journal of Personality, 82*(1), 57–68.

Downey, D. B. (2008). Black/White differences in school performance: The oppositional culture explanation. *Annual Review of Sociology, 34*(1), 107–126.

Dubick, J., Mathews, B., & Cady, C. L. (2016). *Hunger on campus: The challenge of food insecurity for college students.* Retrieved from https://studentsagainsthunger.org /hunger-on-campus/

Dweck, C. S. (2007). The perils and promises of praise. *Educational Leadership, 65*(2), 34–39.

Eison, J. (2010). Using active learning instructional strategies to create excitement and enhance learning. Retrieved from http://citeseerx.ist.psu.edu/viewdoc /download?doi=10.1.1. 456.7986&rep=rep1&type=pdf

Fike, D. S., & Fike, R. (2008). Predictors of first-year student retention in the community college. *Community College Review, 36*(2), 68–88.

Finley, A., & McNair, T (2013). Assessing underserved students' engagement in high-impact practices. Washington, DC: Association of American Colleges and Universities.

Fordham S., & Ogbu, J. U. (1986). Black students' school success: Coping with the burden of "acting white." *The Urban Review, 18,* 176–195.

Frankl, V. E. (1959). The spiritual dimension in existential analysis and logotherapy. *Journal of Individual Psychology, 15,* 157–165.

Gardner, H. (1999). *Intelligence reframed: Multiple intelligences for the 21st century.* New York: Basic Books.

Gallagher, R. P. (2016). *National Survey of Counseling Center Directors.* Arlington, VA: The Association for University and College Counseling Center Directors. Retrieved from https://www.aucccd.org/assets/documents/aucccd%202016%20survey%20press%20release%20final.pdf

Haefner, J., & Ford, D. (2010). The double helix: A purposeful pathway to an intentional and transformational liberal education. *Liberal Education, 96*(2), 50–55.

Hoffman, M., Richmond, J., Morrow, J., & Salomone, K. (2002). Investigating "sense of belonging" in first-year college students. *Journal of College Student Retention, 4*(3), 227–256.

Hongkong and Shanghai Banking Corporation Limited. (2017). *The value of education: The price of success.* Reproduced with permission from the Value of Education, published by HSBC Holdings. Retrieved from https://www.us.hsbc.com/value-of-education/

Hurtado, S., & Carter, D. F. (1997). Effects of college transition and perceptions of campus racial climate on Latino college students' sense of belonging. *Sociology of Education, 70*(4), 324–345.

Hurtado, S., Milem, J. F., Clayton-Pedersen, A. R., & Allen, W. R. (1998). Enhancing campus climates for racial/ethnic diversity: Educational policy and practice. *The Review of Higher Education, 21*(3), 279–302.

Ishitani, T. T. (2003). A longitudinal approach to assessing attrition behavior among first-generation students: Time varying effects of pre-college characteristics. *Research in Higher Education, 44,* 433–449.

Ishitani, T. T., & DesJardins, S. L. (2002). A longitudinal investigation of dropout from college in the United States, *Journal of College Student Retention, 4*(2), 173–201.

Jacoby, B., & Garland, J. (2004). Strategies for enhancing commuter student success. *Journal of College Student Retention: Research, Theory, & Practice, 6*(1), 61–79.

Keeling, R. (Ed.). (2004). *Learning reconsidered: A campus-wide focus on the student experience.* Washington, DC: National Association of Student Personnel Administrators & American College Personnel Association.

Kuh, G. (2009). What student affairs professionals need to know about student engagement. *Journal of College Student Development, 50*(6), 683–706.

Kuh, G. D., Cruce, T. M., Shoup, R., Kinzie, J., & Gonyea, R. M. (2008). Unmasking the effects of student engagement on first-year college grades and persistence. *Journal of Higher Education, 79*(5), 540–563.

Kuh, G. D., Kinzie, J., Buckley, J. A., Bridges, B. K., & Hayek, J. C. (2006, July). What matters to student success: A review of the literature (Commissioned report). *Spearheading a Dialog on Student Success*. Conducted at the National Symposium on Postsecondary Student Success, National Postsecondary Education Cooperative, Washington, DC.

Kuh, G. D., Kinzie, J., Schuh, J. H., Whitt, E. J., & Associates (2005). *Student success in college: Creating conditions that matter*. San Francisco: Jossey-Bass.

Kuh, G. D., Schuh, J. H., Whitt, E. J., Andreas, R., Lyons, J., Strange, C. C., . . . MacKay, K. A. (1991). *Involving colleges: Successful approaches to fostering student learning and development outside the classroom*. San Francisco: Jossey-Bass.

Lipari, R. N., & Jean-Francois, B. (2016). *A day in the life of college students aged 18 to 22: Substance use facts* (The Center for Behavioral Health Statistics and Quality [CBHSQ] report). Rockville, MD: Substance Abuse and Mental Health Services Administration.

Livingston, A., & Wirt, J. (2003). Services and accommodations for students with disabilities. In *The condition of education 2003 in brief* (NCES 2003–068) (Appendix I [Supplemental Tables], Table 34–1, p. 160). Washington, DC: National Center for Education Statistics, U.S. Department of Education. Retrieved from https://nces.ed.gov/pubs2003/2003067.pdf

Lombardi, A. R., Murray, C., & Gerdes, H. (2012). Academic performance of first-generation college students with disabilities. *Journal of College Student Development, 53*(6), 811–826.

Major, B., & O'Brien, L. (2005). The social psychology of stigma. *Annual Review of Psychology, 56,* 393–421.

Maslow, A. H. (1954). *Motivation and personality*. New York: Harper & Row.

Massey, D. S., Charles, C. Z., Lundy, G. F., & Fischer, M. J. (2003). *The source of the river: The social origins of freshmen at America's selective colleges and universities*. Princeton, NJ: Princeton University Press.

McCabe, L., & McCabe, E. R. B. (2000). *How to succeed in academics*. London, England, United Kingdom: Academic.

McFarland, J., Hussar, B., de Brey, C., Snyder, T., Wang, X., Wilkinson-Flicker, S., Gebrekristos, S., . . . Hinz, S. (2017, September). *The condition of education 2017* (NCES 2017-144). Washington, DC: National Center for Education Statistics, U.S. Department of Education. Retrieved from https://nces.ed.gov/pubsearch/pubsinfo.asp?pubid=2017144

Meacham, J., & Gaff, J. G. (2006). Learning goals in mission statements. *Liberal Education, 92*(1), 6–13.

Merikangas, K. R., He, J. P., Burstein, M., Swanson, S. A., Avenevoli, S., Cui, L., Benjet, C., . . . Swendsen, J. (2010). Lifetime prevalence of mental disorders in U.S. adolescents: Results from the National Comorbidity Survey Replication-Adolescent Supplement (NCS-A). *Journal of the American Academy of Child and Adolescent Psychiatry, 49*(10), 980–989.

Molasso, W. (2006). Exploring Frankl's purpose in life with college students. *Journal of College and Character, 7*(1), 1–10.

Musu-Gillette, L., Zhang, A., Wang, K., Zhang, J., & Oudekerk, B. A. (2017). *Indicators of school crime and safety: 2016* (NCES 2017-064/NCJ 250650).

Washington, DC: National Center for Education Statistics, U.S. Department of Education, & Bureau of Justice Statistics, Office of Justice Programs, U.S. Department of Justice.

Murray, C., Goldstein, D., Nourse, S., & Edgar, E. (2000). The postsecondary school attendance and completion rates of high school graduates with learning disabilities. *Learning Disabilities: Research & Practice, 15*(3), 119–127.

Nash, R. J., & Murray, M. C. (2010). *Helping college students find purpose: The campus guide to meaning making.* San Francisco: Jossey-Bass.

National Survey of Student Engagement (NSSE). (2011). *Fostering student engagement campus wide–Annual results 2011.* Bloomington: Indiana University Center for Postsecondary Research.

National Survey of Student Engagement (NSSE). (2016). *Engagement insights: Survey findings on the quality of undergraduate education–Annual results 2016.* Bloomington: Indiana University Center for Postsecondary Research.

Newman, L., Wagner, M., Cameto, R., & Knokey, A.M. (2009). *The post-high school outcomes of youth with disabilities up to 4 years after high school: A report of findings from the National Longitudinal Transition Study-2* (NLTS2), (NCSER 2009-3017). Menlo Park, CA: SRI International. Retrieved from https://nces.ed.gov /pubs2017/2017064.pdf

Palardy, G. (2013). High school socioeconomic segregation and student attainment. *American Educational Research Journal, 50*(4), 714–754.

Pajares, F., Miller, M., & Levin, J. R. (1994). Role of self-efficacy and self-concept beliefs in mathematical problem solving: A path analysis. *Journal of Educational Psychology, 86*(2), 193–203.

Pascarella, E. T., & Terenzini, P. T. (1991). *How college affects students: Findings and insights from twenty years of research.* San Francisco: Jossey-Bass.

Pascarella, E. T., & Terenzini, P. T. (2005). *How colleges affect students: A third decade of research.* San Francisco: Jossey-Bass.

Reker, G. T., Peacock, E. J., & Wong, P. T. P. (1987). Meaning and purpose in life and well-being: A life-span perspective. *Journal of Gerontology, 42*(1), 44–49.

Scholl, L., Seth, P., Kariisa, M., Wilson, N., & Baldwin, G. (2018). Drug and opioid-involved overdose deaths – United States, 2013–2017. *Morbidity and Mortality Weekly Report,* ePub December 21, 2018. Published January 4, 2019; 67, 1419–1427. doi:http://dx.doi.org/10.15585/mmwr.mm675152e1

Schulenberg, J. E., Johnston, L. D., O'Malley, P. M., Bachman, J. G., Miech, R. A., & Patrick, M. E. (2017). *Monitoring the future: National survey results on drug use, 1975–2016: Volume II, College students and adults ages 19–55.* Ann Arbor: Institute for Social Research, University of Michigan,

Schunk, D. (1995). *Social origins of self-regulatory competence: The role of observational learning through peer modeling.* Paper presented at the 61st Biennial Conference of the Society for Research in Child Development, Indianapolis, IN. (ED 281 375). Retrieved from https://files.eric.ed.gov/fulltext /ED381275.pdf

Schunk, D. H., & Pajares, F. (2002). The development of academic self-efficacy. In A. Wigfield & J. Eccles (Eds.), *Development of achievement motivation* (pp. 16–31). San Diego, CA: Academic Press.

Scott-Clayton, J. (2012). *What explains trends in labor supply among U.S. undergraduates,*

1970–2009? (NBER Working Paper No. 1774). Cambridge, MA: National Bureau of Economic Research.

Scott-Clayton, J., & Schudde, L. (2016). Pell grants as performance-based aid? An examination of satisfactory academic progress requirements in the nation's largest need-based aid program. *Research in Higher Education, 57*(8), 943–967.

Shernoff, D. (2010). Engagement in after-school programs as a predictor of social competence and academic performance. *American Journal of Community Psychology, 45*(3-4), 325–337.

Singell, L. (2004). Come and stay a while: Does financial aid effect retention conditioned on enrollment at a large public university? *Economics of Education Review, 23*(5), 459–471.

Smith, R. (2003). Changing institutional culture for first-year students and those who teach them. *About Campus, 8*(March-April), 3–8.

Snell (1982). *The discovery of the mind in Greek philosophy and literature.* New York: Dover. (Original work published 1960).

Stinebrickner, R., & Stinebrickner, J. R. (2003). Working during school and academic performance. *Journal of Labor Economics, 21*(2), 473–491.

Strayhorn, T. L. (2006). Factors influencing the academic achievement of first-generation college students. *NASPA Journal Online, 43*(4), 82–111.

Steele, C. M. (1988). The psychology of self-affirmation: Sustaining the integrity of the self. *Advances in Experimental Social Psychology, 21,* 261–302.

Steele, C. M. (1998). A threat in the air: How stereotypes shape intellectual identity and performance. In J. L. Eberhardt & S. T. Fiske (Eds.), *Confronting racism: The problem and the response* (pp. 202–233). Thousand Oaks, CA: Sage.

Substance Abuse and Mental Health Services Administration. (2014). *Results from the 2013 National Survey on Drug Use and Health: Summary of national findings* (NSDUH Series H-48, HHS Publication No. [SMA] 14-4863). Rockville, MD: Author.

Tinto, V. (1987). *Leaving college.* Chicago: University of Chicago Press.

Tinto, V. (1993). *Leaving college: Rethinking the causes and cures of student attrition.* Chicago: University of Chicago Press.

Tinto, V. (2016, September 26). From retention to persistence. *Inside Higher Education,* Retrieved from https://www.insidehighered.com/views/2016/09/26/how-improve-student-persistence-and-completion-essay

Trevisan, D. A., Bass, E., Powell, K., & Eckerd, L. M. (2017). Meaning in life in college students: Implications for college counselors, *Journal of College Counseling, 20*(1), 37–51.

Trombitas, K. (2012). Financial stress: An everyday reality for college students. Lincoln, NE: Inceptia White Paper. Retrieved from https://www.universitybusiness.com/sites/default/files/Inceptia_FinancialStress_whitepaper.pdf

Turner, A. L., & Berry, T. R. (2000). Counseling center contributions to student retention and graduation: A longitudinal assessment. *Journal of College Student Development, 41*(6), 627–636.

Walton, G., & Cohen, G., (2007). A question of belonging: Race, social fit, and achievement. *Journal of Personality and Social Psychology, 92*(1), 82–96.

Walton, G. M., & Spencer, S. J., (2009). Latent ability: Grades and test scores systematically underestimate the intellectual ability of negatively stereotyped students. *Psychological Science. 20*(9), 1132–1139.

Wessel, R. D., Jones, J. A., Markle, L., & Westfall, C. (2009). Retention and graduation of students with disabilities: Facilitating student success. *Journal of Postsecondary Education and Disability, 21,* 116–125.

Zika, S., & Chamberlain, K. (1992). On the relation between meaning in life and psychological well-being. *British Journal of Psychology, 83,* 133–145.

Zohar, D., & Marshall, I. (2000). *Spiritual intelligence: The ultimate intelligence.* London, England, United Kingdom: Bloomsbury.

Chapter 4

CULTIVATING CAMPUS ENVIRONMENTS TO SUPPORT DIVERSE STUDENT POPULATIONS

Michelle Tyson

As demonstrated in previous chapters, student success is dependent on how institutions are prepared to meet the changing needs of students. Students entering college campuses today are unlike ever before, though the campuses themselves have not evolved alongside this demographic and societal shift, creating a disconnect between the needs of students and what colleges have the capacity to provide. Whereas each institution has its own culture and creates its own environment, the culture and environment of higher education as a whole needs to be examined. Higher education has a responsibility to society to educate and graduate a sufficient number of individuals in order to build and sustain communities, both big and small, that are economically stable (Carnavale, Smith, & Strohl, 2013; Museus & Jayakumar, 2012). Individual institutions have the responsibility to recruit and retain these future graduates by intentionally creating the campus culture that is welcoming to diverse student populations and fostering the inclusive and engaging environments that allow for student success.

This chapter explores the role that campus environments play in student success and identifies strategies for student affairs leaders and educators to influence and create an inclusive and engaging campus environment for the students of today and tomorrow. Beginning with a brief history of the "traditional" college campus and discussion of how this history has created environments that are (under)serving modern student populations, I define key terms used, such as climate, culture, and environment, to introduce models of inclusive and engaging college campuses. Finally, I provide a description of the characteristics of students attending college today and introduce short- and long-term strategies for praxis to meet the changing needs.

Campus Environments

History of Higher Education and Traditional Environments

Though it is important to note that indigenous people were educating within their communities long before colonization, the history of formalized American higher education can be traced to the colonial era, with the founding of the first institution, Harvard, in 1636 (Cohen & Kisker, 2010). From the founding of the original institutions through the eras of institutional growth and the evolution of students accessing higher education, we have come to understand that there are many purposes of higher education for an individual as well as society. The first students to attend college were 14- and 15-year-old boys coming from wealthy white families. Initially, the founding purpose of colleges in the United States was to control these youth by sending them away to the colleges, which would then act as a surrogate parent by instilling character education steeped in morality and discipline within an isolated community, while preparing these young men for life as clergymen (Cohen & Kisker, 2010).

The population attending college and the purpose of higher education expanded greatly in the following century as students from lower and middle classes gained access to college, including some women and small segments of the African American population living in the North (Allen & Jewell, 2002; Cohen & Kisker, 2010; Perkins, 1997). With these changes in demographics, the age of the student attending college increased slightly from the prior generation. Young people continued to leave home to attend college, as the residential nature of college established in the colonial era persisted. The purpose of higher education broadened with this change in access as well, as many students pursued the original intent of preparation for the church, studying classics, such as Greek, Latin and moral philosophy, whereas others began enrolling with the intent to learn specific vocations within the sciences. By 1899, about 4 percent of 18 year olds were attending college (Cohen & Kisker, 2010).

The demand for doctors, lawyers, and other professionals to hold a college degree, combined with the belief that education could be used as a vehicle to move from the lower class to the middle class, led to great expansion in higher education, and by 1940, the percentage of 18 year olds attending college had increased to 16 percent (Cohen & Kisker, 2010). Young white men were greatly represented in this growing number, though more black men and women also found opportunities for higher education. In addition to the potential for social mobility as a purpose for attending college, so was the opportunity to engage in a residential setting and cultivate relationships with faculty and peers, both of which led to shaping societal perceptions of what the purpose of a college education was to be and what a college campus environment was all about. Those perceptions of college continue into the present day, over 100 years later, and have become what is traditionally thought of as higher education. The "traditional" college student in the later part of the twentieth century was a white young adult, aged 18 or 19, whose parents had attended college and held at least a bachelor's degree. These students likely moved away from home, lived in college residence halls, attended college on a full-time basis, engaged in various extracurricular experiences, and often graduated in four years. Additionally, these students were likely full-paying students who relied on a relatively small amount of financial assistance, if any at all, because they remained financial dependents of their parents. College environments were shaped by these traditional students and the needs they had at the time.

The challenge with this traditional view of a college campus and the environments created is that the profile of a typical twenty-first century college student has changed and continues to evolve quickly, as more and more diverse students are accessing higher education (Bound, Lovenhiem, & Turner, 2010; Montiegel, 1999; Museus & Jayakumar, 2012; Ross-Gordon, 2011; Soares, 2013). By 2006, "the eighteen-to-twenty-two-year-old white male attending full-time would never again be the typical college student" (Cohen & Kisker, 2010, p. 470). Kasworm (2014) agreed, stating that 85 percent of the students attending college today do not fit the criteria once established as a traditional college student. The environments these students are stepping into have not changed as quickly.

Characteristics of Inclusive and Engaging Environments

A basic dictionary definition of *environment* is the "circumstances and conditions in which one is surrounded; the aggregate of social and cultural conditions that influence the life of individuals and community" ("Environment," 2018, definition 1, 2b). The campus environments in which students enter and interact with throughout their educational career are heavily shaped by both campus culture and campus climate. It is the professional responsibility of student affairs leaders and educators to create the environments that are both inclusive and engaging to the diverse student populations seeking higher education opportunities today and in the future. Understanding the intersection of culture and climate with today's student population is how we will begin to understand how to develop and cultivate the campus environment.

Campus Culture and Campus Climate

A number of scholars have studied campus climate and campus culture. Bauer (1998) provided a comprehensive summary to define these two terms. *Campus culture* is broadly shaped by the history of the institution, including the physical structures and their symbolism, the imbedded rituals and traditions, the educational mission, and the policies and practices in place. Campus culture examines an institution from a holistic point of view to understand the key components of a campus' identity—the values, beliefs, and assumptions that create the "cultural norms" that guide behaviors. These cultural norms affect the way in which education is approached and delivered (Museus & Jayakumar, 2012) and provide a frame of reference for how outside news and events get interpreted (Kuh & Hall, 1993). *Campus climate,* on the other hand, refers to "the current perceptions, attitudes, and expectations" (Bauer, 1998, p. 2) that are susceptible to change. Climate is best described as the way one might feel at any given time within their environment, based on their observations. It focuses more on individual sections of the institution and is affected by organizational phenomena as well as outside news and events. Both campus culture and climate create the patterns of behavior from institutional actors that can affect how students experience their environment (Museus, Ravello, & Vega, 2012).

Characteristics of Today's Student Population

As introduced above, although the once traditional college student certainly continues to pursue higher education, they are no longer the majority. In 2013, The American Council on Education introduced the term "post-traditional student" to describe and encompass the many faces and the life experiences of twenty-first century college students, and to better reflect the individual needs of those pursuing a college degree (Soares, 2013). Characteristics used to expand the understanding of the post-traditional learner include

- Students who are first-generation college students;
- Students who are first-generation U.S. citizens;
- Students who are not only financially independent from others but also have children or family that are financially dependent on them;
- Students who work full time and take classes part time, causing an increased time to degree;
- Students who are from an historically underrepresented, marginalized population;
- Students who are single parents;

• Students who had or have an affiliation with military service (Gagliardi & Soares, 2017).

In 2017, 60 percent (13.3 million) of all undergraduate students (23.1 million) were either older than 24 years old; working full time; financially independent; or a current or former member, or spouse of a member in the military (Gagliardi & Soares, 2017). Clearly, the depth and breadth of a traditional college student have evolved into those of a post-traditional student population. With this expanded understanding of post-traditional, it is important to emphasize that although much of the post-traditional population is over the age of 23 and an adult learner, an increasing number of traditional-aged students (18 to 22 years old) also meet this post-traditional criteria, given this extended list of characteristics. Specifically understanding the varying post-traditional students' needs and the environments in which they can thrive and successfully complete their educational goals is critical, because higher education leaders accept responsibility for the role of institutional retention and student persistence towards degree.

Inclusive and Engaging Environments

Tinto's (1987) theory of student success is one of the most commonly referenced explanations of why students leave college prior to earning a degree. In short, Tinto proposed that in regard to student success, there are particular characteristics of not only an individual student prior to attending college but also the educational institution, such as climate and culture. Upon the intersection of student and institutional characteristics, an environment is created in which a student would either persist through degree completion, or would leave the institution and perhaps post-secondary education entirely.

Whereas Tinto's (1987) framework puts the onus on the student to fit into and integrate into the institutional culture, Museus and Jayakumar (2012) have argued that the institutional culture is more responsible than individual student factors in retention and persistence. This paradigm shift is indicative of the philosophical question, Whose job is it to retain a student and ensure student success? Kuh (2015) pointed out that throughout most of the twentieth century, the burden was placed on the student to fit into the mold of the institution. This worked well for students for whom higher education was historically designed, however as that student population started to shift toward the end of the century, the numbers applicable to these older models of retention dwindled. Museus (2014) reiterated that the modern traditional college campus and its culture has not evolved along with the needs of the changing demographic of students entering college, which has led to less-supportive campus environments. Tinto's model uses factors, such as family background, student academic skills and abilities, educational trajectory, and prior educational experience, to define pre-entry attributes—those pre-existing conditions that a student carries with them prior to attending college.

Yet, pre-entry attributes are even more developed and often more complex for the diverse populations of students seeking higher education today. For example, students may have a much more complicated family background that could include the economic responsibility and care of dependents, such as children or parents. Many students are leaving high school environments in need of remediation for seemingly basic academic skills as they enter the college environment. Lower-income students may be working full-time jobs or experiencing housing and food insecurities while attending college. Additionally, the academic trajectories may appear unclear. Adult students and veterans demonstrate enrollment patterns that are often seemingly disjointed, with gaps in enrollment, movement among institutions, and assorted coursework that may not be leading toward a specific degree. These increasingly evolving pre-entry factors impact the fit within an institution, especially if the institutional environment is not prepared to recognize, honor, and engage these life experiences that impact how a student fits into the institution's culture.

The current eight-year bachelor's completion rate is less than 40 percent (Bound et al., 2010; Pingel & Sponsler, 2015), which means that at least 60 percent of college students are leaving college without a college degree, indicating a disjuncture in the intersection of students and their college environments. Gladieux and Perna (2005) pointed out that those dropping out of college are more likely to come from low-income backgrounds, more likely to have children, more likely to be independent of parent financial support, and also more likely to have parents who do not have a college degree. A new model for student engagement that supports equity and inclusion for these diverse students is needed to better understand the role of campus environments on student success.

Museus (2014) provided that new model, the culturally engaging campus environments (CECE) model, which also acknowledges the pre-college inputs as a significant factor to student success, as Tinto (1987) suggested, but has expanded on the impact of those factors, specifically for diverse populations. The CECE model suggests that "undergraduates who encounter more culturally engaging campus environments are more likely to (1) exhibit a greater sense of belonging, more positive academic dispositions, and higher levels of academic performance and ultimately (2) be more likely to persist to graduation" (Museus, 2014, p. 210). Institutions have a responsibility to create an environment in which racially and ethnically diverse students can succeed (Museus & Jayakumar, 2012).

Practices That Create Inclusion and Engagement

The American College Personnel Association (ACPA) and National Association of Student Personnel Administrators (NASPA) (2015) stated, "Higher education is a dynamic enterprise facing unprecedented change" (p. 7). One of those significant changes is the demographic diversity of students pursuing higher education in the twenty-first century. Student affairs educators and higher education leaders, particularly those serving in the frontline service positions, such as academic advising, campus life, residential education, financial aid, and student academic services, understand the role they play in shaping the environment and the success of these students. They need to understand how to work with these post-traditional students, because they will continue to be the fastest growing population of college students (Bowl, 2010; Gilardi & Guglielmetti, 2011; Montiegel, 1999; Phillips, Baltzer, Filoon, & Whitley, 2017; Soares, 2013). Student affairs preparation programs play a critical role in preparing graduate students who will lead higher education institutions in the future. Ultimately, the efforts of these preparation programs impact the academic success of the student population, as well as the sustainability of institutions serving the public good mission.

A significant piece of best serving students academically, personally, and socially is to create an inclusive and engaging college campus that is both culturally relevant and responsive. Museus (2014) proposed this in his work on the CECE framework. The CECE framework introduces nine independent indicators of a culturally engaging campus environment that demonstrate a campus' commitment to engaging diverse cultural backgrounds and facilitating their success in post-secondary education. These indicators include (a) the significance of cultural familiarity, (b) connecting the academic experience to this culturally relevant knowledge, (c) cultural community service, (d) cross-cultural engagement, (e) collectivist cultural orientation, (f) culturally validating environments, (g) humanized educational environments, (h) proactive philosophies, and (i) the availability of holistic support. Although not a comprehensive list of engagement strategies, together the following overarching initiatives of class engagement, a culture of care, one-stop shops for student services, and experiential learning opportunities reflect those CECE indicators.

Classroom Engagement

A number of high-impact practices help engage college students in the campus environment and promote the success discussed in previous chapters. Kuh (2011) suggested that some of these practices take place in the classroom, such as (a) faculty having consistent and meaningful contact with students, (b) faculty setting and communicating clear expectations, and (c) instructors providing prompt feedback on assignments. The classroom should be a space that allows for a student to have a physical connection to both students and faculty. The CECE model echoes the importance of this type of engagement, emphasizing the *significance of cultural familiarity* (CECE Indicator #1) in the classroom. It is essential that students connect with those faculty and students who share a common background and similar life experience in an academic setting. These opportunities for *cross-cultural engagement* (CECE Indicator #4) can be achieved through cohort-based learning communities and dedicated time to engage with other students through group work and active experiential learning. Creating diverse learning experiences by considering various cultural perspectives in the development of curriculum and selection of class materials validates student life experiences and cultural backgrounds (Quaye & Harper, 2014).

Connecting the academic experience to this culturally relevant knowledge (CECE Indicator #2) can be achieved through offering specific classes, such as those that focus on ethnic studies. The engagement can also occur in any class that allows students the time and space to connect to their understanding of their communities of origin by acquiring new knowledge that contributes to their lived experience and by reading authors and hearing from speakers who have had a similar lived experience. In addition, students should be invited to share their experience and knowledge about what is important to themselves and to their communities with others. This level of acknowledgment encourages additional participation, which in turn helps sustain increased levels of motivation within the academic setting.

A Culture of Care

Outside the classroom, recommended practices include (a) connecting students with on-campus employment opportunities (Kuh, 2011), (b) providing strong academic advising and support services (Anft, 2018), (c) eliminating the run-around and creating ease in accessing campus services (Anft, 2018; Tyson, 2017), and (d) establishing quality and expansive opportunities to connect with affinity groups are recommended (Museus, 2014). A key responsibility that student affairs leaders play in these practices is ensuring that those on the front lines have what they need to be helpful to students (Tyson, 2017). The frontline professionals I am referring to include resident advisors and hall directors, financial aid counselors, academic advisors, admissions representatives, career counselors, student activity program coordinators, and cashier's office staff, among many others. These staff members need to develop interpersonal and problem-solving skills sets.

Together these skills contribute to a "culture of care." An environment built from a culture of care represents a growing trend among educational fields. In healthcare, the culture of care began as a theory of practice in nursing care that describes a method in which professionals assist patients from diverse cultures in receiving culturally competent and congruent healthcare (McFarland & Wehbe-Alamah, 2014). This method can also be applied to educational environments as one strategy for creating a supportive environment in which students elect to engage. The CECE model expands the idea of culture of care to include the validation of one's cultural background. *Culturally validating environments* (CECE Indicator #6) and *humanized educational environments* (CECE Indicator #7) can be created and sustained by the individuals who hold the student-facing positions listed above. These people in frontline service positions are in a critical role to demonstrate that they value the cultural backgrounds and identities of each student. Grounded in cultural competence, institutions have adopted this culture of care philosophy as a response to the changing personal needs that students are expressing as they enter college—to include students with mental health needs and physical and learning challenges, those experiencing food and housing insecurities, and students who simply want to fit in—or as a way to recognize and honor past experience.

The frontline service professionals and other institutional representatives must have the ability to holistically see and hear the individual in front of them, listening to individual stories, and subsequently be equipped with the tools to help coach or advise a student through a particular situation. If these are not natural skill sets of those serving the frontlines of education outside of the classroom, then institutional leaders need to provide professional development to help frontline professionals in these key areas of service in acquiring those skills, while also building the capacity to develop meaningful relationships with the students they serve. Building and sustaining a culture of care that validates diverse student populations can be a significant step in cultivating an engaged environment, while supporting students through their individual experience.

One-Stop Shops for Student Services

Comprehensive academic advising and "one-stop" shops for student and academic services have recently been identified as two additional starting points for cultivating an inclusive campus environment and are indicative of a *collectivist cultural orientation* (CECE Indicator #5). College students are entering campus with a wide range of diverse needs—from mental health support and healthy food options to tutoring and writing support—and often the assigned academic advisor becomes the university representative to navigate the systems of support with a student. Anft (2018) explained,

Gone are the days when the advising office's mission involved little more than helping students register for next semester's classes or decide on a major. The emerging brand of adviser is still expected to take on those tasks, but also to handle a wider range of student needs—financial concerns, mental-health issues, extracurricular opportunities—and keep students on track. (p. 24)

Clearly, the role of academic advisor has expanded. The *availability of holistic support* (CECE Indicator #9) is a concept that demonstrates an understanding of the student as a whole person and makes room for frontline professionals, faculty, and other staff to work with students as that whole person. Many institutions have recognized this increased expectation on individuals in these positions and have made structural changes to reflect the evolution of the position by training advisors to be academic coaches. Other institutions have increased the academic advising budget to support additional advisors, allowing these advisors (or coaches) to spend significant amounts of time with each student. Due to the significant role the academic advisor has grown to play in student success beyond academics, many institutions have even moved advising responsibilities away from the faculty and developed professional advising staffs or created a co-advisor hybrid model that includes student affairs practitioners as a co-advisor alongside the faculty member. Between 2013 and 2016, the National Academic Advising Association reported a 36 percent increase in institutional funding to support advising staff (Anft, 2018). This increase in student need has necessitated academic advisors to be in constant contact with students and have a coordinated effort with other academic and student service offices, specifically the financial aid staff, in order to ensure that the whole student is being cared for in the institutional environment and avoid the run-around that often occurs on college campuses.

This constant contact between and among institutional offices has also led to a number of campuses adopting a concierge model of support (Anft, 2018), where key student-facing university operations have been brought together in a one-stop shop, similarly reducing the run-around and providing better, comprehensive customer service to students. This model ensures that students receive comprehensive services to meet all of their diverse needs. These one-stop shops look different at different institutions, but tend to include financial aid, registrar, and bill-paying functions. Other institutions have worked to combine opportunities for student involvement, connecting academic classrooms to residence halls or gathering campus involvement opportunities with one another. The key to an effective environment is having qualified, well-trained staff in all of these areas that can support the basic needs of students on campus. Although these types of high-impact practices are often designed to better engage a population that may be deemed at risk, all students can benefit from these changes in practice (Kuh, 2011).

Experiential Learning Opportunities

College students entering college today tend to have a strong commitment to their communities and societal issues. They want to demonstrate that commitment through social change initiatives that allow them to contribute to the bettering of the communities in which they live, by working on long-term systemic change (Museus, 2014; Peck, Seemiller & Sawalich, 2018). In the CECE framework, this *cultural community service* (CECE Indicator #3) can be found when institutions provide students the tools and opportunities to give back and transform their community. Internships, study abroad, and service learning have become important strategies to keep students engaged, particularly for upper-class students in their junior and senior years. Creating an environment where this type of experiential learning is not only available but also incorporated into the curriculum demonstrates an institution's commitment to giving students real-world experience in meaningful engagement on and off campus. Culturally relevant and responsive experiential learning connects students to faculty, staff, and peers; provides opportunities to learn more about their own cultural communities; and validates the identities and knowledge of diverse students, while fostering cultural connections.

Experiences inside the classroom and the opportunity for experiential learning, combined with a culture of care and a culture that reduces the confusion and simplifies procedures, can create an environment that truly puts students from diverse backgrounds first. These are all *proactive philosophies* (CECE Indicator #8) that institutions can put into practice to demonstrate their commitment to valuing students, particularly those who have been historically underrepresented on traditional campuses. These practices are examples of those that allow students to experience an environment that provides meaningful and culturally relevant practices by using the nine indicators of a culturally engaged campus (Museus, 2014).

Assessing Campus Environments

As the population continues to evolve, so must the strategies for assessing campus environments. Creating and sustaining a culture that is both dedicated to continuous assessment and to changing campus practices based on the results of those assessments is the only way institutions can keep up with the changing demography. Although the individual methods of assessment will look different on individual campuses, there are a few overarching key recommendations to assess campus environments.

The first consideration is to understand what is already known about engagement practices on an individual campus. What are the current practices? Who is responsible for them? Who is participating in them? Who is not participating in them? Are they working? How do we know? Asking these questions will help institutional leaders begin to determine what remains unknown about student engagement on their own campus. Often institutions commit to looking at large data sets to assess student success without a full commitment to making sense of the data. Witham and Bensimon (2012) emphasized the importance of developing a culture of inquiry by inviting faculty and practitioners to examine institution-specific data. Defining student success, disaggregating data, involving campus representatives, and establishing an understanding of how the findings will be used must all be considered in creating and sustaining a culture of inquiry. The significance in having representatives from across campus involved in this process cannot be understated. Too often, those involved in this conversation tend to be institutional leaders at the very top. Although it is important to have those individuals included, a culture of inquiry needs to include the perspectives of those who work directly with students as well as those who are paying attention to the national landscape to obtain a truly holistic view of the campus environment, because both qualitative and quantitative data are critical in this effort.

Staff in frontline positions as well as faculty see students on a daily basis, hear the narratives and stories of the student experience, and assist with positive and negative individual academic and social engagement on an individual student level. These two perspectives must be invited and seriously considered when assessing the campus environment because they can share the qualitative data to connect the curricular, co-curricular, and extracurricular experiences of the student population. Leaders from both student affairs and academic affairs can provide broader context to the conversation related to both national trends as well as institutional context. Representatives from institutional research provide key information and data to the conversation because they are able to obtain historical and current data points to benchmark the conversation and should be able to make sense of and translate the quantitative data. The role of student affairs administrators is to bring these groups together and set the tone for what can become a culture of inquiry, including defining student success and facilitating the conversation about long-term goals and outcomes that focus on equity-minded change (Bensimon, Dowd, & Witham, 2016). A successful culture of inquiry can result in changing institutional processes and practices to better meet the needs of today's students. Institutional leaders need to be prepared to take that action.

In addition to the faculty and staff, assessment of campus climates should be focused on measuring students' attitudes, perceptions, observations, and interactions as well (Museus & Jayakumar, 2012). Facilitating periodic campus climate surveys to gauge how students are experiencing their campus culture at different points in time will establish a benchmark and allow institutional leaders to identify not only culturally relevant practices that are effective but also the gaps in existing programming and services. Setting equity goals in terms of engagement and retention and then implementing the actions that will move toward those goals is the next step (Finley & McNair, 2014).

Witham and Bensimon (2012) posed five overarching topics that institutions must consider through this assessment process: (a) evidence, (b) disaggregating the data, (c) assumptions and values, (d) institutional histories, and (e) language.

- *Evidence.* Campus climate surveys are often administered as a method of data collection on campuses. Questions to consider in looking at the results of these assessments as evidence revolve around who has access to the data and how the data will be used. Results of these climate-based surveys cannot be kept locked away in the ivory tower; they must be shared throughout academic and student affairs units. Professional staff as well as faculty must be invited to look at the evidence and share the counter narratives they hear as qualitative evidence.
- *Disaggregating the data.* Institutions have the technology that can result in many data points, but colleges have not mastered using this technology as assessment tools (Anft, 2018). Data produced through the technology should be disaggregated by race/ethnicity and other demographics to truly assess the gaps in student achievement that may exist within the environment and help guide the conversation to equity mindedness (Kuh, 2011; Witham & Bensimon, 2012).
- *Assumptions and values.* When bringing members of campus together to look at the disaggregated evidence, are we too often defaulting to a deficit-minded narrative? Does the group or individuals in the group assume that certain students are not doing well because of their inputs (or lack thereof), as Tinto (1987) suggested? These assumptions could be having a negative impact on the culture. Are leaders willing to question existing institutional policy and practices and acknowledge institutional responsibility in the experience of historically marginalized students?
- *Institutional histories.* Taking responsibility for institutional policies and practices will require leaders to ask, How and why are things done on

this campus? Why do certain policies and procedures exist on this campus? Too often, the answer has been, "Because that is the way it has always been done." This response can no longer be the default. Leaders must be willing to push for changing those historical practices.

• *Language.* Specifically looking at language related to diversity and equity, Witham and Bensimon (2012) encouraged leaders to move away from looking at best practices across institutions and instead focus on the specifics of that particular institution. How is student success defined on campus? Who is held accountable for meeting certain success measures? Are students looked at through a deficit lens, resulting in deficit language?

This strategy of discussing assessment along the lines of these five topics intentionally moves away from looking at student deficits and focuses on institutional responsibility in student success, as recommended above, by naming and interrogating the problems rather than avoiding them. The most important question, however, will always be, Are we committed to acting on the results of these assessments and actually implementing equity-minded change?

The CECE model can also be used as a guide for assessing campus environments through the lens of cultural relevance and cultural responsiveness (Museus, 2014). Indicators of inclusive and equitable environments echo the five topics that Witham and Bensimon (2012) introduced. At the same time, these indicators expanded on the ways in which campus environments can maintain relevance to the cultural backgrounds and communities of diverse students and focus on the ways in which support systems consider and respond to the cultural norms and needs student have.

Challenges and Opportunities

Understanding the National Landscape

It is projected that 65 percent of all jobs in the United States will require a college degree by the year 2020 (Carnavale et al., 2013). Simply educating the once traditional student will not be enough to meet these demands, because there are not enough of such students. According to Bransberger and Michelau (2016), the number of high school graduates is projected to decrease over the next two decades: "No longer will state and postsecondary institutional leaders be able to count on a steadily increasing stream of high school graduates knocking at their door" (p. 43). Additionally, the racial and ethnic demographic of the school-aged population is changing. These changes in both the compositional diversity of the youth and the aging college student population will inevitably have an effect on higher education. By 2030, the number of white high school graduates is projected to decrease by 14 percent compared to what it was in 2013 (Bransberger & Michelau, 2016). With this decrease will come an increase in the number of students of color graduating high schools, primarily Hispanic and Asian populations (Bransberger & Michelau, 2016).

At least 60 percent of college students are leaving college without a college degree (Bound et al., 2010), meaning that in 2017, there were between 36 and 38 million adults who fit this recently defined "near-completer" descriptor—having some college and no degree (Gagliardi & Soares, 2017; Michelau, 2011). Whereas there are a number of factors that may contribute to this retention problem, lack of engagement and feelings of exclusion are significant among them. Addressing these factors will need to be a multipronged approach in not only being proactive in preventing students from leaving but also re-engaging those students who do leave to return and complete their degree. Both of these will become increasingly more critical in fulfilling the public good mission of higher education, bolstering the knowledge base in each individual state as well as the nation as a whole, and filling the job and workforce demands of the twenty-first century. Undoubtedly, institutional leaders must prepare their institutions for these changes by creating culturally engaging campuses to prepare for the students who will be enrolling, primarily students of color and adult learners.

As the twenty-first century continues, more jobs will require the worker's ability to create knowledge, think critically, and communicate effectively (Gagliardi & Soares, 2017)—skills that are acquired through a college education. Particularly as the number of high school graduates plateaus over the next two decades and the once reliable sources of educational funding (e.g., state funding) grow more volatile, institutional leaders will be forced to think more entrepreneurially about how to recruit and retain students (Gagliardi & Soares, 2017). These forces will undermine the viability of many colleges and universities who choose not to address environmental concerns on their campus. Because there are fewer high school graduates to compete for, these institutions will find they need to expand the base of those whom they are serving, for institutional survival. The changes in race, ethnicity, and age of the student population will be an issue of both access and retention at most institutions throughout the current century. Student affairs educators can play a role in advocating for these changes identified above, playing an influential role on their own campuses and in the profession at large.

Implications for Practice

Meeting the needs of today's student cannot be reduced to one or two easy fixes, just as one size does not fit all. The depth and breadth of diverse students accessing, attending, and experiencing higher education are too great. As described, post-traditional students are more likely to be single parents, veterans, immigrants, lower-income individual, students employed full-time, and/or first generation students, all of which are characteristics of an "at-risk" student (Ross-Gordon, 2011). These life experiences have shaped who these students are, before they ever set foot on college campuses, but the experiences are rarely honored or even acknowledged when they enter the college environment. Too often, the policies and practices in place are not only not contributing to student success but also actually serving as a barrier to student success. Although not exhaustive, below is a growing list of the increasing populations that campuses need to consider, along with examples of policies and practices that need to be (re)considered.

First-Generation Students, Low-Income Students, and Students of Color: Family Support. The outdated practice of forcing students to separate from their families and communities as they enter college must be reexamined. Students of color often rely heavily on family support and may not need to break away from those systems, as has been suggested in Tinto's (1987) outdated model. More recent studies have demonstrated that the emotional support from family is essential in student success (Kiyama et al., 2015). Engaging families throughout the academic year can positively impact students' feelings of inclusion and belonging on campus (Whitford, 2018). Student organizations on campus that connect students to culture and identity can often bridge the gaps that exists between home and campus environments. Historically, these organizations and opportunities have not been well resourced, often relying on student fees. Dedicating more funding and staff support to these units is one example of an institutional practice that could be examined. Additionally, housing policies may need to be adjusted to better fit students' needs. Are the residential facilities inclusive of cultural practices? Are they designed to accommodate a student with a family to support? Perhaps not every student needs to live on campus.

Near-Completers. In 2008, The Center for Adult and Experiential Education calculated that there were 38 million adults in the United States with some college and no degree (Michelau, 2011). Michelau (2011), utilizing information from the Lumina Foundation of Education, described these students as "near-completers" instead of dropouts. If and when these near-completers do return to college campuses to complete their degree, the disjuncture between the ideal (i.e., traditional) methods of student engagement and the reality of adult life will continue to persist (Kasworm, 2014). To meet these needs, institutions need to reevaluate and deconstruct transfer and credit requirements as well as dedicate resources to the student affairs educators who have working knowledge on how to best serve their needs. Additionally, a trend among adult education advocates is to promote the practice of recognizing life experience through college credit. Competency-based education and prior learning assessment are two ways that students are earning credit for what they already know, and the prior academic and life experience they bring to the college classroom (Sherman & Klein-Collins, 2015). Institutions need to provide a mechanism to evaluate and award credit for life experiences, which often include knowledge obtained through prior coursework as well as on-the-job real-world work experience.

Adult Students. Gagliardi and Soares (2017) suggested that adult learners are less likely to be enrolled in a traditional four-year institution and can more often be found in the community college setting. However 35 percent of the adult learner population are choosing to attend institutions with bachelor's degree program offerings—those likely to be traditional four-year institutions. The lack of institutional preparation to meet the adult student needs impacts the student's ability to positively intersect with the institution and create the positive relationship that Tinto (1987) would argue leads to student persistence and retention.

Older students are understudied and misunderstood (Hagedorn, 2014), and very few studies have targeted adult student persistence (Kasworm, 2014). Institutional leaders need to disaggregate the data and understand how adults are experiencing the campus. Are classes offered at an opportune time to meet their needs? Are student service offices open and accessible beyond traditional business hours? Adult students are likely to "swirl," moving in and out of different educational environments. This is both a sign that institutions are not offering what is needed to keep them, and a characteristic that demonstrates their adult students' enrollment patterns. In a system-wide sample using National Education Longitudinal Study data, Goldrick-Rab (2006) discovered many students are exhibiting multi-institutional attendance patterns, because 47 percent of students in the twenty-first century have attended more than one institution over a six-year span, and 15 percent attended more than two institutions. These students may be enrolled in a community college one term, transfer to a four-year institution in the following term, yet go back to the community college to complete a course in a subsequent term. At any point, they may also need to take a term off from school and not enroll anywhere. How are institutions preparing to engage these students?

Transfer Students. In a study of college students who entered college for the first time in 2008, Mangan (2015) found that one-third of students had transferred institutions at least once by 2014, 6 years after initial point of entry. Half of these students actually transferred more than once. Institutions need to examine the policies and practices related to accepting transfer credit. Are students taking the same course content over and over again at different institutions because their initial work is not being valued with credit by a new institution? Reviewing the policies and practices within an institution that are used to evaluate transfer credit and ensuring that students are correctly awarded credit they have already earned will also allow for a friendlier campus, because that is one way to demonstrate that the campus values the students' previous experience. Is there an opportunity for these students to connect and engage with other students who are transferring into the school?

Recommendations for Practice

Role of Institutions

Whereas Tinto's theory of student departure (1987) would indicate that students are leaving their institutions because they did not exhibit the characteristics to persist at that institution, Museus and Jayakumar (2012) insisted that institutions have responsibility in establishing a climate and culture that better fit the needs of today's college student. The demographics of students continue to change, and institutions need to be prepared to engage and retain them. An institutional goal must be a multi-pronged approach, the first of which is to work on additional retention measures to prevent attrition of the traditional-aged student. If institutions are not successful in retaining these students as traditional-aged students, they will leave. When they leave the institution prior to degree completion, they become the near-completers described above, and the institution must also be prepared to welcome them back and retain, matriculate, and graduate them as well.

Institutional policies and practices need to be nimble enough to do this continuously, evolving with the populations that are inevitably going to continue to change. Deflecting responsibility of educating the twenty-first century post-traditional student will eventually have an impact on enrollment at four-year schools. As consumers of the educational product, students will either never select or will choose to leave the institutions that are not meeting their needs in search of those that can. It is in the best interest of institutions to think of both short-term and long-term solutions in creating the engaging campus environment that meets the needs of post-traditional students.

Short-term solutions could help retain the students that are currently pursuing degrees, whereas long-term planning could assist with the access and persistence for the populations moving forward. In general, Ely (1997) found that students have an increasingly higher expectation for quality customer service and support in every aspect. Ensuring that campus representatives, particularly frontline professionals who tend to be student affairs educators, are equipped with basic customer service skills is a short-term improvement that could go a long way in creating an engaging environment for students, as discussed above. Specific skills in active listening, asking probing questions, and going the extra mile are basic elements of customer service that must be extended to all students. Lack of this basic customer service may have a particularly negative impact on some populations—making them feel unwelcome when such services are not performed. An unfriendly campus culture often contributes to student attrition (Museus & Jayakumar, 2012). These small adjustments to current practices can begin the evolution of the campus environment and could have a large impact on post-traditional student success in the short term. Student service staff must understand the unique needs that exist, and faculty need to understand how to incorporate the life and work experience of students into course curriculum for more culturally relevant classroom discussion.

Institutional leaders should think proactively about creating a long-term strategy to meet the anticipated needs of their students in the future. These changes will need to take place within both academic and student service functions within the institution. Alternative delivery models for both in-person and online learning environments, truncated courses that may not fit into a typical semester or quarter term, and the offering of courses that meet on evenings and weekends may provide additional flexibility for students who have employment, family, and community commitments. Again, it will be critical to educate faculty through professional development opportunities about the growing populations, with special attention on how students of today and tomorrow learn and how to engage the life experience of students in a way that is both culturally relevant and culturally responsive. This will help prepare individual faculty members for effectively teaching all students in the classroom.

Role of Student Affairs Educators

The *Professional Competency Areas for Student Affairs Educators,* produced through an ACPA and NASPA (2015) joint publication, encourages those entering the field to think about the knowledge, skills, and dispositions that connect the history, philosophy, and values of the student affairs profession to current professional practice. Demonstrating this understanding through the ability to both work directly with and serve the students enrolling in our institutions as well as working through the administrative ranks within higher education to advocate for and make change for the post-traditional population represent a key responsibility of student affairs educators.

Student affairs educators play an important role in building and sustaining campus environments that engage diverse student populations. They are the conveners of campus representatives, the facilitators of conversations, and the ones who can move in, among, and between academic and student affairs units—from listening to the frontline staff, responding to faculty who are identifying student co-curricular needs, and connecting to the many student populations and individual stories of challenges and success. These leaders set the tone for culturally relevant and responsive campus engagement. Student affairs educators and leaders can build the skills of frontline service professionals, acknowledging and valuing the significant role they play in the student experience.

Individuals who choose to enter higher education need to be prepared to contribute to or lead the institutional practices that create inclusion and engagement, both inside and outside of the classroom. This competency area embodies the foundations of the profession from which current and future research, scholarship, and practice will change and grow. According to ACPA/NASPA (2015), "The commitment to demonstrating this competency area ensures that our present and future practices are informed by an understanding of the profession's history, philosophy, and values" (p. 18). Connecting to the history of the profession requires us to acknowledge what is not working.

Conclusion

Higher education public policy, institutional policies, and the structures of college campuses were created for the traditional college student many years ago. It is the growing number of post-traditional students who benefit the least from the more traditional policies and practices that still shape campus environments. This should concern higher education scholars, policymakers, and practitioners. With a changing population, institutional survival will depend on meeting the needs of diverse students. Because student needs are changing rapidly, institutions must be nimble. There are benefits to both short-term and long-term efforts to adapt our college environments through changing attitudes, policies, and practices to meet the needs addressed throughout this chapter. Student affairs professionals must commit to leading and facilitating the changes to campus policies that will allow for change to occur within institutional environments more quickly. Educational environments have been in a position of reacting to new student trends, rather than being proactive. Student affairs preparation programs and professional development programs should prepare educators to work with diverse student populations. Projections of Generation Z students show that they are more reliant on peer support, enjoy small group activities, and prefer face-to-face communications (Peck et al., 2018). Understanding the current and future gaps in how learners can access different institutions and persist through their goals of degree completion will help allow student affairs educators to determine how they can fill those gaps and be better advocates for the equity-minded change needed at every institution.

Reflection Questions

1. Who are the frontline professionals at institutions with whom students engage most often? How can those individuals contribute to the creation of a culture of care?
2. How do universities assess the environment on campus? Are frontline professionals included in the collection and analysis of student-level and institutional data?
3. Are there institutional policies that stand in the way of creating an inclusive and engaging campus environment? What are they? What purpose did they once serve? How can they be updated to serve modern students?
4. What are the short-term strategies that can be implemented to help make the college campus more engaging for all students?
5. What are the long-term changes that your college or university will need to make to improve the campus environment for future students?
6. How can you develop and institute a professional development program for your institution to teach faculty and staff about the needs of today's college students and their many roles in meeting those needs?

References

The American College Personnel Association (ACPA) and National Association of Student Personnel Administrators (NASPA). (2015). *Professional competency areas for student affairs educators.* Retrieved from https://www.naspa.org/images/uploads/main/ACPA_NASPA_Professional_Competencies_FINAL.pdf

Allen, W. R., & Jewell, J. O. (2002). A backward glance forward: Past, present, and future perspectives on historically black colleges and universities. *The Review of HigherEducation, 25,* 241–261.

Anft, M. (2018, July). Students needs have changed. Advising must change, too. *Chronicle of Higher Education, 64*(37), 24. Retrieved from https://www.chronicle.com/article/Student-Needs-Have-Changed/243797

Bauer, K. (1998). Editor's notes. *New Directions for Institutional Research, 98,* 1–5.

Bensimon, E. M., Dowd, A. C., & Witham, K. (2016). Five principles for enacting equity by design. *Diversity and Democracy, The equity imperative, 19*(1, winter).

Bound, J., Lovenheim, M., & Turner, S. (2010). Why have college completion rates declined? An analysis of changing student preparation and collegiate resources. *American Journal of Applied Economics, 2,* 129–157.

Bowl, M. (2010). Experiencing the barriers: Non-traditional students entering higher education. *Research Papers in Education, 16*(2), 141–160.

Bransberger, P., & Michelau, D. K. (2016). *Knocking at the college door: Projections of high school graduates* (9th ed.). Boulder, CO: Western Interstate Commission for Higher Education.

Carnavale, A. P., Smith, N., & Strohl, J. (2013). *Recovery: Job growth and education requirements through 2020.* Washington, DC: Georgetown Policy Institute, Georgetown University.

Cohen, A. M., & Kisker, C. B. (2010). *The shaping of American higher education: Emergence and growth of the contemporary system.* San Francisco: Jossey-Bass.

Ely, E. E. (1997, April). *The non-traditional student.* Paper presented at the American Association of Community Colleges Annual Conference (77th), Anaheim, CA.

Environment. (2018). In *Merriam-Webster Dictionary.com.* Retrieved from https://www.merriam-webster.com/

Finley, A., & McNair, T. (2014). *Assessing underserved students' engagement in high impact practices.* Washington, DC: Association of American Colleges and Universities. Retrieved from https://files.eric.ed.gov/fulltext/ED582014.pdf

Gagliardi, J., & Soares, L. (2017, Dec. 6). Serving post-traditional learners [Web log message]. *Higher EducationToday.* Retrieved from https://www.higheredtoday.org/2017/12/06/serving-post-traditional-learners/

Gilardi, S., & Guglielmetti, C. (2011). University life of non-traditional students: Engagement styles and impact on attrition. *Journal of Higher Education, 82*(1), 33–53.

Gladieux, L., & Perna, L. (2005). *Borrowers who drop out: A neglected aspect of the college student loan trend* (National Center Report #05-2). San Jose, CA: National Center for Public Policy and Higher Education.

Goldrick-Rab, S. (2006). Following their every move: An investigation of social class differences in college pathways. *Sociology of Education, 79*(1), 67–79.

Hagedorn, L. S. (2014). Engaging returning adult learners in community colleges. In S. J. Quaye & S. R. Harper (Eds.), *Student engagement in higher education: Theoretical approaches and practical approaches for diverse populations* (pp. 307–322). New York: Rutledge.

Kasworm, C .E. (2014) Paradoxical understandings regarding adult undergraduate persistence. *The Journal of Continuing Higher Education, 62*(2), 67–77.

Kiyama, J. M., Harper, C. E., Ramos, D., Aguayo, D., Page, L. A., & Riester, K. A. (2015). Parent and family engagement in higher education. *ASHE Higher Education Report, 41*(6), 1–94.

Kuh, G. D. (2011). What educators and administrators need to know about college student engagement. In S. R. Harper & J. F. L. Jackson (Eds.), *Introduction to American higher education* (pp. 189–212). New York: Routledge.

Kuh, G. D. (2015). Foreword. In S. J. Quaye & S. R. Harper (Eds.), *Student engagement in higher education: Theoretical perspectives and practical approaches for diverse populations* (pp. ix–xii). New York: Rutledge.

Kuh, G. D., & Hall, T. D. (1993). *Cultural perspectives in student affairs work* (American College Personnel Association Series). Lanham, MD: University Press of America.

Mangan, K. (2015, July 7). Despite hurdles, students keep switching colleges. *Chronicle of Higher Education.* Retrieved from https://www.chronicle.com/article /Despite-Hurdles-Students-Keep/231397

McFarland, M. R., & Wehbe-Alamah, H. B. (2014). *Leninger's culture care, diversity, and universality.* Burlington, MA: Jones & Bartlett.

Michelau, D. K. (2011). *Crossing the finish line: Helping adults with significant college credit get back on track to a college degree* (Complete to Compete Briefing Paper). Washington, DC: National Governors Association.

Montiegel, K. (1999). *Gaining a foothold: Women's transitions through work and college.* Washington, DC: American Association of University Women. Educational Foundation DYG & Lake Snell Perry & Associates.

Museus, S. D. (2014). The culturally engaging campus environments (CECE) model: A new theory of success among racially diverse college student populations. In M. B. Paulsen & L. W. Perna (Eds.), *Higher education: Handbook of theory and research* (pp. 189–227). Dordrecht, Netherlands: Springer.

Museus, S. D., & Jayakumar, U. M. (Eds.). (2012). *Creating campus cultures: Fostering success among racially diverse student populations.* New York: Routledge.

Museus, S. D., Ravello, J. N., & Vega, B. E. (2012). The campus racial culture: A critical race counterstory. In S. D. Museus & U. M. Jayakumar (Eds.), *Creating campus cultures: Fostering success among racially diverse student populations* (pp. 28–45). New York: Routledge.

Peck, A., Seemiller, C., & Sawalish, S. F. (2018). Student engagement revisited. *Leadership Exchange, 16*(2), 20–24.

Perkins, L. M. (1997). The impact of "the cult of true womanhood" on the education of Black women. In L. E. Goodchild & H. S. Weschler (Eds.), *The history of higher education* (ASHE Reader Series, pp. 173–182). Boston: Simon & Schuster.

Phillips, L. A., Baltzer, C., Filoon, L., & Whitley, C. (2017). Adult student preferences: Instructor characteristics conducive to successful teaching. *Journal of Adult and Continuing Education, 23*(1), 49–60.

Pingel, S., & Sponsler, B. (2015). *Redesigning state financial aid: Principles to guide state aid policymaking.* Denver, CO: Education Commission of the States. Retrieved from http://statefinancialaidredesign.org/

Quaye, S. J., & Harper, S. R. (Eds.). (2014). *Student engagement in higher education: Theoretical perspectives and practical approaches for diverse populations.* New York: Routledge.

Ross-Gordon, J. M. (2011). Research on adult learners: Supporting the needs of a student population that is no longer nontraditional. *Peer Review, 13*(1), 26–29.

Sherman, A., & Klein-Collins, R. (2015). *State policy approaches to support prior learning assessment.* Chicago: Council for Adult and Experiential Learning.

Soares, L. (2013). *Post-traditional learners and the transformation of postsecondary education: A manifesto for college leaders.* Washington, DC: American Council on Education.

Tinto, V. (1987). *Leaving college: Rethinking the causes and cures of student attrition.* Chicago: University of Chicago Press.

Tyson, M. (2017). *The long and unconventional road: Stories of financial challenges and system barriers in college completion of adult women undergraduate students* (Unpublished doctoral dissertation). University of Denver, Denver, CO.

Whitford, E. (2018, July 11). Parental support key to student success. *Inside Higher Ed* (Digital media company). Retrieved from https://www.insidehighered.com /news/2018/07/11/emotional-support-families-makes-difference-low-income -students

Witham, K. A., & Bensimon, E. M. (2012). Creating a culture of inquiry around equity and student success. In S. D. Museus & U. M. Jayakumar (Eds.), *Creating campus cultures: Fostering success among racially diverse student populations* (pp. 46–67). New York: Routledge.

Chapter 5

UNDERSTANDING THE NEEDS OF VARIOUS DIVERSE POPULATIONS

Lorenzo Baber

In 2014, the two largest student affairs professional associations in the United States—The American College Personnel Association (ACPA) and the National Association of Student Personnel Administrators (NASPA)—collaborated on reviewing and revising the established set of competency areas for professional preparation and practice in student affairs (ACPA & NASPA, 2015). Among the most significant changes was the revision of the *equity, diversity, and inclusion* competency, renaming it *social justice and inclusion.* Drawing from a synthesis of social justice concepts from Bell, the ACPA-NASPA committee sought to reconceptualize this competency away from a static, non-participatory perspectives implied by theoretical definitions of diversity, towards an emphasis on professional and personal actions that "integrate the concepts of equity, diversity, and inclusion within the active framework of social justice" (as cited in ACPA & NASPA, 2015, p. 5). As part of the social justice and inclusion competency, student affairs educators are expected to understand, acknowledge, and actively deconstruct oppression and privilege rooted in existing campus practices, policies, and structures. Further, reflective applications of social justice and inclusion require interconnection between administrative leadership responsibilities and active support for equity and collective liberation. As a revised competency, social justice and inclusion supported not just the acknowledgement of cultural domination but a professional ethos to confront and deconstruct systems of oppression on college campuses.

For educators in student affairs, active engagement with social justice and inclusion is critical for the development of a campus environment that supports healthy success for all students. As products of broad ideological debates, colleges and universities reflect both the historical legacy and contemporary characteristics of American society. For many institutions, historical legacy includes extensive practices of exclusion and marginalization for the comfort of a privileged identity—white, male, heteronormative, cisgender, and/or wealthy. The result is covert normalization of structures and practices that appear to be culturally neutral but systematically disadvantage non-conformists. Post-secondary institutions are also used as spaces to express overt forms of oppression, including acts of aggression and hostility targeting non-conformists. Contemporary sociopolitical discourse appears to have contributed to the frequency and intensity of such actions, placing targeted students in physical and emotional danger.

To support the needs of a diverse student population[1] in the midst of increasing sociocultural hostility and division, educators in student affairs should consider utilizing their professional status to advance social justice and inclusion at their campus. Navigating this path requires the understanding of how past practices in our field contribute to current campus norms around diversity, as well as knowledge of analytical tools that support ongoing disruption and collective reimagination of campus place—physical areas, such as classrooms, residence halls, and student unions, that foster dynamic meaning-making experiences among students, faculty, and administrators (Baber, 2010).

The purpose of this chapter is to provide support for educators in student affairs working towards reshaping campus environments to support diverse student populations. Following the general outline for this volume, I start with an examination of contemporary issues that are shaping current practices and policies in higher education. Next, I focus on identifying challenges and potential strategies for student affairs educators as they engage in equity and social justice work on their college campuses. Finally, I conclude with specific recommendations and actions for practice.

There are a few considerations for educators in student affairs who seek to embrace activism around social justice and inclusion. First, there are no all-encompassing solutions for resolving structural oppression occurring on college campuses. The purpose of this chapter is very broad: to serve as an initial resource for the exploration and reimagination of institutional practices that better serve the increasing racial, sexual, gender, and differently abled diversity in contemporary American society. The hope is that readers will consider the general perspective offered in this chapter and, more importantly, explore the cited references for specific consideration and discussion within their own unit and campus.

---

1. Acknowledging the various forms of diversity across the human experience, this chapter focuses on the demographic diversity within student populations. This includes socially constructed identities connected to race, ethnicity, ability, gender expressions, and sexuality.

Second, this chapter should not be viewed as a blueprint for the "saving of others," especially by those with privileged identities. This rationale, even if well-intentioned, serves to exacerbate cultural deficit perspectives and undermine the agency of marginalized populations. As Australian Aboriginal activist Lila Watson stated, "If you have come here to help me you are wasting your time, but if you have come because your liberation is bound up with mine, then let us work together" (as cited in Briskman, 2016, p. 111). Supporting diverse student populations as an act towards collective liberation necessitates mindfulness towards constant reflection on personal positionalities, especially in relation to the established sociocultural hierarchies existing on campus (Patton & Bondi, 2015).

A third consideration to maintain when reading this chapter is the difficulty, if not impossibility, of engaging in social justice work without personal commitment and sacrifice. When challenging structures that uphold the status quo and interrupting everyday acts of oppression, one will quickly realize the depth of aggressive opposition to progressive change. Even independent of a practice-focused evaluation, educators in student affairs that hold social justice perspectives should prepare to be unfairly labeled (naïve, impatient, hostile, or much worse), systematically silenced, and/or actively marginalized. Lorde (1984) reminded us that social justice work includes moments when one must learn "how to stand alone, unpopular and sometimes reviled, and how to make common cause with those others identified as outside the structures in order to define and seek a world in which we can all flourish" (p. 112). The risk of taking an educator-activist approach is particularly heightened for those from diverse backgrounds, whose resistance is often connected to identity (Quaye, Shaw, & Hill, 2017). Even with commitment, there is no guarantee for scaled transformation or long-term sustainability. To maintain a hopeful approach, however, it is important to consider the words from law professor and educator-activist Bell (2007):

> But knowledge of the fragility and impermanence of life is precisely what we must keep in mind as we seek to rise to the challenge of these diabolically complex injustices that seem beyond repair—racial, sexual, economic, religious—and all the human misery they cause. With a firm understanding of our real role, these challenges are not less welcome simply because there are all manner of indications that we will not be able to eliminate or even dent the evils of racism, poverty, and inadequacy. For again, our mandate is not to guarantee reform, but to recognize evils in our midst and commit ourselves to ending them. (p. 530)

To align professional and personal investment in equity and justice for students, practitioners must start with addressing internalized forms of oppression within ourselves—our routine language, perceptions, and conclusions, presented to us as customary but reflect embedded structures of domination, including whiteness, patriarchy, and heteronormativity (to name a few). An examination of self includes a continuous revisit of the following questions: What privileges do I hold/maintain? How do these privileges operate to provide unearned advantages across multiple contexts? How can I use my place of privilege to reduce domination and unearned advantages, at both individual and structural levels?

This final question connects us to professional reflection around campus policies and practices (both hidden and explicit) that operate to structure domination, amplify unearned advantages, and marginalize particular student populations. Thus, we are led to engaging with proactive actions around questions articulated most recently by Stewart (2017): What student populations have limited (or no) presence on campus and why? Are there institutional practices that support and maintain cultural dominance at our institution? Who or what is being protected by current institution policies, and who or what is being systematically harmed? These are some of the questions that support the process towards alignment of the individual and collective actions to transform campus environments.

Contemporary Issues

Colleges and universities in the United States face the challenge of supporting various outcomes for graduates, including healthy psychosocial development, skills for success in a professional field, and tools for civic engagement in a participatory democracy (Bok, 2015; Kezar, Chambers, & Burkhardt, 2015). A unique feature of American higher education, the multifaceted mission reflects the consistent placement of colleges and universities as a core social institution to encourage the development of knowledge and expand intellectual curiosity. In return, larger society benefits through the practical application of new knowledge; economic vitality, driven by a creative workforce; and progressive social movements, often initiated on college campuses.

Not surprisingly, the broad range of functions for post-secondary institutions tends to invite as much conflict as harmony, particularly because external stakeholders encourage institutions towards a particular mission priority (St. John, Daun-Barnett, & Moronski-Chapman, 2018). As a result, the higher education environment also reflects the inconsistent practices in American society. Post-secondary institutions have supported democratic aspirations, while replicating de jure and de facto forms of racial segregation; mediated pathways to the middle-class status, while managing academic ambitions within particular communities; and encouraged collaborative research and scholarship, while isolating minoritized students from specific fields of study. These contradictory positions represent recurring debates about the purpose of post-secondary education, levels of access, and responsibility for funding.

A contemporary conflict, one that educators in student affairs face consistently, is the increasing emphasis on individual economic benefits for post-secondary attainment, as institutions experience a significant increase in cultural diversity among the student population (Harper, Patton, & Wooden, 2009). This individual emphasis is connected to decreasing support for higher education, notably declining state appropriations for public institutions and shifting federal financial aid policies that emphasize unsubsidized loans rather than grants for individuals. As such, post-secondary institutions are increasingly focused on institutional practices that align with market-based student outcomes. Perhaps not-so-coincidently, the focus on individual economic results in postsecondary education overlaps with a significant increase in diversity among the student population. Civil rights movements in the 1960s and 1970s pressured legislative and institutional actions to broaden post-secondary access across all institutional types. Once on campus, student leaders from historically marginalized populations demanded institutional structures—student organizations, cultural centers, and academic programs— for a sustained and scaled presence on campus. Such social, cultural, and intellectual activities challenged societal norms, particularly around constructs of race, ability, gender identities, and sexuality (Andersen & Collins, 2007).

Further complicating current post-secondary environments is the substantial increase in hate crimes on campus over the last decade (Bauer-Wolf, 2017; Bauman, 2018). The National Center for Education Statistics (2017) defined the term *hate crime* as "a criminal offense that is motivated, in whole or in part, by the perpetrator's bias against the victim(s) based on their race, ethnicity, religion, sexual orientation, gender, gender identity, or disability" (p. 128). Between 2011 and 2016, the number of hate crimes reported on a college campus increased 37 percent, with a significant spike between 2015 (1,043 reported incidents) and 2016 (1,300). Of all reported incidents, the most common type of hate crime was vandalism (38%), followed by intimidation (38%), and assault (16%). Racial bias was the most common and fastest growing motivation for reported hate crimes, followed by religion and sexual orientation. As Ahamdi, Cole, Castellanos, Manson, and Zhou (2017) suggested, the number of reported hate crimes on campus may reflect just a portion of actual incidents of hostility. Many acts go unreported or may not be classified as a hate crime due to the high burden of proof associated with proving perpetrator's bias as motivation for the crime. A set of research has examined associations between campus characteristics and frequency of reported hate crimes, with a specific focus on acts related to racial bias.

Stotzer and Hossellman (2012) found that increased enrollment of African American and Latino students predicted decreases in reported hate crimes on campus. Similarly, Van Dyke and Tester (2014) found an association between moderate students-of-color enrollment and high levels of racially motivated hate crimes.

In addition to being targets of increasing hate crimes on campus, minoritized students continue to experience everyday microaggressions that signal more subtle forms of privilege and power (Solorzano, Ceja, & Yosso, 2000; Sterzing, Gartner, Woodford, & Fischer, 2017; Sue, 2010). *Microaggressions* refer to expressions, behaviors, or visual cues that communicate derogatory signals, whether intentionally or unintentionally, to individuals or groups based on cultural identity. Sue (2010) defined three types of microaggressions: microassaults, microinsults, and microinvalidation. *Microassaults* are specific actions that purposefully discriminate against a particular social identity. For example, an administrator who refuses to acknowledge non-Christian holidays during the academic year is performing a microassault. *Microinsults* refer to demeaning or insensitive messages, purposeful or not, that target specific individuals based on social identity. The praising of a successful student, followed by the words, "despite their disability," is considered a microinsult because it presumes a personal deficit. *Microinvalidations* involve denying or dismissing the lived experiences of a marginalized population. Defining all restrooms in a building or campus only by binary gender labels is a form of microinvalidation. Whereas much of the research has focused on racialized forms of microaggressions, scholars have also examined microaggressions related to sexuality (Woodford, Chonody, Kulick, Brennan, & Renn, 2015), gender (Yang & Carroll, 2018), gender expression (Seelman, Woodford, & Nicolazzo, 2017), and disability (Kellar & Galgay, 2010). Common themes across studies have supported the finding that experiences with microaggressions are related to higher rates of depression and anxiety, decreased academic self-efficacy, and lower levels of persistence.

Despite evidence of overt and covert forms of hostility in post-secondary environments, campus practices supporting diverse student populations remain focused on individual actions rather than contextual environments (Abes, 2016; Patton, Renn, Guido, & Quaye, 2016; Quaye & Harper, 2014). Specifically, student affairs practices tend to address individual adjustment to the campus context rather than a centering of post-secondary environments as sites of oppression. The primary focus on individual adjustment is problematic because it supports the view that post-secondary environments are apolitical, ahistorical, and acultural spaces. For example, early persistence frameworks, in an attempt to bridge the ideological divide between individual agency and structural determinism, encouraged practices that fostered student integration into the established institutional values and norms (Spady,

1971; Tinto, 1975, 1993). Spady (1971) postulated that students withdraw from institutions due, in part, to the lack of shared values, whereas Tinto (1993) stated, "The first stage of the college career, separation, requires individuals to disassociate themselves, in varying degrees, from membership in the communities of the past" (p. 95). Subsequent scholarship challenged both the lack of consideration for students from diverse backgrounds and the assumptions that institutional values and norms were unbiased and culturally neutral (Guiffrida, 2006; Swail, Redd, & Perna, 2003). Elaborating this point, Rendón, Jalomo, and Nora (2000) stated, "Absent from the traditional social integrationist view are the distinctions among cultures, differences among students with regard to class, race, gender, and sexual orientation, and the role of group members and the institutions in assisting students to succeed" (p. 139).

Moving toward centering the contextual environment, scholars advanced the concept of diversity as a framework for supporting the development and persistence of students from various backgrounds (Hurtado, Milem, Clayton-Pederson, & Allen, 1999; Milem, Chang, & Antonio, 2005; Smith, 2015). A diversity lens suggests that a numerical increase in students from diverse backgrounds fosters an environment that supports various cultural expressions and opportunities to learn from each other. Further, the presence of a critical mass of minoritized students serves as a crucial feature for the development of an equitable campus.

Unfortunately, evidence has suggested that the diversity frame co-opted to serve as an end goal rather than an initial stage of structural transformation (Garces & Jayakumar, 2014; Stewart, 2017). Manning (2009) stated,

> Simply increasing the numbers of diverse people on a college campus does not change the power structure to more equitable forms. In fact, such a redistribution of power is rarely addressed by those who express a diversity perspective. Because it works in their favor, the power structure is typically not identified as a problem by those in charge of institutions. Access and equal opportunity regarding entry into the existing power structure are the primary concerns of those seeking social justice. But equity (for example, being admitted into a college) does not mean equality (for example, having that college adequately respond to your needs). (p. 14)

Much like the "deliberate speed" of desegregation in secondary education, the power of a diversity framework in higher education is often diluted by interest-convergence perspectives (Taylor, 2000). Generally applied, *interest-convergence* (Bell, 2003) suggests that progress towards equality is accommodated only when it serves the interest of the privileged (e.g., white, male, heteronormative, and cisgender) and is abandoned at the point it threatens their dominant status. Scholars defined increasing compositional diversity as the initial stage of institutional transformation. However, reconceptualized as a tool for dominant self-interest, the diversity framework has been reduced to quantitative assessment of individual presence.

Challenges and Opportunities

Faced with contemporary challenges to the democratic purpose of higher education as well as the use of college campuses for expression of covert and overt acts of sociocultural hostility, educators in student affairs must advance the practice of social justice and inclusion. The first step towards doing this is to challenge the default assumption in the campus engagement literature that socially produced patterns on campus are rooted in individual characteristics (Bensimon, 2007; Kaufman & Feldman, 2004). Whereas student affairs educators should not subscribe to structural determinist paradigms that eliminate consideration of individual agency, reducing the sociocultural environment to, at best, a secondary influence on student experience is problematic for practice. Harper and Quaye (2009) pointed out that even with a critical mass of students from diverse backgrounds, environments should not be treated with benign neglect. The onus for healthy student development and engagement remains on the institutional actors responsible for campus structures and policies.

Student affairs professionals may look to serve as validating agents as an initial step towards supporting campus engagement among minoritized students (Rendon, 1994; Rendón Linares & Munoz, 2011). *Validation* refers to a confirmatory process, which includes active intervention, initiated by institutional administrators, staff, and/or faculty, that fosters engagement and belonging on campus. Educators in student affairs are positioned to provide *interpersonal validation,* actions that support sociocultural adjustment to institutional settings. Validating actions include proactive encouragement, consistent conversations that offer both positive and constructive feedback, and demonstrated attention to and care for a student's communities (both within and external to the institution). Validation stands in opposition to deficit thinking because it assumes student success rather than failure. Validating agents stand between a student's cultivated self-efficacy and existing institutional norms that often demand sociocultural repositioning as part of successful engagement on campus.

To develop validating skills, student affairs practitioners may start by expanding their historical and contemporary understanding of conditions that shape experiences and perceptions of particular student populations, asking such questions as What are the histories of LGBTQ communities in U.S. society? How is the current sociopolitical environment reshaping LGBTQ experiences? The next step is to consider the unique experiences of diverse student populations at the specific campus, with such questions as What are the histories of LGBTQ students at this college/university? How does campus climate shape contemporary experiences of LGBTQ students at this institution? Final development of validating skills includes fostering connections with individual students and collective communities, asking questions, such as How can I work with LGBTQ students and communities in support of educational equity and justice? In what ways can I cultivate personal and professional relationships to amplify success among LGBTQ students?

By moving the onus for engagement from student to the practitioner, validation theory offers an initial path for supporting success with students from diverse socio-demographic backgrounds. However, the process remains focused on the individual level and does little to address the ways campus environments shape incongruence between healthy sociocultural identity and engagement. To address the challenge of initiating structural and systemic changes to campus environments, educators in student affairs may consider engaging in a cyclical process of revelation, deconstruction, and reconstruction (Kezar, 2010). The process of revelation provides an opportunity to confront hidden assumptions and privileges that are normalized in the institutional culture. Part of the revelation process is the acknowledgment that campus structures are not apolitical when shaping recognition of knowledge or proximity to valuable resources. Instead, campus structures mirror the preferences—language, customs, and socially constructed imagination—of dominant cultures. The process of deconstruction seeks to dismantle policies and practices that uphold forms of privilege, intentionally or unintentionally. Deconstruction may be the toughest part of a transformative process because it draws attention from external constituents with important forms of power: alumni, politicians, and partisan organizations. Therefore, educators in student affairs may consider coupling the process of deconstruction with a reconstruction of policies that reflect equity and social justice principles.

It may be useful to map deconstructive/reconstructive considerations with conceptual frameworks that center macro-level transformation. For example, Museus (2014) conceptualized the culturally engaging campus environment (CECE) model. Focusing on students of color populations, the CECE model offers several indicators of a culturally engaging campus environment, including collectivist rather than individualistic cultural norms, holistic support systems, opportunities for service within historically marginalized communities, and structures that proactively foster meaningful cross-cultural engagement. The CECE model, Museus explained, is based on evidence that when students "frequently encounter elements of culturally engaging campus environments . . . they are less likely to perceive those environments as exclusionary, experience hostile climates, and feel excluded within the cultures of their respective campuses" (p. 217).

Similarly, the diverse learning environment (DLE) model offers a frame to examine multiple influences that shape campus climate: sociohistorical context, policy context (federal and state), and local community contexts (Hurtado, Alvarez, Guillermo-Wann, Cuellar, & Arellano, 2012). Each of these contexts operates to shape micro-level interactions, embed preferred practices within curricular and co-curricular spaces on campus, and define the influence of external commitments. The CECE and DLE models are similar in that they offer analytical tools for a comprehensive assessment of institutional structures and actors (faculty, staff, and administrators) that shape engagement, development, and success among students from diverse backgrounds. The application of these models within a cycle of revelation, deconstruction, and reconstruction provides student affairs professionals with an opportunity to consider these theoretical components within the unique context of their campus structure.

The initial process may include an assessment of the visibility of diverse student populations on campus, using such questions as How many student from low-income backgrounds reside in our residence halls and/or attend campus programming? How might current practices limit access and/or active engagement for students from low-income communities? Such questions should be followed by an assessment of (in)congruence between current practices and conceptual developments in the scholarship, asking, for example, How does contemporary scholarship amplify the understanding of experiences for diverse students from low-income communities in postsecondary education? Do our policies and norms reflect updated scholarship on students from low-income communities? Finally, student affairs practitioners may consider reconstruction of policies and practices framed and assessed by concepts of inclusion, justice, and equity, using such questions as: In what ways do our reconstructed policies and practices reflect conceptual underpinnings of inclusion, justice, and equity? Do our intentions match outcomes related to inclusion, justice, and equity? Why or why not?

Nevertheless, even the most comprehensive assessment of practitioners' actions and campus environments cannot adequately address evolving forms of inequality produced by contemporary political and sociocultural turmoil. Recurrent acts of marginalization, harassment, and violence are stark reminders that oppression is a common rather than unique feature of American society. Although the theoretical frameworks support practices around developing an engaging community for increasing culturally diverse student populations, the increased pace and intensity of current social discourse requires student affairs educators to compress theory-to-practice translation. To support this process, student affairs educators may consider embracing a practitioner-as-researcher perspective to "produce knowledge within a local context in order to identify local problems and take action to solve them"

(Bensimon, Polkinghorne, Bauman, & Vallejo, 2004, p. 105). Building off elements of action-oriented research, the practitioner-as-researcher model empowers institutional agents to move theoretical concepts from abstract to concrete and context specific. Whereas this model suggests collaboration with researcher scholars, it encourages pairing the contextual experiences and knowledge of practitioners with empirically validated theoretical constructs.

Bensimon (2007) outlined several principles of the practitioner-as-researcher model. Foremost, the process raises questions based on an understanding of existing modes of power and privilege. Secondly, the inquiry activities are context dependent and sensitive. Third, there is an emphasis on making existing inequality concrete and solvable. Fourth, the inquiry aims to foster equity mindedness among practitioners through open discussion of sense making, increasing awareness of perspectives and taking responsibility for addressing inequalities. Finally, the process views institutional transformation as multidimensional, promoting change to individual actions and spaces of interaction, as well as macro-level structures, policies, and practices. When applied, the practitioner-as-researcher model buffers against the practice of wholesale application of theory, which often overlooks conceptual variability of student success, especially as shifting social discourse reshapes campus environments.

Addressing similar concerns about the theory-to-practice process, Reason and Kimball (2012) outlined a scholarship-context-reflection framework that emphasizes four components: (a) formal theory, (b) institutional context, (c) informal theory, and (d) practice. The understanding of *formal theoretical frameworks,* grounded in empirical research, provides a basis for shared knowledge, including common language and definitions. *Institutional context* refers to the observation of explicit (e.g., the socio-demographic background of the student population) and implicit (e.g., the practitioner's values and beliefs) characteristics that shape campus culture. *Informal theory* refers to the contextual consideration of formal theory through the experiential lens of a reflective campus practitioner, whereas *practice* is the application of such considerations in everyday encounters with students, colleagues, and institutional structures. The model stresses the importance of reflective feedback loops between informal theory considerations and success of practical applications and transformation of institutional contexts.

Both the practitioner-as-researcher and scholarship-context-reflection models are useful when considering the development of practices and structures that support diverse populations. Foremost, they offer clarity for a theory-to-practice process that often promotes a reductive assessment of student experiences (e.g., attempting to place an African American student into a stage of black identity development). The model also addresses a common trend in the field of higher education to give absolute status to theoretical frameworks. A classic example is the aforementioned student departure theory (Tinto, 1975; 1993), which served as a standard model for decades before alternative scholarship was formally recognized in the field. Given the pace of social discourse and related reconstruction of everyday realities for minoritized students, a broad application of existing theories may unintentionally serve to reinforce inequalities rather than guide social justice practices. As part of the theory-to-practice process, educators in student affairs would benefit from staying attuned to more critical forms of scholarship emerging from the traditional academic gatekeeping processes.

Recommendations for Practice

The challenges and opportunities for reshaping campus environments to support diverse student populations offer several potential pathways for everyday practice. Foremost, practicing critical forms of reflexivity supports both validating agent and practitioner-as-researcher roles. A common feature of qualitative research, the reflexivity process has significant value for continuous exploration of one's understanding of knowledge, constructed realities, and labeled identities within a particular context (Alevesson, Hardy, & Harley, 2008; Pillow, 2003). Cunliffe (2016) noted that the practice of *critical reflexivity* encourages examination of the personal and theoretical assumptions shaping our actions; the impact of our actions on others and the community; and the philosophical (dis)connection between actions, perceptions, and practices. As part of professional practice, senior-level educators in student affairs should promote consistent individual reflexivity and support collective reflexivity discussions during both formal and informal meetings. As part of this practice, educators should engage in real-time documentation of reflexive moments for self-comparison over time and intentional sharing with mentors, colleagues, and (when appropriate) students. The individual and collective processes serve to center practitioner experience as a catalyst for institutional transformation, while also countering the potential of "undesirable assumptions about student experience, development, and learning that foster negative outcomes" (Reason & Kimball, 2012, p. 363).

Critical reflexivity serves an increasingly important practice because campus environments (physical and virtual) experience incredible rates of change, leading to the second recommendation for practice in student affairs: more consistent opportunities and expectations to read, discuss, and analyze empirical research and theoretical frameworks related to diverse student experiences. Continuous adult learning among practitioners is a feature of standards from ACPA-NASPA and the Council for the Advancement of

Standards in Higher Education. However, this activity often fades into the background due to the immediacy of daily responsibilities. In addition, reduction of university budgets has impacted support for professional development opportunities, including travel to professional conferences where much of the boundary-pushing scholarship is first presented and discussed. As emerging scholarship in the field expands understanding of student experiences through interdisciplinary frameworks, a practitioner's lens is valuable for discussion on informing theoretical considerations from their everyday experiences and actions. Aligned with both multi-disciplinary frameworks and empirical data, the practitioner's expertise would only broaden understanding of current realities and future possibilities for equity-driven outcomes.

From the practitioner perspective, continuing to engage with researchers and scholars encourages practices beyond dominant paradigms presented during graduate school training. Because the most widely cited student success theories focus on individual experiences rather than the institutional environment, educators in student affairs may tend to shape their interactions with students from this perspective. Bensimon (2007) spoke to this point as follows:

> When practitioners have been socialized to view student success from the perspective of the dominant paradigm, what do they notice? What might they fail to notice? What do they expect to see and what happens when their expectations are not met? Might the know-how derived from the dominant paradigm be inimical to the needs of minority students? Might it lead to misconceptions? (p. 451)

Understanding and participating in research grounded in non-dominant paradigms, notably critical theory and poststructuralism, serve to broaden scholarly perspectives of practitioners in the field (Abes, 2016). For example, expanded scholarly understanding of critical theory would allow educators in student affairs to interrogate interest-convergence trends in diversity work on their campus. Post-structuralist frameworks would support the revelation-deconstruction-reconstruction of ingrained policies and practices that uniquely shape marginalization of minoritized students on campus. Combined with reflexive practices, interaction with scholars who utilize critical theory and post-structuralist frameworks provides practitioners with opportunities to consider their positionality as they work to create equitable learning and living environments for students.

A last recommendation for practice is for educators in student affairs to work with academic units on campus or external consultants in creating longitudinal assessments of institutional environments, with specific attention to understanding campus environments as sociocultural places (Baber, 2010). *Campus place* refers to the individual and collective investment of meaning and value of an occupied physical space that is, in the presence of diverse populations, both flexible in meaning and dynamic over time (Gieryn, 2000). The active and malleable composition is an important, yet underrated consideration for educators in student affairs. For example, although the physical space of a residence hall may be consistent, as a place it is constructed and reconstructed with significant historical, social, and cultural meaning for students (positively or negatively). Further, the meaning of a campus place may change year to year (or semester to semester) as incoming students enter the campus community. Ongoing research projects that situate the university as an active agent in shaping student experiences, development, and learning may inform understanding of this constant evolution of campus places (Hunter, Abelmann, Cain, McDonough, & Prendergast, 2008).

For practitioners at institutions in need of a starting point for a longitudinal project on campus place, the aforementioned culturally engaging campus environment (CECE) and diverse learning environment (DLE) models provide strong initial frameworks. From these models or other similar frameworks, practitioners can work with colleagues across campus to build sustainable activities around data collection and assessment to inform institutional change. Data collection may include individual reflections on experiences in a campus place or set of places, visual representation (e.g., drawings or photos) of inclusive and exclusive places on campus, collective feedback from students with shared identities, or direct observations of interactions within a campus place. Assessment includes archiving (with proper protections) collected data for comparison across time, evaluating the connection between institutional practices and documented experiences, and linking individual experience and institutional practices to theoretical and conceptual frameworks. Most importantly, the continuation of collaborative data collection and assessment must be sustained beyond the tenure of a practitioner or set of practitioners at the institution.

To support recommendations for practice, student affairs practitioners may consider several actionable items. For example, research and scholarship on intergroup dialogue are useful resources to support activities around critical reflexivity (Nagda, Gurin, & Rodriguez, 2018; Patton et al., 2016; Quaye & Baxter Magolda, 2007; Zúñiga, Lopez, & Ford, 2016). *Intergroup dialogue* is a facilitated engagement that helps a collective group "build skills for developing and maintaining relationships across differences and enhance their ability to work together toward social justice" (Zúñiga, Nagda, & Sevig, 2002, p. 7). Whereas practitioners are often positioned as facilitators of intergroup dialogue, participation is a valuable tool for both individual development and collegial engagement. Further experiencing intergroup dialogue as a participant provides practitioners with the opportunity to model self-reflection, group collaboration, and collective responsibility towards social justice and equity.

To encourage the transition of dialogues to transformation of policy, practices, and campus norms, Poon et al. (2016) suggested development of participatory action research projects on campus. *Participatory action research* is "a collaborative research process that involves collective co-construction of knowledge that collapses traditional hierarchies of power between the researcher and researched, critical self, and group reflection and awareness" (Poon et al., 2016, p. 26). Through this research process that centers a critical perspective, practitioners have the opportunity to support exploration of empirical research and theoretical frameworks related to diverse student experiences, assess applicability of such scholarship to institutional context, and collaborate with both faculty colleagues and students to plan research projects, collect and analyze data, and disseminate findings across campus. Over time, participatory action research projects have the potential to evolve into an ethnographic understanding of campus space and place, institutionally supported by further collaborations with the campus Institutional Review Board (IRB) and senior-level administrators to archive projects and encourage future practitioners and students to understand and build upon past participatory action research projects. One such example is the Ethnography of the University Initiative (EUI) at the University of Illinois, Urbana-Champaign. Started in 2002 by campus anthropologists Nancy Abelmann and Bill Kelleher, EUI supports training in ethnographic method across multiple campus units. As of 2016, the initiative has archived over 1,200 research projects investigating a broad range of topics related to student experience across campus environments (EUI, n.d.).

Conclusion

To support the reshaping of campus environments to support diverse student populations, this chapter provides educators in student affairs with a perspective on contemporary issues shaping current practices in higher education, challenges and potential strategies for engaging in equity and social justice work, and specific recommendations for practice. As a former full-time practitioner, I hold tremendous respect and value for the work of current educators in student affairs, particularly those who take the lead in developing inclusive environments for minoritized students at their institution. Although challenging forms of systematic oppression ingrained in institutional policies and practices may initially invoke individual frustration and collective pessimism with resistance to rapid campus transformation by institutional leaders and policy makers, we may consider advice from historian Zinn (2009):

> Revolutionary change does not come as one cataclysmic moment (beware of such moments!) but as an endless succession of surprises, moving zigzag toward a more decent society. We don't have to engage in grand, heroic actions to participate in the process of change. Small acts, when multiplied by millions of people, can transform the world. (p. 13)

At the campus level, leading revolutionary change in student affairs requires consistent practices around reflexivity, validation of students, and engagement with scholarship and research. Eventually, these practices lead to development of inclusive communities, both on campus and across the profession, that build and sustain consideration of social justice and inclusion as part of everyday practice. For evidence of success, consider the decision by ACPA and NASPA (2015) to revise competencies around social justice and inclusion, a conversation that started on the margins of the field and now is included as part of the framework for practice. For current practitioners, the challenge remains to identify and collaborate with researchers on identifying new frameworks for practices that improve healthy success for all students.

Reflective Questions for Student Affairs Practitioners

1. How do your personal identities shape your perspective on justice and equity for diverse populations? What are important considerations as you align your professional commitment to justice and equity with your personal identities and positionalities?
2. What are the histories of diverse student populations on your campus? How is your unit positioned to initiate, develop, and/or maintain practices that support holistic development and engagement of student populations historically marginalized at your institution?
3. Do current policies, norms, and practices within your department align with principles of justice and equity? Are these actions specifically aligned to empower diverse student populations? If not, what are the institutional processes and collaborative opportunities for deconstruction and redeveloping policies, norms, and practices towards justice and equity?
4. Identify innovative strategies from research and scholarship that serve to support diverse student populations. How can they be implemented, sustained, scaled, and assessed at your institution?

References

Abes, E. S. (Ed.). (2016). *Critical perspectives on student development theory: New directions for student services*. Hoboken, NJ: John Wiley & Sons.

Ahamdi, S., Cole, D., Castellanos, M., Manson, S., & Zhou, J. (2017). Hate speech and hate crimes on campus. In J. L. Jackson, L. J. Charleston, & C. Gilbert (Eds.), *Advancing equity and diversity in student affairs: A festschrift in honor of Melvin C. Terrell* (pp. 113–132). Charlotte, NC: Information Age.

Alvesson, M., Hardy, C., & Harley, B. (2008). Reflecting on reflexivity: Reflexive textual practices in organization and management theory. *Journal of Management Studies, 45*(3), 480–501.

American College Personnel Association (ACPA)—College Student Educators International & National Association of Student Personnel Administrators (NASPA)—Student Affairs Administrators in Higher Education. (2015). *Professional competency areas for student affairs educators*. Retrieved from https://www.naspa.org/images/uploads/main/ACPA_NASPA_Professional_Competencies_FINAL.pdf

Andersen, M., & Collins, P. H. (2007). *Race, class and gender: An anthology*. Belmont, CA: Wadsworth.

Baber, L. D. (2010). Beyond structural diversity: Centrality of campus "place" in shaping experiences of African American students at predominately white institutions. In T. E. Dancy II (Ed.), *Managing diversity: (Re)visioning equity on college campuses* (pp. 221–242). New York: Peter Lang.

Bauer-Wolf, J. (2017, September 22). A September of racist incidents. Inside *Higher Education*. Retrieved from https://www.insidehighered.com/news/2017/09/22/racist-incidents-colleges-abound-academic-year-begins

Bauman (2018, November 14). Hate crimes on campuses are rising new FBI data show. *Chronicle of Higher Education*. Retrieved from https://www.chronicle.com/article/Hate-Crimes-on-Campuses-Are/245093

Bell, D. (2003). Diversity's distractions. *Columbia Law Review, 103*(6), 1622–1633.

Bell, D. (2007). What's diversity got to do with it? *Seattle Journal for Social Justice, 6*, 527–532.

Bensimon, E. M. (2007). The underestimated significance of practitioner knowledge in the scholarship on student success. *The Review of Higher Education, 30*(4), 441–469.

Bensimon, E. M., Polkinghorne, D. E., Bauman, G. L., & Vallejo, E. (2004). Doing research that makes a difference. *The Journal of Higher Education, 75*(1), 104–126.

Bok, D. (2015). *Higher education in America*. Princeton, NJ: Princeton University Press.

Cunliffe, A. L. (2016). Republication of "On becoming a critically reflexive practitioner." *Journal of Management Education, 40*(6), 747–768.

Ethnography of the University Initiative (EUI). (n.d.). EUI website. Retrieved from http://www.eui.illinois.edu

Garces, L. M., & Jayakumar, U. M. (2014). Dynamic diversity: Toward a contextual understanding of critical mass. *Educational Researcher, 43*(3), 115–124.

Gieryn, T. F. (2000). A space for place in sociology. *Annual Review of Sociology, 26*(1), 463–496.

Guiffrida, D. A. (2006). Toward a cultural advancement of Tinto's theory. *The Review of Higher Education, 29*(4), 451–472.

Harper, S. R., Patton, L. D., & Wooden, O. S. (2009). Access and equity for African American students in higher education: A critical race historical analysis of policy efforts. *The Journal of Higher Education, 80*(4), 389–414.

Harper, S. R., & Quaye, S. J. (2009). Beyond sameness, with engagement and outcomes for all: An introduction. In S. R. Harper & S. J. Quaye (Eds.), *Student engagement in higher education* (pp. 29–44). New York: Routledge.

Hunter, G., Abelmann, N., Cain, T. R., McDonough, T., & Prendergast, C. (2008, September). Interrogating one archival the university, entry at a time. *Change: The Magazine of Higher Learning, 40*(5), 40–45. doi:10.3200/CHNG.40.5.40-45

Hurtado, S., Alvarez, C. L., Guillermo-Wann, C., Cuellar, M., & Arellano, L. (2012). A model for diverse learning environments. In J. C. Smart & M. B. Paulsen (Eds.), *Higher education: Handbook of theory and research* (Vol. 27, pp. 41–122). Dordrecht, Netherland: Springer.

Hurtado, S., Milem, J., Clayton-Pedersen, A., & Allen, W. (1999). Enacting diverse learning environments: Improving the climate for racial/ethnic diversity in higher education. *ASHE-ERIC Higher Education Reports, 26*(8).

Kaufman, P., & Feldman, K. A. (2004). Forming identities in college: A sociological approach. *Research in Higher Education, 45*(5), 463-496.

Keller, R. M., & Galgay, C. E. (2010). Microaggressive experiences of people with disabilities. In D. W. Sue (Ed.), *Microaggressions and marginality: Manifestation, dynamics, and impact* (pp. 241–268). Hoboken, NJ: John Wiley & Sons.

Kezar, A. (Ed.). (2010). *Recognizing and serving low-income students in higher education: An examination of institutional policies, practices, and culture.* New York: Routledge.

Kezar, A., Chambers, A. C., & Burkhardt, J. C. (Eds.). (2015). *Higher education for the public good: Emerging voices from a national movement.* Hoboken, NJ: John Wiley & Sons.

Lorde, A. (1984). *Sister outsider: Essays and speeches.* Trumansburg, NY: Crossing Press.

Manning, K. (2009). Philosophical underpinnings of student affairs work on difference. *About Campus, 14*(2), 11–17.

Milem, J. F., Chang, M. J., & Antonio, A. L. (2005). *Making diversity work on campus: A research-based perspective.* Washington, DC: Association of American Colleges and Universities.

Museus, S. D. (2014). The culturally engaging campus environments (CECE) model: A new theory of success among racially diverse college student populations. In M. B. Paulsen (Ed.), *Higher education: Handbook of theory and research* (pp. 189–227). Dordrecht, Netherlands: Springer.

Nadal, K. L., Erazo, T., Fiani, C. N., Parilla, M. C. M., & Han, H. (2018). Navigating microaggressions, overt discrimination, and institutional oppression: Transgender and gender nonconforming people and the criminal justice system. In C. L. Cho, J. K. Corkett, & A. Steele (Eds.), *Exploring the toxicity of lateral violence and microaggressions* (pp. 51–74). London, England, United Kingdom: Palgrave Macmillan.

Nagda, B. R. A., Gurin, P., & Rodríguez, J. (2018). Intergroup dialogue: Education for social justice. In P. L. Hammack (Ed.), *The Oxford handbook of social psychology and social justice*. Oxford, England, United Kingdom: Oxford University Press.

National Center for Education Statistics (2017). *Indicators of school crime and safety: 2016* (NCES 2017-064). Washington, DC: Author, U.S. Department of Education.

Patton, L. D., & Bondi, S. (2015). Nice white men or social justice allies?: Using critical race theory to examine how white male faculty and administrators engage in ally work. *Race, Ethnicity and Education, 18*(4), 488–514.

Patton, L. D., Renn, K. A., Guido, F. M., & Quaye, S. J. (2016). *Student development in college: Theory, research, and practice*. Hoboken, NJ: John Wiley & Sons.

Pillow, W. (2003). Confession, catharsis, or cure? Rethinking the uses of reflexivity as methodological power in qualitative research. *International Journal of Qualitative Studies in Education, 16*(2), 175–196.

Poon, O. A., Squire, D. D., Hom, D. C., Gin, K., Segoshi, M. S., & Parayno, A. (2016). Critical cultural student affairs praxis and participatory action research. *Journal of Critical Scholarship on Higher Education and Student Affairs, 3*(1), Article 2.

Quaye, S. J., & Baxter Magolda, M. B. (2007). Enhancing racial self?understanding through structured learning and reflective experiences. In S. R. Harper & L. D. Patton (Eds.), Responding to the realities of race on campus. *New Directions for Student Services, 120,* 55–66). San Francisco: Jossey-Bass.

Quaye, S. J., & Harper, S. R. (Eds.). (2014). *Student engagement in higher education: Theoretical perspectives and practical approaches for diverse populations.* New York: Routledge.

Quaye, S. J., Shaw, M. D., & Hill, D. C. (2017). Blending scholar and activist identities: Establishing the need for scholar activism. *Journal of Diversity in Higher Education, 10*(4), 381–399.

Reason, R. D., & Kimball, E. W. (2012). A new theory-to-practice model for student affairs: Integrating scholarship, context, and reflection. *Journal of Student Affairs Research and Practice, 49*(4), 359–376.

Rendon, L. I. (1994). Validating culturally diverse students: Toward a new model of learning and student development. *Innovative Higher Education, 19*(1), 33–51.

Rendón, L. I., Jalomo, R. E., & Nora, A. (2000). Theoretical considerations in the study of minority student retention in higher education. In J. M. Braxton (Ed.), *Reworking the student departure puzzle* (pp. 127–156). Nashville, TN: Vanderbilt University Press.

Rendón Linares, L. I., & Munoz, S. M. (2011). Revisiting validation theory: Theoretical foundations, applications, and extensions. *Enrollment Management Journal, 2*(1), 12–33.

Seelman, K. L., Woodford, M. R., & Nicolazzo, Z. (2017). Victimization and microaggressions targeting LGBTQ college students: Gender identity as a moderator of psychological distress. *Journal of Ethnic & Cultural Diversity in Social Work, 26*(1-2), 112–125.

Smith, D. G. (2015). *Diversity's promise for higher education: Making it work.* Baltimore: Johns Hopkins Press.

Solorzano, D., Ceja, M., & Yosso, T. (2000). Critical race theory, racial microaggressions, and   campus racial climate: The experiences of African American college students. *Journal of Negro Education, 69*(1-2), 60–73.

Spady, W. G. (1971). Dropouts from higher education: Toward an empirical model. *Interchange, 2*(3), 38–62.

St. John, E. P., Daun-Barnett, N., & Moronski-Chapman, K. M. (2018). *Public policy and higher education: Reframing strategies for preparation, access, and college success* (2nd ed.). New York: Routledge.

Sterzing, P. R., Gartner, R. E., Woodford, M. R., & Fisher, C. M. (2017). Sexual orientation, gender, and gender identity microaggressions: Toward an intersectional framework for social work research. *Journal of Ethnic & Cultural Diversity in Social Work, 26*(1-2), 81–94.

Stewart, D.-L. (2017, March 30). Language of appeasement. *Inside Higher Education.* Retrieved from https://www.insidehighered.com/views/2017/03/30/colleges -need-language-shift-not-one-you-think-essay

Stotzer, R. L., & Hossellman, E. (2012). Hate crimes on campus: Racial/ethnic diversity and campus safety. *Journal of Interpersonal Violence, 27*(4), 644–661.

Sue, D. W. (2010). *Microaggressions in everyday life: Race, gender, and sexual orientation.* Hoboken, NJ: John Wiley & Sons.

Swail, W., Redd, K., & Perna, L. (2003). Retaining minority students in higher education: A framework for success. *ASHE-ERIC Higher Education Report, 30*(2). Washington, DC: George Washington University.

Taylor, E. (2000). Critical race theory and interest convergence in the backlash against affirmative action: Washington State and Initiative 200. *Teachers College Record, 102*(3), 539–560.

Tinto, V. (1975). Dropout from higher education: A theoretical synthesis of recent research. *Review of Educational Research, 45*(1), 89–125.

Tinto, V. (1993). *Leaving college: Rethinking the causes and cures of student attrition.* Chicago: University of Chicago Press.

Van Dyke, N., & Tester, G. (2014). Dangerous climates: Factors associated with variation in racist hate crimes on college campuses. *Journal of Contemporary Criminal Justice, 30*(3), 290–309.

Woodford, M. R., Chonody, J. M., Kulick, A., Brennan, D. J., & Renn, K. (2015). The LGBQ microaggressions on campus scale: A scale development and validation study. *Journal of Homosexuality, 62*(12), 1660–1687.

Yang, Y., & Carroll, D. W. (2018). Gendered microaggressions in science, technology, engineering, and mathematics. *Leadership and Research in Education, 4,* 28–45.

Zinn, H. (2009). The optimism of uncertainty. *Amass, 13*(4), 12–13.

Zúñiga, X., Lopez, G. E., & Ford, K. A. (2012). Intergroup dialogue: Critical conversations about difference, social identities, and social justice: Guest editors' introduction. *Equity & Excellence in Education, 45*(1), 1–13.

Zúñiga, X., Nagda, B. R. A., & Sevig, T. D. (2002). Intergroup dialogues: An educational model for cultivating engagement across differences. *Equity & Excellence in Education, 35*(1), 7–17.

Chapter 6

CREATING A CULTURE OF INCLUSION IN THE CLASSROOM

Raquel Wright-Mair

> The academy is not paradise. But learning is a place where paradise can be created. The classroom, with all its limitations, remains a location of possibility. In that field of possibility, we have the opportunity to labor for freedom, to demand of ourselves and our comrades an openness of mind and heart that allows us to face reality even as we collectively imagine ways to move beyond boundaries, to transgress. This is education as the practice of freedom.
>
> —bell hooks (1994, p. 207)

One of the most discussed topics in higher education today is the need for inclusive classroom cultures that affirm and validate the diverse identities and experiences of students (Danowitz & Tuitt, 2011; Kumar, Zusho, & Bondie, 2018; Linder, Harris, Allen, & Hubain, 2015). Of specific interest is the notion that professors need to be inclusive in their pedagogical approaches and also in their understanding of the changing demography of students entering their classrooms. Beliefs of a "one size fits all" attitude towards teaching continue to permeate the field of higher education and in turn contribute to classroom environments that are not affirming or relevant to the experiences of diverse student populations. Of particular concern is the idea that in the absence of an inclusive classroom culture, current and future student affairs practitioners are not being exposed to innovative and inclusive ways of thinking and learning. The word *inclusion* can be defined as a set of practices that promote meaningful engagement among groups of people who come from varied identities and experiences (Kumar et al., 2018). Specifically, inclusion in the classroom takes into account different perspectives and includes appreciation and value for said perspectives and experiences in a way that supports the growth and development of all students.

One of the 10 professional competency areas for student affairs educators includes social justice and inclusion (American College Personnel Association [ACPA] & National Association of Student Personnel Administrators [NASPA], 2015). Understanding and implementing principles of equity, diversity, and inclusion allows student affairs professionals to demonstrate that they have the necessary skills, abilities, and knowledge needed to create learning environments that seek to examine and address issues of oppression, power, and privilege (ACPA & NASPA, 2015). As such, this chapter is intended to be used as a resource for faculty members in higher education and student affairs programs nationally, as well as provide context for what graduate students in these programs should expect and think about with regards to inclusive classroom cultures.

The discussion in this chapter is divided into six sections. In the first section, I discuss my personal and professional experience with inclusive classroom cultures. Within that context, the chapter is heavily influenced by the inclusive pedagogical approaches I employ in the classroom and serves as an account of those experiences. I then recount some of my own experiences as a professor who intentionally sets the tone for an inclusive classroom environment. In the sections following, I highlight the impact of inclusion on learning, inclusion as a shared responsibility in the classroom, the engaging of multiple perspectives in the classroom, and problematic assumptions in the classroom. This chapter also outlines some recommended practices that contribute to the development of inclusive and affirming classroom cultures. It is my hope that this chapter will be beneficial to those in the field of higher education who seek to create inclusive classroom spaces for all students and useful for practitioners who engage in the development and delivery of trainings and instruction across different issues that impact college students. Additionally, this chapter can inform practitioners on how classroom experiences contribute to students' sense of inclusion on campus.

From Banking to Co-Constructing: An Educator's Transformation

Creating a culture of inclusion in the classroom is essential to learning and development. In my educational experiences, I have been on the receiving end of both inclusive and exclusive classroom environments and have experienced firsthand the benefits and drawbacks of both. In my role as an assistant professor of higher education and student affairs leadership, I strive to create inclusive classroom cultures that foster transparency, vulnerability, honesty, inclusivity, and equity, essential elements that characterize inclusion.

These are not easy processes and inherently challenge how our institutions of higher education condition us to teach and learn.

Almost always, we are taught the opposite of liberatory ways of approaching the classroom. Growing up in the Caribbean, specifically in Jamaica, I was a product of the banking system of education. Freire (1993) described this way of teaching and learning as a philosophical concept where teachers see themselves as the holder of knowledge and students as ignorant, non-creative beings who exist simply to absorb knowledge from their instructors. This style of education is not unique to my home country, Jamaica, and is quite pervasive globally across a variety of educational systems. The banking system, as Freire posited, in many ways maintains the professor's power and control in the classroom, with the teacher holding all autonomy in regard to curriculum development and execution. Freire also acknowledged the problematic nature of this system of education, which, as he stated, exists to uphold power and oppression by giving the teacher the ultimate responsibility for teaching and reproducing knowledge, while taking away any agency from students to be part of the knowledge production process.

In my own life, I rarely experienced classroom environments that required my input in the context of the co-construction of learning, particularly throughout my primary and secondary education. In fact, the few teachers that I did encounter whose pedagogy did not center the banking system engaged a fire within me for learning in ways that I was never able to explain. Feeling as if I mattered and that my perspective was important to the learning process was a crucial part of my educational success. Freire (1993) referred to this form of liberating education as "problem-posing" education, which seeks to transform rather than dictate. Problem-posing education, as examined by Freire, describes an approach to education that fosters active engagement with both instructor and student. This method of teaching and learning, allows the student and instructor to be in constant dialogue, open to the co-construction of knowledge and the emergence of a conscious educational awakening together. In practice, problem-posing education cultivates a learning environment in which both practitioners and students can participate in reciprocal dialogic processes. Such interactions can produce transformative agents of change within higher education and student affairs leadership.

During my undergraduate years at Ithaca College, a mid-size, liberal arts four-year institution in the United States, I developed a passion for learning that was never there before. At the time, I do not think I attributed my love for learning to the intentional and engaged pedagogical approaches of my faculty, though I noticed an obvious difference in general and specific approaches to teaching and learning. Back then, I credited my new love for learning to my newfound independence several thousand miles away from my homeland, family, and friends. In college, I did experience a few classrooms that were more "banking"-like in nature, but the vast experiences I had were very focused on co-constructing knowledge. My faculty provided space for students to interrogate the material assigned in readings and taught lectures in a way that developed critical thinking. This was also the case during both my master's and doctoral programs as well.

With classroom spaces that supported thinking outside the box, I was able to contribute constructively to classroom discussions and assignments; I engaged with learning in a more intentional and meaningful way. Additionally, my faculty allowed me to bring my authentic self to the classroom. Because they all knew I was an international student from Jamaica, they were interested in the global lens that I brought to the classroom and asked probing questions that allowed for me to contextualize my experiences. This, of course, was a specific experience in a liberal arts college environment. Many of my professors encompassed an inclusive and engaged pedagogy that centered student growth and success.

Furthermore, an example from my college years that resonates with me is that none of my faculty members corrected my use of British spelling in my academic papers and presentations—something that took me years to eventually realize. After wondering why and speaking with these faculty members many years later, I recognized that this was a conscious and intentional attempt on their part to be culturally engaging and affirming to my specific culture and ethnic background. This made a difference in how I performed in the classroom, because there was no external pressure on me from my faculty to assimilate to a culture that was new to me. Additionally, I was not *othered* because of my own cultural background. Othering or othered refers to the experiences marginalized groups face when they are considered to be different or subordinate to dominant groups in society (Kumashiro, 2000). As such, many marginalized groups who experience discrimination are treated in ways that reinforce power and oppressive ways of thinking; they are othered because they are seen as different. Although I did get a heads up from one professor many years after, it never felt punitive in nature; the professor was simply making me aware that if I planned on submitting work to journals or official publishing entities, my spelling would probably need to be in accordance with American English standards. I appreciated such conversations because they were honest and purposeful in nature. As a student, I grew tremendously from the attention my faculty paid to inclusive practices that centered my own growth and success.

As a professor, my own pedagogical approaches are deeply rooted in my personal and educational experiences and my strong passion and love for teaching. I reject the banking system of teaching and learning and strive to uphold a classroom culture that is heavily focused on the co-construction of knowledge, inclusivity, and equity, along with the disruption and interrogation of normative discourse. When students first enter my classroom, they go through a period of shock, wondering whether my pedagogy is a real and sustainable approach. I see and hear them asking, "So what is the answer?" To which I respond, "What do you think?" It is often in these moments that the stares begin and the "We've never had a professor push us to think in this way" comments start. I gently remind them that in my classrooms, their learning will often look very different from the status quo. My students tell me all the time that my classes are very different from others they have taken; they specifically discuss that *how* and *what* they learn is very different.

I am unapologetic for how I show up in my classroom, bringing not only my authentic self but also a pedagogical approach that encourages and supports students' varying views and challenges dominant ways of thinking. I refer to showing up as the way in which I utilize personal experiences to anchor my pedagogical delivery. I invite my students to take part in their learning as well, and as such, hold very high expectations of them that they produce quality work that seeks to examine deeply rooted systemic issues in society. At the end of the semester, my students share with me, both privately and publicly (and also by way of teaching evaluations), that they are stunned with my consistency in the classroom. Although I acknowledge that I am an expert in some areas, I am unashamed in admitting that I, too, learn from them, and essentially become a better professor because I do *not* claim to know it all. I am also honest in my utilization of what hooks (1994) described as critical pedagogical approaches to learning, which center a conscious disruption of dominant ideologies around traditional ways of teaching and focus on concepts of community building, inclusion, and different ways of knowing.

Impact of Inclusion on Learning

Higher education scholarship has documented that practices of inclusivity in the classroom contribute to more positive and meaningful experiences for all students (Danowitz & Tuitt, 2011; Linder et al., 2015). Juxtaposed with the notion that exclusive classroom environments and pedagogical approaches lead to feelings of isolation and a deterioration in motivation to learn, the need for inclusive classrooms and pedagogies is increasing in our field (Linder et al., 2015). Transforming classrooms to be more inclusive, although challenging, is not impossible. It often requires educators to rethink our roles and responsibilities in the classroom, while also interrogating our own biases and the ways in which we show up in these spaces. How we approach the classroom and choose to *show up* sets the tone for how students will learn and engage with each other.

Oftentimes when discussing issues of inclusivity, many limit its definition to issues of race and ethnicity. Although important and relevant to this chapter, topics of inclusion are not just limited to issues pertaining to race and ethnicity. Inclusion also encompasses the recognition that people of differing gender identities, sexual orientations, socioeconomic status, political thought, educational attainment, age, nationality, and ability will experience the classroom differently. Therefore, leaving room to create a classroom environment that takes students' backgrounds, identities, and experiences into account is crucial, because it empowers students and enables a certain kind of agency that is atypical for students in more traditional classroom settings. In my experience, when students feel valued, included, and respected, they are more likely to find their own voice and utilize that voice in ways that inherently transform their educational experiences.

The impact of inclusion on learning and development is undeniable. Museus (2014) pointed out that when students feel a greater sense of belonging and feel as if they matter in the classroom, they are more likely to perform at higher academic standards, connect more meaningfully with their home communities, and experience high levels of motivation. Pascarella and Terenzini (2005) iterated that when students believe that their faculty care about them and engage with them intentionally in ways that validate their identities, there is an increase in persistence rates and stronger engagement inside and outside the classroom. I have witnessed firsthand the successful impacts of inclusion on learning. By ensuring that students feel as if they matter, classroom dynamics shift greatly, as is the case if students feel their experiences do not matter (Schlossberg, 1989). As such, it is important that professors create classroom environments that provide students with the tools to develop in significant ways academically, personally, and professionally.

Furthermore, for many students from minoritized backgrounds, the classroom may be the only place on campus where they can contextualize and unpack their identities and experiences and engage in theoretical ways with their home communities, while understanding greater systemic issues. Though there are many accounts I can recall, one specific student's story comes to mind. I met Krista[1] during the second semester of her master's program. Krista identified as a queer woman of color who often discussed feelings of loneliness, isolation, and hostility in her program of study. On the first day of class when I met Krista, I knew she was experiencing feelings of exclusion based on her body language, which indicated frustration and agitation. Not only did she verbally express her frustration to me and her peers in class on the first day, but very often I could tell from her body language

---

1. Pseudonym used.

that she was on the defensive. After getting to know Krista, who was also one of my graduate advisees, I recognized that prior to my arrival, she never felt validated, affirmed, or "seen" in her classes. She mentioned to me that she enjoyed my classes because of my intentionality in creating a curriculum that encapsulated the experiences of all kinds of people. She explained further that in other classes, very rarely did she get to read materials from authors of different racial, ethnic, ability, sexual, and gender identities. She found solace in my class, because she felt that a less dominant and more transformative agenda was being pushed, and that by my careful selection of readings and nontraditional assignments, she was truly able to critically analyze social inequities and understand different perspectives.

Initially, Krista was reserved and concerned about what others thought about her. As time progressed, Krista developed confidence and was able to more confidently articulate her own experiences through connecting with relevant, applicable literature in which she saw herself represented. Everything about Krista changed within one semester—her writing changed, her confidence soared, and she started to complicate her intersecting identities and make meaning of them within an academic context. She later met with me and told me she was confident she wanted to pursue a Ph.D. and become a professor, because she finally saw herself represented in the classroom in a way that she had not before. Krista was one of the first students I intentionally talked with, as a new professor, about inclusion and inclusive pedagogy. Later that academic year, I began realizing similar instances happening with other students across the board, regardless of their identities.

Although students of color and white students experience the classroom in different ways (Danowitz & Tuitt, 2011; Linder et al., 2015), both groups have outlined to me the benefits of an inclusive and student-centered classroom environment. Some of these benefits include being able to be reflexive, critical, and more aware of their experiences and the experiences of others. For example, students of color have shared with me that they found a connection to me personally because of my racialized identities, in addition to seeing themselves reflected in the curriculum and in assignments that required nontraditional approaches to academic writing and assessment. White students shared that the opportunity to be presented with alternative discourses and ways of thinking not only allowed them to challenge their privileged identities but also provided context for them to understand their privilege in relation to power and oppression. Many white students also acknowledged that they felt more willing to confront bias and discrimination as well as better equipped with tools to discuss difficult topics around equity, inclusion, and social justice.

Utilizing an inclusive pedagogical style in the classroom reaffirms all students can be seen and heard, and this is a goal I attempt to accomplish in my own teaching. *Inclusive pedagogy,* as described by Tuitt (2003), refers to practices that account for holistic ways of teaching and learning that embrace the whole student and consider the varying components that comprise their individuality, including but not limited to their identities and experiences. Tuitt discussed the value added when teachers are able to make classrooms meaningful and transform their own level of consciousness. Oftentimes, the benefits of such transformed consciousness on the part of the teacher lead to highly engaged and motivated students, willing to step outside the confines of their comfort zones and willing to explore and expand knowledge inside and outside the classroom.

Thus, developing and maintaining a culture of inclusion in the classroom has several implications for student growth and development:

- Students are exposed to different ways of thinking and can contextualize and interrogate ways of knowing and being, in more constructive and critical ways.
- Students from all backgrounds can start to feel a sense of belonging and understand that the classroom is a space that must embrace people from different backgrounds.
- Students become more open and aware and are able to engage in dialogue and activities that encourage a multidimensional and more complicated way of processing.
- Students feel more comfortable to make mistakes in environments that are less punitive and concerned with a one-dimensional way of thinking, and therefore they become less ashamed to engage in the unlearning and relearning process.
- Students become better equipped to have critical conversations outside their classroom and start to consider inclusion more broadly in spaces that require more practical approaches (e.g., graduate assistantships and full-time practitioner jobs).

Many of the implications above are informed by previous scholarship that has examined equity-oriented pedagogies and their unique impact on student learning (hooks 1994; Museus, 2014; Tuitt, 2003). Specifically, these pedagogies call for learning environments that recognize and validate the unique value that students bring with them to their classrooms. Such approaches to learning potentially transform perspectives and critique systems of oppression, and thus have a greater impact on society as a whole.

In the field of higher education and student affairs, learning to create inclusive, affirming, and supportive environments transcends the classroom. Oftentimes, students in master's and doctoral programs take the formal and informal knowledge conveyed to them in the classroom into other areas in their lives. For example, students who are full-time student affairs professionals often cite examples of how they use the knowledge and exchanges in their classrooms to revamp existing policies and/or practices in their department. In fact, in many instances, these students share how their relationships with colleagues improved after being able to apply theoretical knowledge practically. My experience has been that when students feel included or start to think in inclusive ways, they inevitably start applying these ways of learning in varied capacities. For example, in-class activities and discussion can influence students to think more meaningfully about their roles in specific departments. Students have previously shared that they utilized many of the prompts and in-class activities in their own departments to get their students and colleagues thinking in critical and inclusive ways to achieve goals outlined for their departments. Frequently, students tell me they are stronger practitioners because of the ways inclusion, or lack thereof, has appeared in their lives and/or in the classroom.

Moreover, when students experience inclusion or exclusion, they become more likely to re-create environments focused on more positive experiences for others in their professional, academic, and personal communities (Linder et al., 2015). Professors who center inclusion in their pedagogy and model inclusive ways of being connect more meaningfully with students (Linder et al., 2015). In many ways, these pedagogical approaches and practices make instructors more intentional and relatable, leading to more solid relationships between students and their professors.

As Tuitt (2003) posited, many of the components necessary for a successful pedagogical style anchored in inclusive practices include the use of the following tenets: (a) faculty-student interaction, (b) shared power, (c) dialogical student-professor interaction, (d) activation of student voice, and (e) utilization of personal narratives. I incorporate these tenets into my own teaching and in the following sections, offer tangible examples of how I do this and how these tenets are applicable to practice.

Faculty-Student Interaction

Relationships and communication are important to me, and fundamental to effective teaching. Guided by my prior experience as a student affairs professional, I am motivated to create opportunities for students to be their best selves by fostering environments that encourage frequent and significant interaction. Making myself available to students during office hours and in many instances outside of assigned office hours via digital communication allows meaningful interactions to take place between faculty and students. Whereas the classroom provides an important space for faculty-student interaction, it is important to connect with students outside the classroom in an effort to get to know them better and understand their individual needs and experiences (Stewart, 2016; Tuitt, 2003). This often sheds light on in-class interactions and helps both faculty and students understand each other in different ways. This form of interaction also facilitates proactive mentoring and advising, as well as allows students to feel a sense of belonging (Museus, 2014). This is especially the case for students who struggle with public communication and prefer private conversations to effectively process their thoughts and/or feelings. In practice, these interactions serve similar purposes: to generate conversations and build relationships with students and colleagues. Establishing trust between professionals and students is also an important component for creating inclusive spaces. In order to achieve these goals of building trust, student affairs professionals can engage with students through one-on-one conversations, staff meetings, professional development workshops, or time designated outside of typical work hours. This may include attendance at student-run events and/or activities that are led by peers.

Sharing Power

It is important to incorporate students in the execution of the curriculum in the classroom. In my own work, I challenge students to be active agents in their own learning. This usually manifests in students teaching or facilitating a portion of the designated lesson plan for the day. Students are given the opportunity to experience being the instructor by presenting information, engaging with the class, asking thought-provoking questions, and providing meaningful feedback. Sharing power, though frightful for many students, helps develop confidence and confront their own biases about power in the classroom. Additionally, students get the opportunity to learn with and from each other and take "greater responsibility for their own learning" (Stewart, 2016, p. 15). For student affairs professionals, sharing power looks like collaborative efforts that encourage both students and colleagues to take part in their own learning and development. This could be the administration of a self-evaluation between a supervisor and employee, or an intentional conversation between advisor and advisee about the trajectory of a student's academic journey. Student affairs professionals must also be willing to confront their own biases in an effort to better assist students in reaching their educational goals. Sharing power in this respect is beneficial to all involved, because this approach encourages ownership and active involvement in decision making.

Dialogical Professor-Student Interaction

In my classroom, I offer students the opportunity to really be honest and critical, both of myself and their peers. The structure of my classes allows for consistent open and engaged dialogue, where I encourage students to feel free to disagree with my perspectives but present their opposing views and explain their positionality and stances in ways that facilitate active engagement. As outlined by Stewart 2016, many students find this difficult because of traditional rules that govern the classroom environment; they consistently defer to me, although I encourage alternative ways for them to respond. In practice, this translates to communicating honestly with students, inviting them to not just agree with the perspective presented, but also bring multiple views to the table that foster open dialogue and encourage active participation and engagement in their varying roles within student affairs. Student affairs professionals can reinforce what is learned in the classroom and structure their functional areas in ways that create opportunities for students to become active agents in their learning by practicing reflection, engaging in difficult dialogues, and sharing power in decision making about student programs and services.

Activation of Student Voice

Many students enter the classroom feeling as if their voices do not matter. Acknowledging and encouraging students to utilize their voices in the classroom is important to their own growth but also adds richness and depth to the classroom environment (Darder, 1996; Tuitt, 2003). By utilizing their voice, students bring to the classroom their experiences as they have lived them. These experiences allow for vulnerability and authenticity, which helps to create humanizing conditions for learning to occur for all. When student voices are in fact activated, it is important that instructors offer support and not dismiss their individual experiences. For student affairs practitioners, this requires challenging and supporting students in ways that not only bring their voices to the table but also make space for them to include their perspectives and experiences.

Utilization of Personal Narratives

Through free write exercises, journaling, and sharing personal stories, students participate in their own learning by incorporating and deconstructing their own experiences in the classroom. Often this is new and different for students but allows them to bring their individual identities and experiences into a space designated for learning. In student affairs, this can be utilized with teambuilding activities that intentionally call for inclusion of personal stories from students and their connection with practice.

These tenets foster inclusion through co-creation of knowledge in the classroom, and in turn, redistribute power in the classroom. The next section addresses the importance of shared responsibility in the classroom and discusses reasons why shared responsibility is a crucial component of an inclusive classroom environment.

Inclusion as a Shared Responsibility in the Classroom Community

In order to have inclusive classroom cultures, together faculty members and students should be part of a collective effort in the classroom. *Inclusion* encompasses the notion that everybody coming to the classroom brings a different perspective and a valid one. Being inclusive goes beyond limited conceptions, such as being "politically correct" and "not hurting feelings," in a way that centers the experiences and perspectives of various populations who differ by gender, sexuality, race, socioeconomic status, ability, age, and so on. Inclusion encourages the deconstruction of one's own beliefs in order to truly understand and contextualize the experiences of others in and around our classrooms.

There are many ways that I incorporate inclusion into my pedagogical style in a way that lends itself favorably to a collaborative learning environment in which my students are also active drivers in the process. Inspired by the work of Dr. Bianca Williams, I create an inclusive space at the beginning of each semester by utilizing a *radical honesty* statement. Williams (2016) defined radical honesty as "a concept that describes a pedagogical practice of truth-telling that seeks to challenge racist and patriarchal institutional cultures in the academy" (p. 72). As suggested by Williams, this statement incorporates many of my personal and professional experiences as well as perspectives I have of the world. I start by explaining my various identities and how they contribute to my pedagogical practices and approaches in the classroom. I have found that the vulnerability that results from this exercise for both myself and my students sets the tone for the rest of the semester. As Williams suggested by sharing a radically honest positionality statement, I invite my students to partake in and co-construct learning with me. In addition, students are introduced to the "politics of education and learning" (p. 76) as we learn about and contextualize our various identities and experiences. The co-construction of knowledge, as explained by Danowitz and Tuitt (2011), encourages students to also take responsibility for their learning. This style of learning creates a foundation for the classroom that is foregrounded in honesty and authenticity. Whereas I do not ask students to craft their own radical honest statement, they share information throughout the semester that encompasses radical honesty.

An excerpt from my own radical honesty statement is included below. The entire statement includes additional information about my whole self, including my personal and professional interests and my research agenda, as well as my overall expectations for my students and for myself as the instructor.

> My teaching philosophy centers students, as many of you who have taken classes with me previously know. By our second class, I will know your name and refer to you as such for the rest of our lives together. I truly love my job and believe that co-constructing knowledge with my students is essential to learning. Because I grew up in an environment that centered the banking system of education, a system of learning focused on the instructor as the holder of all knowledge and the student as the mere receptacle of said knowledge, I reject that kind of teaching and learning in all its forms. If you are looking for a professor who "deposits" knowledge, I am not that. I have high expectations of students and will commit to challenging and support-ing you no matter what. As an educator, my goal is to provide students with conceptual tools that allow you to analyze how things work in higher edu-cation and understand your own positionality within these systems. We are here to ask hard questions and work intentionally to become stronger and more aware scholar-practitioners. Everyone's experiences are different, and regardless of how we feel, we must respect each other's perspectives and respond in a way that encourages learning. Radical honesty, as Williams (2016) suggested, means that we not only speak truth, but also illustrate that truth through our actions. I will always expect that you all will bring your genuine selves to this space and be brave and open as we navigate this jour-ney together.

When I first decided to utilize Dr. William's radical honesty statement, I was fearful for weeks leading up to the start of the semester. Although I have always been a very open and transparent person and professor, I was now challenging myself to disclose personal pieces of information about my life on the first day of class to new students; traditionally this has been a process that takes months, sometimes years for me to disclose. I recognized that the information I disclose is relevant for the courses and topic areas that I teach, and for the type of engagement I hope students will take part in during the semester. I see value in this approach and know that if I truly want my stu-dents to show up as their true selves, I needed to model this as well.

So, on the first day of class, I introduce myself, discuss the syllabus and dive straight into my radical honesty statement. As Williams (2016) shared, silence usually permeates the room thereafter. In the spirit of valuing and honoring silence in classroom spaces, I have become comfortable resisting the desire to interrupt silence in the classroom and feel it necessary to honor silence and allow students the space they need to process. I have become comfortable honoring silence in my classroom, much to the dismay of my students who desperately look at me to "say something." In these "uncomfortable moments," I practice mindfulness, knowing I put my vulnerable self out there, and do a general check-in to see if anyone has thoughts, concerns, or suggestions. Much like William's experience, after moments of silence, students start to comment that they have never experienced such openness from a faculty member. They also often discuss the impact the statement has on how they are thinking about the class and their own perspectives towards learning. Such statements reaffirm the importance of showing up authentically in classroom spaces and assure me that radical honesty is indeed a crucial component of inclusion. Many students remain shocked at my vulnerability and openness to establish such a learning environment and marvel at the notion of radical honesty long after the first day of class. I understand that this approach is very new to many students and not everyone will jump on board or know how to readily process such nontraditional ways of connecting in the classroom. I am still very aware of the rawness of my vulnerability in the moments after my statement but honor its value and importance in establishing an open and inclusive classroom environment.

Throughout the semester, I see a major difference in how my students showed up for class, how they participated and eagerly learned, bore their bare selves, and shared their own radically honest experiences with me. Being vulnerable has indeed shifted the entire energy in my classrooms and engaged a different type of teaching and learning. As the semester progresses, I am often reminded about the value and impact of my statement when my teaching evaluations are released. I am often shocked to see that the vast majority of students were so impacted by my statement that on my evaluations, they comment that what they experienced in my class is very different. This radical honesty approach can be utilized by student affairs professionals by engaging in open, transparent, and authentic conversations about their varying identities and experiences and discussing openly how they might integrate themselves into practice. This approach also requires professionals to be comfortable and open to sharing personal stories and engage in critical self-reflexivity.

Other ways that I strive to create an inclusive classroom space and encourage collectivist approaches to inclusion include setting community-learning expectations with students. In fact, this is an activity that I simply facilitate, with the purpose of students' developing a set of expectations that serve as an accountability tool focused on respect, support, validation, and responsibility in the classroom. This differs from traditional ground rules in that I allow students to be an active part of the process, rather than imposing my ideas of what I think the norm is. Additionally, the term *ground rules* carry a perception of authority that comes solely from the professor. Instead, in my own work, I challenge those practices by establishing community guidelines where students are active participants in the process and have the opportunity to learn without the historical restrictions of normative education. Periodically throughout the semester, we revisit these expectations; usually, it is students who remind their peers about these expectations. Often, this revisiting of expectations occurs when difficult conversations and situations arise in the classroom. I normally discuss these expectations throughout the semester, especially before I facilitate an activity that requires students to be open about their varying identities and perspectives. In addition to setting expectations, I encourage students to work in groups to analyze theory and make connections to practice. This includes working on a variety of in-class and out-of-class assignments in both small and large groups.

My classes are structured in ways that encourage group discussions of case scenarios. The scenarios are heavily informed by actual events across higher education and student affairs, both nationally and globally. These scenarios encourage students to unpack real-life situations and apply theory to practice within small groups. Processing in smaller groups and then reconvening as a larger class often yields very different perspectives on topics. Students are able to share their thoughts on different topics and collectively engage in dialogue. In these moments, the exchange of ideas on certain topics becomes a shared responsibility, and each student actively plays a role in the others' learning processing. In the spirit of creating an inclusive classroom, I strive to encourage students to share their experiences and engage in constructive dialogue with each other in order to start the process of thinking outside the traditional boxes of learning. Whereas students undoubtedly learn from me, they also learn from each other in very distinct and meaningful ways.

Another tool that encourages inclusion as a shared responsibility is a values continuum activity. The purpose of this type of activity is to create a space in which students can communicate their thoughts and feelings on diversity, both verbally and nonverbally. In addition, this activity is useful to spark self-reflection and self-disclosure, both of which are essential to becoming better intercultural communicators. For this activity, four areas are identified in the room, based on the following responses: (a) strongly agree, (b) agree, (c) disagree, and (d) strongly disagree. Students are asked to move to the area that best reflects their opinion in response to statements, such as "I am comfortable having hard conversations with my colleagues about systemic inequities and asking them to be accountable where necessary." This type of activity allows students to be honest in their assessment of their growth and learning in an environment that supports them at their particular stage. This process is twofold: It allows students to not only understand their own perspectives but also work closely with others on a variety of issues. During this activity, students learn to hear the perspectives of others in the class and are encouraged not to comment on or interrupt the learning process of those who volunteer to express their opinions. This sets the stage for processing in deep and reflective ways without always having to comment or analyze a specific student's perspective.

Despite all the work I do to construct a classroom environment that is inclusive, students come to the classroom in different ways, which means they can or might express opinions that are not inclusive and that emphasize ways of thinking about policies, practices, and behaviors that promote exclusion. In these instances, students have to commit to doing their own work to deconstruct how and why policies, practices, and behaviors are exclusive. My responsibility as an instructor is not to do their work for them, but to provide resources and tools for them to continue to do the work required to be inclusive.

In recognizing and appreciating the different learning styles of students, I provide room for other activities that allow students to work on a more individual level and process their thoughts and feelings by themselves. These opportunities usually include journaling, free writing, and reflection papers that require analysis of theory and practice, while recognizing how one's self influences those ideals. Although assignments vary in my classes, my assignments typically center inclusion and allow students, whether in groups or alone, to incorporate an application piece into their lives, departments, or roles in their fields. In one specific class, I asked students to bring a relevant current event to discuss in class. Students were expected to talk about the current event and its implications for higher education and student affairs to unpack the deeper meaning of the specific current event. Students had a chance to bring in relevant material that incorporated many of their interests and were able to examine the structural and systemic underpinnings of their chosen topic. An example of this was a story making national news about two roommates, which involved a hate crime in a residence hall at a four-year institution. Students were able to thoroughly discuss and analyze how they would have dealt with such a situation as a student affairs administrator. This provided an excellent opportunity for students to apply their theoretical knowledge of the field to a difficult practical example that involved many layers of systemic inequity. The conversations that ensued about this case were difficult but meaningful and encouraged students to think in ways that were critical. An inclusive classroom also allows for conflict to transpire.

Because conflict is usually generated due to a difference of opinions, embracing difficult moments in the classroom provides an opportunity for myself and students to navigate the identities and experiences of others in supportive and respectful ways. Although this is easy in theory, conflict in the classroom is not only inevitable but also sometimes hard to negotiate when students expect that it is only the instructor's role to "fix things."

Conflict rears its head in various forms, and depending on the type of conflict that arises, faculty should expect conflict and be prepared to facilitate discussions with students to achieve a productive resolution. When conflict emerges in my classroom, I quickly evaluate if there needs to be immediate action, that is, a discussion with the class, individual meetings with involved parties, or if external help is required from a mediator. I also carefully and honestly assess my role in the conflict at hand and humbly take responsibility if and when I have contributed to the development of conflict. It is a strong component of my pedagogy to always follow up immediately after any conflict occurs in the classroom, as uncomfortable as it may feel. Even in instances where I do not have an immediate resolution, I walk students through my thinking and acknowledge my need to process the situation at hand, while working towards a solution. Of course, no one is perfect; and students, like faculty colleagues, will have their own view of how faculty should or could have handled a situation rooted in conflict. In those instances, it is important to acknowledge that there will be times that conflict is handled in ways that seem most appropriate at the specific moment. Conflict in the classroom provides an opportunity for healthy debate, proactively working towards resolution with others, and emulates future issues that may arise in practice (Tuitt 2003).

I also administer mid-semester reviews to allow students to share their thoughts on how they are experiencing my class, and what, if anything, they would change. These assessments have allowed me to make many changes to the existing format of my classes, to incorporate viewpoints and perspectives that were not previously accounted for. Students also appreciate the opportunity to make suggestions that will contribute further to more critical and engaged learning.

Finally, I find that engaging in self-reflection allows me to ask important questions about how I, as the instructor, am transforming my teaching to be more inclusive. These questions include

1. Am I offering a healthy balance of support and challenge to my students?
2. Am I providing space to address difficult conversations?
3. Are there opportunities for students to examine their own perspectives and the perspectives of others?
4. Is my curriculum diverse, equitable, and engaging?
5. How am I incorporating student voice into the classroom?
6. How am I cultivating and reinforcing student agency?
7. How am I presenting and discussing my own viewpoints?
8. How am I challenging my own perspectives?

Expecting and allowing for students to self-reflect also allows for them to be active in their learning process and centers their personal journeys as future professionals. In my experience with teaching, it is evident that to truly have an inclusive space, there has to be a focus on the collective. Not everyone will get it or appreciate it. In fact, I sometimes have students who are still navigating, unlearning, and relearning their own beliefs and attitudes. To be honest, some see inclusion as lofty and unattainable. Nevertheless, the majority of students I interact with see the value in creating and maintaining environments that center practices of inclusion and strive for equity in higher education. These values established in the classroom then translate into their work as student affairs professionals. I recognize that the culture I create in my classroom is transferable to practice, because learning does not stop once you leave the classroom; rather it is the entry point for practitioners to disrupt the binary of theory and practice.

Engaging Around Multiple Perspectives in the Classroom

As a racially minoritized immigrant faculty member, it is important to me to engage a variety of perspectives in my classroom. This is important, because when students are exposed to different ways of thinking and knowing, they are able to learn how to interact with others who are different from themselves. Students are also able to recognize that there are people who are marginalized primarily because of systemic oppression. As such, engaging multiple perspectives offers students different ways to think about people and come up with varied solutions to support them. Another benefit is that students begin to confront their own biases and contextualize their thoughts and beliefs. What I have seen is that when students start to unlearn their own biases, they start engaging in intentional self-reflection and reflectivity, which is essential to the success of any student affairs practitioner. Without a doubt, this starts the process of engaging students in a critically conscious way of viewing and showing up in the world. At the core of engaging multiple perspectives in the classroom is familiarizing students with different knowledge and presenting them with additional viewpoints. In the field of higher education and student affairs, this is important in order to support students holistically and support their varying identities and experiences, as well as understand that their lives outside the classroom heavily impact how they perceive the world and act in it. When practitioners engage with students, they must consider all aspects of the students' experience; and thus, inclusion in the classroom can have an impact on students' sense of belonging and success.

The specific ways in which I engage multiple perspectives in the classroom include the intentional designing of a syllabus that not only incorporates readings from an array of scholars from various backgrounds, identities, and perspectives on the topic area, but also embodies inclusion. Additionally, I assign work that allows students to incorporate theory, practice, and their individual skills, identities, and backgrounds. In class, I engage with students in a variety of ways that affirm their learning styles by incorporating clear learning outcomes and the corresponding ways of learning (Davis & Arend, 2013). Because we understand that students learn in different ways, different modes of delivery are pertinent to a student's developmental process. As such, much of my teaching includes opportunities for students to (a) build new skills and expand their knowledge base, (b) develop a critical and conscious way of reasoning, (c) expand problem-solving capabilities, (d) examine their own experiences and perspectives, (e) apply theory to practice, and (f) reflect on their own growth (Davis & Arend, 2013). By designing assignments and providing ample engagement opportunities in the classroom, students learn these skills through instructional strategies, including the use of visual, audio, closed-caption, and kinesthetic tools. These approaches invite students to share differing perspectives on complex issues that might emerge in the classroom by engaging in ways that are better suited for their learning styles and preferences. For example, students who are visual learners benefit from videos, in class role play, and diagrams that clearly explain theoretical concepts and allow them to make important connections to practice.

Problematic Assumptions in the Classroom

There are several barriers that can interrupt how a culture of inclusion is created in the classroom environment. As noted by Freire (1993), students show up to classrooms with presumptions of what learning should look and be like. Additionally, Tuitt (2003) highlighted that when professors of these "inclusive" classroom settings are from minoritized identities, a layer of complexity is added. This is so because many students come in with assumptions that if their instructor is of a particular race, ethnicity, nationality, sexual orientation, gender identity, or ability, they will only focus on issues of social justice and equity. Whereas this is certainly the case for many of us with minoritized and marginalized identities, our greatest challenge becomes trying to teach in innovative ways that get students to understand that the notion of equity and inclusion is everybody's business and not just relevant to those of us who experience everyday discrimination. The acknowledgement that these assumptions exist is the first step in the direction of recognizing that building an inclusive classroom is a two-way street and not just the sole responsibility of the instructor. Professors can try to address these assumptions in the classroom, but students also have to be willing to engage and disrupt these patterns as well.

Some of the problematic assumptions made by students that exist in classrooms today include

- Discounting knowledge and assuming that the knowledge the faculty member brings is irrelevant or not important. This is especially true for faculty members who belong to minoritized groups;
- Tokenizing those from marginalized identities and expecting that it is the job of professors and students with minoritized identities to educate dominant identity students on their experiences;
- Subscribing to the idea that the only one with knowledge in the classroom is the instructor;
- Believing it is the sole responsibility of the instructor to discipline and be authoritative; that it is the role of the professor to hold everyone accountable;
- Believing that all students or all professors come from the same background and have the same experiences;
- Viewing learning as complete after the semester is over, followed by a resistance to challenging one's self to learn more;
- Buying into the idea, "This is the way it's always been done, so why do we have to change it?"

In order to confront and unlearn these assumptions through an inclusive lens, both students and professors have to be willing to challenge themselves and their perspectives to contextualize the experiences of others. Below I explain some recommendations that contribute to the creation of inclusive classrooms.

Recommendations for Creating Inclusive Classrooms: Planning and Instructional Strategies

In this chapter, I have outlined various ways in which inclusive classrooms are beneficial to students. Many of these practices have been informed by scholars in our field who center equity and inclusion. Freire (1993), hooks (1994), Tuitt (2003), and Stewart (2012) emphasized the importance of intentionality before entering a class, as well as the need to be honest and true in an effort to foster a culture of inclusion. When considering the creation and development of an inclusive classroom environment, the following factors should be considered:

- Engage intentionality behind curriculum prep (syllabi, approach to teaching, readings, and assignments);

- Set the stage in the first class: sharing of a positionality statement, developing community expectations, and incorporating student perspective about aspects of the syllabus;
- Vary the structure of classes and be willing to be flexible if a particular method does not work for students' needs (e.g., small groups, large groups, and discussion prompts designed by both instructor and student); provide activities that encourage vulnerability, honesty, and interrogation of preexisting assumptions, and include students' perspectives in all classes, calling on students who seem quiet to also contribute. These strategies allow students with different learning styles to utilize their strengths and push themselves in meaningful and constructive ways;
- Commit to challenge and support as well as facilitate conversations with students, especially in the face of difficult discussions (inside and outside the classroom);
- Incorporate difficult and critical conversations that help students move beyond the confines of their presuppositions;
- Utilize a variety of delivery styles (e.g., visual, audio, and journaling) that speak to the different learning styles of students;
- Practice reflexivity through activities and assignments that give students space to reflect on their learning, for example, written reflections;
- Maintain implementation of expectations and classroom guidelines.

Conclusion

In conclusion, inclusive environments are necessary for growth, learning, and development to take place on college campuses. Faculty and student affairs professionals are tasked with fostering and contributing to these environments in very different yet similar ways. In order to be successful in creating inclusive campus environments, both faculty and student affairs professionals must incorporate resistance to normative ways of teaching and learning as a means to empower and transform. We must all interrogate long-held beliefs about the way we educate and interact with our students. As faculty and administrators, we should challenge ourselves to learn to utilize inclusive concepts to bridge the gap between our informal understanding of student development, and a systematic approach to establishing inclusive environments, thereby linking theory to practice. In my experience as a faculty member, many of my students have expressed to me in person as well as in teaching evaluations that they grew to appreciate the critical lens I utilize in my classrooms because it pushed them to think deeply about issues for the first time and reflect upon their own engagement with systems of oppression. Nevertheless, as hooks (1994) reminded us, those of us who dare to teach in ways that counter normative pedagogy often face negative consequences, including lower and more disparaging course evaluations, pushback in the classroom, and resistance by faculty colleagues and students.

Inclusion in the classroom has several pedagogic benefits not only applicable to the classroom; inclusion also contributes to students' overall experience and sense of belonging across the broader institution. Inclusive practices that begin in the classroom can permeate other college contexts. Students have taught me how to enact and embrace grace and compassion in ways that quite frankly I never knew were possible. I have learned that humanizing myself and encouraging students to do the same has been an important factor in this quest of creating inclusive and supportive classroom environments. Faculty members and student affairs professionals play a crucial role in creating inclusive, affirming, and relevant environments for students. It is important to recognize and understand that students do not check their varying identities at the door when they enter our institutions of higher learning. When we are able to see these traits as positive and beneficial to the learning process of all students and faculty, there will be a drastic change in how we approach the classroom and the profession—and how we foster environments that are supportive and inclusive for all students.

Reflection Questions

1. How does inclusion impact the student experience?
2. How do you create an inclusive environment for students and professionals?
3. How are some of the concepts discussed in this chapter applicable to your department?
4. What are some barriers that inhibit your ability to create inclusive environments?
5. How can you utilize existing campus resources to supplement your own learning about creating inclusive environments?
6. How can you apply inclusive concepts learned in the classroom in more practical ways?
7. How can you engage with other campus constituents to create and maintain inclusive, equitable, and affirming campus environments?

References

American College Personnel Association (ACPA)–College Student Educators International & National Association of Student Personnel Administrators (NASPA)–Student Affairs Administrators in Higher Education. (2015). *Professional competency areas for student affairs practitioners.* Washington, DC: Author.

Danowitz, M. A., & Tuitt, F. (2011). Enacting inclusivity through engaged pedagogy: A higher education perspective. *Equity & Excellence in Education, 44*(1), 40–56.

Darder, A. (1996). Creating the condition for cultural democracy in the classroom. In C. Turner, M. Garcia, A. Nora, & L. I. Rendon (Eds.), *Racial and ethnic diversity in higher education* (pp. 134–149). Needham Heights, MA: Simon & Schuster.

Davis, J., & Arend, B. (2013). *Facilitating seven ways of learning.* Sterling, VA: Stylus.

Freire, P. (1993). *Pedagogy of the oppressed.* London, England, United Kingdom: Penguin Books.

Harven A.M., & Soodjinda D. (2016). Pedagogical strategies for challenging students' world views. In R. Papa, D. M. Eadens, & D. W. Eadens (Eds.), *Social justice instruction: Empowerment on the chalkboard* (pp. 3–14). Cham, Switzerland: Springer.

hooks, B. (1994). Teaching to transgress: Education as the practice of freedom. *Journal of Engineering Education, 1,* 126–138.

Kumar, R., Zusho, A., & Bondie, R. (2018). Weaving cultural relevance and achievement motivation into inclusive classroom cultures. *Educational Psychologist, 53*(2), 78–96.

Kumashiro, K. K. (2000). Toward a theory of anti-oppressive education. *Review of Educational Research, 70*(1), 25-53.

Linder, C., Harris, J. C., Allen, E. L., & Hubain, B. (2015). Building inclusive pedagogy: Recommendations from a national study of students of color in higher education and student affairs graduate programs. *Equity & Excellence in Education, 48*(2), 178–194.

Museus, S. D. (2014). The culturally engaging campus environments (CECE) model: A new theory of success among racially diverse college student populations. In M. B. Paulsen (Ed.), *Higher education: Handbook of theory and research* (Vol. 29, pp. 189–227). Dordrecht, Netherlands: Springer. doi:10.1007/978-94-017-8005 -6_5

Pascarella, E. T., & Terenzini, P. T. (2005). *How college affects students: A third decade of research* (Vol. 2). San Francisco: Jossey-Bass.

Schlossberg, N. K. (1989). Marginality and mattering: Key issues in building community. *New Directions for Student Services, 48,* 5–15.

Stewart, S. (2012). Problematizing racism in education. In M. Vicars, T. McKenna, & J. White (Eds.), *Discourse, power, and resistance down under* (pp. 199–213). Rotterdam, Netherlands: SensePublishers.

Stewart, S. (2016). Advancing a critical and inclusive praxis: Pedagogical and curriculum innovations for social change in the Caribbean. In F. Tuitt, C. Haynes, & S. Stewart (Eds.), *Race, equity, and the learning environment: The global relevance of critical and inclusive pedagogies in higher education* (Ch. 1). Sterling, VA: Stylus.

Tuitt, F. (2003). Afterword: Realizing a more inclusive pedagogy. In A. Howell & F. Tuitt (Eds.), *Race and higher education: Rethinking pedagogy in diverse college classrooms* (pp. 243–268). Cambridge, MA: Harvard Education Press.

Williams, B. (2016). Radical honesty: Truth telling as pedagogy for working through shame in academic spaces. In F. Tuitt, C. Haynes, & S. Stewart (Eds.), *Race, equity, and the learning environment: The global relevance of critical and inclusive pedagogies in higher education* (pp. 71–82). Sterling, VA: Stylus.

Chapter 7

PREPARING SCHOLAR PRACTITIONERS TO ASSESS CAMPUS ENVIRONMENTS TO MAXIMIZE SUCCESS OF DIVERSE STUDENT POPULATIONS

Lucy A. LePeau

Scholar practitioners—student affairs professionals, faculty, online instructors, and graduate paraprofessionals—need to use assessment to understand what diverse student populations learn and experience in different campus environments. The term *diverse* as applied to student populations is related to race, ethnicity, class, ability, gender identity/expression, sexual orientation, country of origin, and religion. Upcraft and Schuh (1996) defined assessment as "any effort to gather, analyze, and interpret evidence which describes institutional, departmental, division, or agency effectiveness" (p. 18). Further, Schuh, Biddix, Dean, and Kinzie (2016) extended this definition of assessment by adding information about program effectiveness or "the extent to which an intervention, program, activity, or learning experience accomplishes its goals, frequently linked to how student learning is advanced" (p. 5). In short, assessment is used for the purpose of accountability and improvement in student affairs practice (Ewell, 2009; Schuh et al., 2016). For scholar practitioners, then, *accountability* pertains to educators actively demonstrating that the objectives they have articulated vis-a-vis learning outcomes or accreditation standards are met; *using assessment for improvement* means using data to inform ways to improve educational practices and initiatives to better meet the needs of and learning opportunities for diverse student populations. Yet, how rising scholar practitioners are prepared to create and assess learning opportunities to optimize success for diverse student populations needs more attention.

I am a faculty member at Indiana University in the Higher Education and Student Affairs program. My research and teaching focus on academic affairs and student affairs partnerships for creating more equitable campus environments, pursuing organizational change for equity and inclusion, and improving student affairs teaching and practice. My first encounter designing and implementing an assessment project occurred as a master's student, when I worked with peers to assess students' perceptions and use of a black cultural center. My peers and I created a quantitative survey to administer to student users of the center because we all happened to be white people assessing a space that was not created for us. I was learning, being questioned, making mistakes, and working to consider how identities, such as my race, influenced my approaches to conducting assessment. As I progressed in the field of student affairs, I practiced as Assistant Dean for New Student Programs, where I directed new student orientation programs. In that role, I continued developing and applying my skills by assessing how orientation leaders met learning outcomes as student educators as well as by collaborating with an institutional researcher to design survey instruments to assess orientation programming effectiveness. My own learning has continued to shift and deepen as I have extended my work as a researcher and professor, learning alongside graduate students who are the next generation of scholars and practitioners in the field.

I open with this glimpse into snippets of my trajectory to acknowledge that developing professional competencies is lifelong work (American College Personnel Association [ACPA] & National Association of Student Personnel Administrators [NASPA] (2015). Because leaders in the two primary student affairs professional associations—College Student Educators International—ACPA and Student Affairs Administrators in Higher Education—NASPA—have outlined professional competencies rooted in social justice and inclusion, as well as assessment, evaluation, and research, I deliberately strive to design learning opportunities to integrate these and additional professional competencies in my approaches to teaching and engagement (ACPA & NASPA, 2015).

In this chapter, I describe ways scholar practitioners can engage with graduate students in two-year professional preparation programs to prepare them to create and assess educational opportunities to maximize success for diverse student populations. I share examples from two courses designed to encourage students to use asset-based and equity-minded approaches to understanding and creating conditions to support student success. In turn, budding scholar practitioners can enter the field poised to collaborate with institutional stakeholders (e.g., faculty, alumni, fellow practitioners, and institutional research) to use data and evidence to not only systemically conduct assessments but also cultivate more equitable campus environments where *all* students can thrive.

The Need for Equity Mindedness and Asset-Based Approaches to Conceptualizing Student Success in Campus Environments

Equity in higher education can be defined as a campus environment where students, faculty, and staff from diverse backgrounds are given the conditions they need to thrive in culturally relevant and responsive ways (Bensimon & Malcolm, 2012; LePeau, Hurtado, & Davis, 2017; Museus, 2014). In this definition, *campus environment* refers to any type of educational institution, including but not limited to minority serving institutions (e.g., Asian American and Native American/Pacific-Islander serving institutions), historically black colleges and universities, Hispanic serving institutions, tribal colleges and universities, predominantly/historically white colleges and universities, community colleges, and religiously affiliated institutions. Furthermore, and importantly, in an equitable campus environment, faculty, staff, and students have an equal voice in decision making and experience multiple forms of educational success, such as classroom experiences and co-curricular engagement, moving beyond persistence, retention, and degree attainment as the only measures of student success (Harper & Quaye, 2009).

Scholar practitioners have work to do to in order to enhance educational achievement and environments for *all* students. For example, the current #MeToo movement has reinforced the pervasiveness of rape culture and sexual assault in workplace environments that include campus environments (Hurtado, 2018; Ropers-Huilman, Williamsen, & Hoffman, 2016). Additionally, in the aggregate who matriculate into four-year institutions, although approximately 42 percent of white students and 61 percent of Asian/Pacific Islander students graduate, only about 23 percent of black, 19 percent of Latinx, and 16 percent of American Indian/Alaska Native students graduate (National Center for Education Statistics [NCES], 2018). These statistics mask the fact that far fewer black, Latinx, Native American, and Pacific Islander students matriculate into four-year institutions (NCES, 2018). These are only a few of the inequities in higher education. Much of the literature continues to focus on the factors that influence low enrollment, persistence, and completion rates for underrepresented students and the need to improve student success, but they only reveal part of the picture when examining equity issues in higher education and take a myopic view of what student success entails (Bensimon & Malcolm, 2012; Harper & Quaye, 2009; Museus, 2014; Pérez & Sáenz, 2017).

Many campus cultures (e.g., norms, practices, and ideas about the "way things are done here") privilege the backgrounds and experiences of dominant groups (i.e., white, heterosexual) without representing and engaging communities and identities of students of color (Kuh & Whitt, 1988; Museus & Jayakumar, 2012). Scholars, such as Bensimon and Malcolm (2012) and

Dowd and Bensimon (2015), have encouraged practitioners to transform *deficit-thinking*– subscribing to ideas that educational attainment gaps for students of color are based on lack of preparedness or motivation—into an equity-mindedness approach. This approach leads scholar practitioners to use evidence and pedagogy to disrupt and challenge inequitable systems and practices that may hinder students' success, replacing them with practices and educational opportunities that enhance success for students from minoritized backgrounds by allowing them to see their cultures and backgrounds meaningfully reflected within the campus environment (Bensimon, 2005; Bensimon & Malcolm, 2012; Museus, 2014).

For instance, Pérez and Sáenz (2017) employed Schreiner's (2010) "thriving quotient" or TQ as an anti-deficit framework to examine how 21 Latino males thrived in two predominantly white institutions (PWIs). The term *thriving* in this context pertains to students who are "intellectually, socially, and emotionally engaged in college" (Pérez & Sáenz, 2017, p. 166). Pérez and Sáenz conducted interviews with students to learn how the participants define collegiate success and what motivated them. One student, Lupe, took an African literature course with a professor who encouraged peers sharing narratives from their own backgrounds. Lupe found this experience powerful, and it motivated him to enroll in ethnic studies so that he could take classes where he could learn more about his own Puerto Rican culture, thereby thriving academically (Pérez & Sáenz, 2017). I chose to highlight this finding from the study because of Pérez and Sáenz's (2017) critique that participants often had to initiate the relationships with faculty that led to growth in confidence and academic thriving. These researchers illustrated that faculty members at PWIs are not expected to facilitate the conditions for thriving, and this dominant norm needs to be challenged. Again, this critique opens up the need to prepare rising scholar practitioners to not only study and assess ways they can create the conditions for diverse student populations to thrive but also investigate their own responsibilities and identities in that process, both when sharing similar identities as particular student populations and across differences.

Assessment in higher education is critical, because policy makers, practitioners, and educators need to demonstrate whether or not students are achieving the outcomes they purport individuals garner through participating and engaging in higher education environments. Yet, the process of using assessment for improvement or accountability is not always tied to critically examining the theoretical framing used to conduct assessment, which may itself obscure the way data are presented. Historically in higher education, the ideas of student success and integration have related to students accommodating or adjusting to the campus culture by becoming academically and socially engaged (e.g., Tinto, 1975). Such frameworks, however, do not account for the unique cultural and social backgrounds students contribute to campus environments (e.g., Harper & Quaye, 2009; Museus, 2014; Pérez & Sáenz, 2017; Rendón et al., 2000; Yosso, 2005). Further, it is critical to think about what campus educators can do to cultivate success for diverse student populations (e.g., Museus, 2014; Harper & Quaye, 2009; Pérez & Sáenz, 2017; Rendón, Jalomo, & Nora, 2000; Yosso, 2005). This asset-based approach dictates that campus educators contemplate and design educational opportunities for students that are both culturally relevant and responsive to who these people are and the experiences they possess (Museus, 2014). When the concept of student success is framed in this way, it then becomes imperative for graduate students and budding professionals to continue investigating (a) who they themselves are, (b) how this influences the way they interact with students who identify both similarly and differently than themselves, and (c) the conditions they can create to support student success.

This is the approach I take in my teaching. I learn with graduate students enrolled in my courses, with graduate students co-instructing or serving as teaching assistants, and with stakeholders in order to collectively engage in striving to create the conditions to maximize success for diverse student populations. In particular, in order to engage graduate students in this journey, I have been teaching two courses back-to-back for graduate students in the Higher Education and Student Affairs program at Indiana University. The first course, Diverse Students on the College Campus, is offered to graduate students in the spring of their first year in the program. The students then often apply the theory learned in this and their other first-year courses to practice through summer internship and assistantship experiences at different institutional types and regions of the country.

By the time the graduate students reach the second of my two courses, Environmental Theory and Assessment, in the fall of their second year, they have the capacity to frame assessment projects from an asset-based approach. That is, they are prepared to think through ways to understand how scholar practitioners create the conditions to promote student success for diverse student populations and assess what is working in the environment or not. In the next two sections of this chapter, then, I outline the theoretical underpinnings of the Diverse Students on the College Campus course and the subsequent Environmental Theory and Assessment course.

Learning Framework for the Diverse Students on the College Campus Course

In the Diverse Students on the College Campus syllabus, I explain that the students, myself, and the co-instructors (i.e., doctoral student instructors doing supervised college teaching) will focus on learning how to have conversations about systemic oppression, power, issues of privilege, current issues in higher education, and being informed about the needs of various groups on campus. This course also serves as a venue through which graduate students are both learners and teachers, requiring all participants to think deeply about their own positionality in relation to diversity and social justice and the extent to which they are prepared to advocate for creating more equitable environments to promote success for diverse student populations. After describing these objectives, I then introduce the learning framework for the course.

The current course is designed and rooted in process elements for creating inclusive campuses, presented in the book *Why Aren't We There Yet?: Taking Personal Responsibility for Creating an Inclusive Campus* (Arminio, Torres, & Pope, 2012) and the culturally engaging campus environments (CECE) model (Museus, 2014). The book emanated from Dr. Vasti Torres's 2008 ACPA Presidential Task Force, named "Walk the Talk." I participated in this task force, which was comprised of both graduate-preparation faculty and scholar practitioners in the field. The meaning behind "walk the talk" was that as long as the student affairs profession continues to espouse commitments to diversity and inclusion, Dr. Torres wanted to continue pushing the profession to actively grapple with what enacting these values includes and the fact that this work is never done. One primary initiative of the task force included conceptualizing and writing the *Why Aren't We There Yet* text. At the time of this task force, I was a scholar practitioner applying to doctoral programs. I worked collaboratively with colleagues on two chapters in this book, one pertaining to the influence of institutional context and culture on the ways campus constituents experience campus spaces (Pope & LePeau, 2012) and the other applying case studies from practice, where readers are introduced to the reflective practices of applying the framework for the text (Weigand & LePeau, 2012).

The framework, then, for the Diverse Students On The College Campus course includes (a) seeking self-awareness, (b) reconciling the tension between self and the other in relationships, (c) considering history, (d) considering institutional context, (e) initiating dialogue as a precursor to action steps, and (f) transforming educational practices to maximize success for diverse student populations (Arminio et al., 2012; Museus, 2014). The beginning elements of this framework reflect the design of *Why Aren't We There Yet:* "These elements, combined, help practitioners understand their own and the institution's role that must be developed to create space for difficult dialogues" (Arminio et al., 2012, p. 188).

The creating or transforming promising practices component of the learning framework is where students are introduced to the CECE model (Museus, 2014). The CECE model posits that there are ways scholar practitioners can cultivate culturally relevant and responsive environments so that all students can thrive. Museus (2014) based this model on over 20 years of research related to conditions that positively and negatively contribute to students of color finding cultural validation within campus environments. Museus critiqued aspects of previous student success literature (e.g., Astin, 1984; Tinto, 1975) that emphasize what students must do to adjust academically and socially in order to be retained within a campus environment without explicitly taking the diversity of students into consideration. The CECE model is based on nine indicators that reflect what scholar practitioners can do to bolster cultural relevance and responsiveness within campus environments (Museus, 2014).

The first five indicators relate to *cultural relevance* or the ways learning environments are pertinent to the cultural backgrounds and communities of diverse student populations (Museus, 2014). These five indicators include (a) *cultural familiarity* or spaces where students can connect with institutional agents who have similar backgrounds to theirs; (b) *culturally relevant knowledge,* the extent to which students have opportunities to learn and exchange knowledge about their cultural communities; (c) *cultural community service,* that is, opportunities for students to give back to and positively transform their cultural communities; (d) *meaningful cross-cultural engagement,* opportunities to engage in positive and purposeful interactions with peers from different cultural backgrounds; and (e) *culturally validating environments,* opportunities when students feel validated by educators about their background and experiences.

The four *culturally responsive* indicators of the model reflect the ways institutional agents enact systems and cultural norms in the campus environment that respond to the needs of diverse student populations. These remaining four CECE indicators include (f) *collectivist cultural orientations,* ways institutional agents and norms reflect that students seek to value shared success rather than only individual success; (g) *proactive philosophies,* where institutional agents go above and beyond to not only provide information about available support but also actively reach out to students to encourage participation in support initiatives; (h) *holistic support,* that is, students have confidence that they can count on at least one institutional agent to provide them with the support and information they need or that this person will connect them with someone who does can do so; and (i) *humanized educational environments,* the extent that students know that there are institutional agents who care about them in meaningful ways and are committed to their success. Altogether, when students are able to find experiences with scholar practitioners who support the actualization of these nine indicators in practice, they are more likely to persist and find sense of belonging in the campus environment (Museus, 2014).

I situate the journey I embark on with students in this course as a type of formative assessment. For example, I have the opportunity to identify ways students understand theories and concepts, such as social justice, culture, privilege, and oppression, in early class sessions through discussion of readings and classroom dialogues. We discuss why having dialogue about issues of power, privilege, and oppression can be difficult and subsequently work through pedagogical techniques to understand and sit with discomfort. I also structure assignments, such as photo-elicitations and critical reading journals, to contribute to this process and elicit storytelling. In the photo-elicitation project, students are able to share pictures and descriptions of their choosing related to concepts, such as culture, sense of belonging, oppression, and social justice, to demonstrate how their lived experiences and previous educational experiences shape their differing perspectives. We engage with each other to learn about how peers construct these concepts and questions we have for each other. I can also adjust class discussions and activities related to what students share in their journal entries. As a professor, I then connect with students and they also learn about me to understand who we are and what they believe with regard to student success, particularly in light of systems of power, privilege, and oppression within society.

In alignment with the active orientation to the social justice and inclusion professional competency, I aim to co-construct with students learning opportunities that manifest an orientation to social justice as both a process and a goal (ACPA & NASPA, 2015; Bell, 2013), with "a vision for society in which the distribution of resources is equitable and all members are physically and psychologically safe and secure" (Bell, 2013, p. 21). Thus, the second prominent piece of the course relates to students' investigating of promising practices to support success for diverse student populations through enacting the processes in the learning framework.

In this assignment, student teams work in groups they select to create or transform a practice that fosters conditions to support the success for a particular minoritized student population on one of four institutional environments (i.e., Butler University, Indiana University, Indiana University-Purdue University Indianapolis [IUPUI], and Marian University). We stray away from the term "best practices" and use promising practices because the term "best" assumes that campus educators (without taking into consideration their own identities and unique strengths) can replicate the same set of strategies and conditions in any campus environment and gain the same results for a diverse student population. The term, best practices, also assumes that someone has determined which practices are best, and this is often a claim that is too strong, and one made without sufficient evidence to back it (Indiana University, 2018a). This project is divided into four interconnected parts: (a) prospective for a particular population/projects, (b) meeting with instructors to discuss the prospective, (c) dialogue constructed with peers for half of a class session about the population and why they may be minoritized in society or in a particular campus environment, and (d) a final report to stakeholders about their projects.

Students have examined particular initiatives or populations related to practices, such as a program designed to create a cohort or mentoring group for students who identify as former foster youth, campus climate/initiatives for international students from Muslim-majority countries in light of the Trump administration's travel ban, international student orientation programs, and initiatives designed to support students who identify as parents.

Students conduct a literature review about the particular population and history, meet with stakeholders who construct and operate particular programs, and learn about a promising practice or educational approach to support a particular student population through this lens. This course provides students with opportunities to deeply reflect on not only who they are in relation to students and colleagues who identify differently than themselves but also what conditions can be created to foster culturally relevant and responsive campus environments (Museus, 2014).

Learning Framework for the Environmental Theory and Assessment Course

When students then approach the Environmental Theory and Assessment course, they can integrate what they learn here with learning from the Diverse Students on the College course, additional courses, and their assistantships/practica. In this course, I outline the learning and goals as follows:

> This course provides an overview of different environmental theories applicable to higher education settings. It introduces and encourages the use of multiple perspectives to better understand and more fully appreciate the influence of college and university environments on student development and achievement. The purpose of this course is to familiarize you with the literature on campus environments, give you an opportunity to maximize your critical thinking with regard to strategies for enhancing campus environments, and offer you an opportunity to conduct an environmental research/assessment project. The course also provides foundational knowledge about the practice of assessment in higher education. Throughout the course, attention will be paid to the influence of the campus environment on diverse student populations and variety of student groups. (Indiana University, 2018b)

This course provides students with a venue to connect educational purposes and place (Strange & Banning, 2015). For decades, scholars, such as

Moos (1986) and Pascarella and Terrenzini (2005), have argued that a powerful technique for influencing human behavior rests on what educators do to create environments. In this class, students are challenged to not only understand environmental theories that relate to how diverse student populations may experience campus environments but also assess how well objectives outlined for practice by scholar practitioners are met. Strange and Banning (2015) offered overarching questions that we delve into in this course: "What makes a college or university successful in attracting, retaining, and challenging students? What are the patterns and design characteristics of supportive educational environments, and are some designs appropriate only for certain students?" (p. xi). We examine environmental theories through the four frames offered by Strange and Banning: the influences of physical environments (e.g., place of buildings, arrangement, and messages/symbols to direct students), human aggregate (e.g., person-environment ideas about personality types and patterns), organizational (e.g., anatomy of organizations related to decision making), and socially constructed (e.g., campus culture and climate).

Whereas we investigate the underpinnings of environmental theories, we also critique the ways researchers apply these theories in assessment and research designs. Students are exposed to fundamental design elements of constructing assessment projects, such as practicing ethical decision making, using theoretical frameworks in research/assessment, formulating research questions, and systematically designing the methodology and corresponding methods used to address research questions. We investigate the similarities and differences in purposes for conducting research versus conducting assessment. It is imperative for students to acknowledge that they have particular assumptions and beliefs about specific campus environments. Because they have deeply considered the ways systems of power and privilege in society (e.g., racism, classism, sexism, and other isms) have been manifested in the origins of higher education through previous learning opportunities, such as the Diverse Students on the College Campus course, they recognize that these systems must be considered when cultivating campus environments for diverse student populations that are both relevant and responsive to students' backgrounds (Museus, 2014).

A hallmark of this course, which has been prevalent for many years in the Indiana University Higher Education and Student Affairs master's program, is the Group Assessment Project. This assignment is partially described in the syllabus as follows:

> Students in the class will form teams of 5 or 6 persons to study how a defined environment (department, academic unit or program, residence unit, advising unit, library, academic support services, etc.) affects the behavior

or perceptions of one or more groups. The goal of the assignment is to complete a paper ready for submission (e.g., to a journal or to the setting studied) by the end of the course. The assessment can be conducted in various ways. For example, a combination of material collection, observations, interviews and other data collection methods (questionnaires, electronic surveys) can be used. Each team will (a) identify a problem or issue to explore; (b) choose environmental theories or frameworks appropriate for the study of that problem or issue; (c) choose a setting or settings in which to examine the problem or issue; and (d) identify appropriate groups within the setting to study. (Indiana University, 2018b)

The student teams initiate their own topics and projects. They also have the opportunity to work with a doctoral student mentor to talk through ideas and receive feedback on their project drafts before submitting assignments to me. When students initiate their proposals, we discuss the impetus for their projects. I then learn how students are considering their own positionalities, meaning the ways their identities, experiences, and knowledge base inform why they care to conduct a particular assessment project and why they plan to use particular methods. We engage in conversations about how they hope stakeholders will be able to use the information to improve and inform practice. We discuss together why theories, previous literature, and perspectives drive their decision making. The doctoral student mentors and I often ask questions, such as How do you know what the particular office or unit on campus already collects in terms of data? Why is it a problem if this particular assessment does not get conducted? If they choose to conduct an assessment about a population of students they do not identify with, how will they consider the limitations of that design? If they identify similarly as the population they are investigating, what are possible strengths or considerations before determining what methods to use for data collection? We outline and discuss what political implications might be important considerations and ways to build relationships with campus stakeholders who might connect students with participants or share data they have already collected, which directly ties to tenets of the assessment, evaluation, and research professional competency (ACPA & NASPA, 2015). In these conversations and processes, I am able to see how students are applying the content from the Diverse Students on the College Campus course to practice.

After students have conducted an initial literature review and have outlined the significance of their projects, they move to planning out their methods. Because the students have conceptualized and received feedback about the methods used to collect data for the projects, we have opportunities to pilot or test out particular techniques in class. Students can share their instruments, such as interview protocols, surveys, and physical environment observation rubrics, to get feedback from each other. We also have opportunities to try out their focus group protocols or run a pilot prior to the group's actual data collection. For the purpose of this chapter, I share the following two examples of projects that have emerged from this course to demonstrate how students can integrate learning across the curriculum.

Integrating and Applying Learning About Student Success Through Assessment

Many group assessment projects have emerged from this course. Some projects can be accessed in the peer-reviewed *Student Personnel Association Journal* at Indiana University. The following two examples demonstrate how students are able to apply the knowledge and skills acquired in the Diverse Students on the College Campus course, different courses, and practice experiences to assessment strategies learned in the Environmental Theory and Assessment course. These examples also illustrate how students conceptualize student success matters when they strive to assess campus environments.

Example One

A team of six students sought to assess the physical environments as indicators of cultural validation in Counseling and Psychological Services (CAPS) and the Center for Human Growth (CHG) at Indiana University, a research institution in the Midwest (Al-Hassan et al., 2018). CAPS is a health center staffed by certified and trained mental health professionals, and CHG is staffed by graduate students enrolled in the Department of Counseling and Educational Psychology. In the previous semester, some of the students in the CHH group focused attention on investigating why black-identifying students report sexual assaults at a much lower rate than their white counterparts. Through this formative project, they learned that some of the students of color did not see themselves reflected in the counseling services available on campus. Thus, part of the impetus for this project was that the student researchers wanted to extend their learning through an environmental assessment project related to this topic.

As the student researchers, Al-Hassan et al. (2018) outlined gaps in underrepresented students seeking psychological support in campus environments and noted that mental health spaces were often originally created to support White students. They also indicated they had heard that students of color tended to utilize on-campus counseling centers more frequently than others, but they wanted evidence to support these anecdotes. For these reasons, they wanted to understand how particular campus spaces *can* facilitate cultural validation for students inhabiting minoritized identities and thereby support their mental health wellness. In order to conduct their assessment, the student researchers focused on pursuing an observational assessment, using the CECE model as their framework, and in particular, the fifth indicator of *cultural validation*—the appreciation of diverse backgrounds and identities (Al-Hassan et al., 2018; Museus, 2014). When describing cultural validation in relation to physical environments, Al-Hassan et al. stated that "educators in the environment are responsible for valuing the perspectives of their diverse student populations through their actions and the physical environments they construct" (p. 44). They also asserted, "Assessment of culturally engaging spaces is one of the most powerful ways that psychological support services can engage students who otherwise may not benefit from resources which were originally constructed for a majority clientele" (p. 42).

These student researchers created their own rubric to list what to observe, details of the observation, and client identities to consider when they were making their notes about the physical environments. They wanted to link what they observed to what could contribute to diverse student populations' feeling "culturally validated and thereby affect their engagement or desire to use this service" (Al-Hassan et al., 2018, p. 44). In collaboration with the directors of both counseling centers, the student researchers were given access to the assessment sites after hours, so they could take time to make observations and write notes about the explicit and implicit messages in the physical spaces without being disruptive, altering the daily experiences of clients within the spaces, or risking breaches in confidentiality. Both directors were interested in learning the results of their assessments so that they could consider ways to potentially enhance or change the physical environments of their respective counseling centers.

Al-Hassan et al. (2018) integrated literature about the influence of physical cues on experiences diverse student populations may have in spaces with the fifth CECE indicator of cultural validation. Thus, they examined the spaces for what works well to support cultural validation, while outlining opportunities for improvement that may further support students' experiences within the centers. In both spaces, they examined entrances and exits, waiting rooms, intake rooms, hallways, bathrooms, and individual and group session rooms. The students also used the research to consider how to take notes and pictures of posters on the walls, color schemes, furniture options, and signage in order to connect their observations with themes in the literature.

Again, choosing a framework emphasizing how cultural validation is occurring and in what ways makes it possible to outline opportunities to capitalize on strengths and plan for improvement. For instance, they noted that within the floor of the building of CAPS space where most of the services are located, there are three bathrooms with the following characteristics:

> Two are representative of the gender binary labeled as men and women and one bathroom is labeled simply as "Restroom." While the presence of a gender-neutral restroom helps alleviate the pressure of choosing a bathroom, it is not located near the waiting rooms and there was no signage directing students to it. Having to ask if a gender neutral restroom exists and where it is located may cause anxiety and add stress to the student's experience at CAPS because they may feel that they have to expose and explain a personal part of their identity (Kirk et al., 2008). (Al-Hassan et al., 2018, p. 50)

In their call to action, the Al-Hassan et al. (2018) team, connecting to the literature from work by Herman, then suggested that CAPS create signage to direct students to the gender neutral bathroom as a way that might reduce anxiety in transgender or non-binary students who may want to use the restroom but do not want to ask, out of fear of discrimination.

In another instance, Al-Hassan et al. (2018) noted that in the CHG, the staff included pictures and bios about themselves on the walls to humanize the space, and they noticed that the staff members represented multiple underrepresented racial identities within the campus environment (Museus, 2014). Al-Hassan et al. (2018) affirmed this practice by CHG staff and integrated their point with the literature that "racial, ethnic, and national representation within an environment can validate the identities of students who share those underrepresented identities" (p. 51). In sum, Al-Hassan et al. were creative in their approach to designing and implementing a physical environmental assessment. In turn, they can incorporate what they learned to observing and assessing other work environments where they can contribute to creating culturally validating spaces.

Example Two

Azevedo, Howell, Mora, Thomas, and Tovar (2018)—a student research group—conducted a project at IUPUI, an urban research institution, about how high-achieving students involved in the Norma Brown Diversity and Leadership Scholars Program (NBDLSP) find sense of belonging within the program or in different spaces on campus. The leaders of this scholarship program strive to "recruit, retain, and prepare serious, academically gifted students who have demonstrated a commitment to social justice" (IUPUI, 2017). Applying learning from previous courses and their assistantships, the student research group voiced frustration about deficit-oriented approaches to understanding and researching students of color. For this reason, the Azevedo et al. team opted to study high-achieving students of color and the conditions that supported their success. They were interested in studying the NBDLSP program because of its reputation and because it serves historically underrepresented populations. (The 2017–2018 enrollment demographics included 94 students: 42 identified as black, 17 as Asian, 16 as Hispanic/Latino/a, 7 as white, 2 as American Indian/Alaska Native, and 10 as unknown [Azevedo et al., 2018].) The research team argued, with supporting evidence from Fries-Britt (2004) and Museus (2014), that "students of color persist when they feel as though they belong to a group and can identify with peers within the group" (p. 4) and that there is a problem because fewer students of color participate in high-achieving scholarship programs. Furthermore, they claimed there is less research about their participation.

The Azevedo et al. (2018) team collaborated with the director of the program to share their assessment project idea, also establishing a relationship with the director to get access to recruiting participants. The research team interviewed 10 participants (i.e., six first-year and four second-year students) comparable to the racial composition of the participants in the program (i.e., 7 black, 2 Hispanic, and 1 Asian American/Pacific Islander), focusing on addressing the questions: Where, if at all, do Norman Brown Scholars at IUPUI find sense of belonging and how does the program contribute to students' sense of belonging? Again, because the student research team coupled asset-based approaches to student success from the CECE model and research about the construct of sense of belonging with their assessment project by asking interview questions based on the tenets of the CECE indicators, they were able to understand both what institutional agents are doing well to support success and where there are areas for ongoing improvement. They treated their assessment project as a holistic case study to understanding how and why students are finding sense of belonging.

Azevedo et al. (2018) learned about ways the program supported students' sense of belonging. For example, participants discussed how interacting with peers who identified similarly as themselves supported their cultural familiarity (Museus, 2014). One participant elaborated that they could then learn that there are peers going through the same difficulties as they are and realize that they are not alone. The participants discussed how being a part of NBDLSP made them recognize that they belong to something bigger than they themselves and can share in the collective successes of the group. The program director creates conditions to support this collectivist cultural orientation by providing group t-shirts, grouping students by major to intentionally cultivate opportunities to learn about study strategies or opportunities for internships, and sharing stories about their backgrounds and experiences when the team meets for regular meetings (Azevedo et al., 2018).

Additionally, participants discussed how they had exposure to culturally relevant knowledge through the director promoting cultural heritage events at IUPUI and facilitating their engagement with culturally based student organizations, such as the African Student Association or Latino Student Association (Azevedo et al., 2018; Museus, 2014). The research group was able to generate data that illustrated what specific conditions the NBDLSP staff incorporated that ultimately buoyed the student participants' sense of belonging on campus. At the same time, Azevedo et al. (2018) utilized their assessment to offer recommendations for ongoing improvement for the program, such as continuing to take a student-centered approach to programming and monthly meetings, without uniformly doing the same thing for all students. The team also recognized that, although the director created opportunities for students to share stories about their backgrounds, the participants did not mention that they experienced much structured meaningful cross-cultural engagement between peers in NBDLSP (Azevedo et al., 2018; Museus, 2014). Thus, they encouraged the program director to consider how to deepen or design additional ways to incorporate cross-cultural engagement within the scholarship program moving forward or how to encourage students to participate in different opportunities within the campus environment, if interested (Azevedo et al., 2018).

Both of the aforementioned examples illustrate how students designed assessment projects that interested them, collaborated with scholar practitioners to implement the projects, and incorporated asset-based theoretical frameworks when assessing how well a particular program or physical space supports the success of diverse student populations. Both teams of students also identified opportunities for the stakeholders to continue improving upon their services and educational initiatives.

Recommendations for Practice

Although the information I presented in this chapter is merely scratching the surface on the possibilities for using assessment and data to maximize success for diverse student populations, there are some important takeaways for practice. Scholar practitioners can benefit from engaging with graduate students who may be well versed in cutting-edge theories that take asset-based approaches to student success. Graduate students may also be able to share with you how particular practices have provided them with cultural validation as undergraduate students or paraprofessionals. Scholar practitioners can consider how early graduate students can be co-creators of innovative assessment projects within your particular campus environments. Invite them to share how they use current literature about student success to frame their practices. Graduate students who desire to build coalitions on campus may continue building their own expertise, while supporting a culture of assessment within your campus environment when they arrive as early career professionals.

The conversation above is not limited to graduate preparation. As lifelong researchers and scholar practitioners, this description of framing student success dialogues and assessment opportunities can be mirrored in practice as well. Simultaneously, as a reflective researcher and teacher, I recognize that some of what I have written above will lose relevance as I evolve and students continue to push me to be innovative in my teaching as well. I hope that graduate students who read this chapter consider how the work they are exposed to in graduate preparation programs can ultimately influence the competencies they build and practice as scholar practitioners.

Conclusion

In this chapter, I revealed how, in the assessment course, I facilitate students' learning so that they can draw on what they know from the Diverse Students on the College Campus course and other settings (assistantship, practica, courses, etc.) to meaningfully design and enact group assessment projects. By sharing some of my own experience as a researcher and scholar practitioner, coupled with the learning frameworks and initiatives in the courses, I demonstrated how institutional transformation and assessment/research are messy, iterative processes that are just as important to attend to as the outcomes.

I strive to prepare students to work with stakeholders, understand how their positionalities influence their perceptions and interactions in campus environments, use dialogue as a precursor to action, elevate current promising practices that are promoting student success, and use evidence to make data-driven decisions, while building expertise with designing and implementing assessment projects. I think, as is reinforced by the professional competencies for the field (ACPA & NASPA, 2015), that reflecting on one's own identities and positionalities in relation to the theories and frameworks is essential when creating and sustaining environments where all students can thrive.

Reflection Questions

- What guiding frameworks do you use to make meaning of student success and why? How are those frameworks rooted in relation to examining systems of power, privilege, and oppression?
- Who is involved in designing assessment projects at your institution? How do you collaborate with stakeholders in designing assessment initiatives?
- What measures of student success, in addition to persistence and graduation, do educators use at your institution? How are educators disaggregating information about social identities of students (e.g., race, ethnicity, and gender identity/expression) in relation to participation in particular student success initiatives?

- How, as a scholar practitioner, are you considering the ways your identities and perspectives influence your approach to designing and implementing student success initiatives?
- How are campus educators regularly discussing and understanding how what they do in the environment supports student success and why?
- What is one way you might conduct a needs assessment in your respective department?

References

American College Personnel Association (ACPA)–College Student Educators International & National Association of Student Personnel Administrators (NASPA)–Student Affairs Administrators in Higher Education. (2015). *Professional competency areas for student affairs educators.* Washington, DC: Authors.

Al-Hassan, K., Hornell, K., Moon, A., Pasternak, M., Scott, D., & Simon, J. (2018). Physical environment as an indicator of cultural validation in counseling and psychological services and the center for human growth at Indiana University. *Student Personnel Association at Indiana University Journal,* 42–67.

Arminio, J., Torres, V., & Pope, R. (2012) *Why aren't we there yet? Taking personal responsibility for creating an inclusive campus.* Sterling, VA: Stylus.

Astin, A. W. (1984). Student involvement: A developmental theory for higher education. *Journal of College Student Personnel, 25,* 297–308.

Azevedo, J. A., Howell, S. M., Mora, L., Thomas, P., & Tovar, D. (2018). Fulfilling the promise through sense of belonging: Experiences of Norman Brown diversity and leadership scholars at IUPUI. *Student Personnel Association at Indiana University Journal,* 1–18.

Bell, L. A. (2013). Theoretical foundations. In M. Adams, W. Blumenfeld, C. Castenada, H. W. Hackman, M. L. Peters, & X. Zuniga (Eds.), *Readings for diversity and social justice* (3rd ed., pp. 21–25). New York: Routledge.

Bensimon, E. M. (2005). Closing the achievement gap in higher education: An organizational learning perspective. In A. Kezar (Ed.), *What campuses need to know about organizational learning and the learning organization* (Vol. 131, pp. 99–111). San Francisco: Jossey-Bass.

Bensimon, E. M., & Malcolm, L. E. (Eds.). (2012). *Confronting equity issues on campus: Implementing the equity scorecard in theory and practice.* Sterling, VA: Stylus.

Dowd, A. C., & Bensimon, E. M. (2015). *Engaging the "race question": Accountability and equity in U.S. higher education.* New York: Teachers College Press.

Ewell, P. T. (2009). *Assessment, accountability, and improvement: Revisiting the tension.* Champaign, IL: National Institute for Learning Outcomes Assessment.

Fries-Britt, S. (2004). The challenges and needs of high-achieving black college students. In M. C. Brown II & K. Freeman (Eds.), *Black colleges: New perspectives on policy and practice* (pp. 161–176). Westport, CT: Praeger.

Harper, S. R., & Quaye, S. J. (2009). Beyond sameness, with engagement and outcomes for all. In S. R. Harper & S. J. Quaye (Eds.), *Student engagement in higher education* (pp. 1–15). New York: Routledge.

Hurtado, S. S. (2018). *Addressing sexual violence on campus: Exploring the role and respon-sibility of faculty members* (Doctoral dissertation). Available from ProQuest Dissertation and Theses database. (UMI No. 10824680)

Kuh, G. D., & Whitt, E. J. (1988). The invisible tapestry: Culture in American col-lege and universities. *ASHE-ERIC Higher Education Report Series, 1.* Washington, DC: Association for the Study of Higher Education.

Indiana University-Purdue University Indianapolis (IUPUI). (2017). *Norman Brown Diversity & Leadership Scholars Program.* Retrieved from: https://diversity.iupui .edu/norman_brown/index.html

Indiana University (2018a). *U546: Diverse students on the college campus course syllabus.* Bloomington, IN: L. LePeau.

Indiana University (2018b). *U549: Environmental theory and assessment course syllabus.* Bloomington, IN: L. LePeau.

LePeau, L., Hurtado, S. S., & Davis, R. (2017). What institutional websites reveal about diversity-related partnerships between academic and student affairs. *Inno-vative Higher Education.* https://doi.org/10.1007/s10755-017-9412-0.

Moos, R. H. (1986). *The human context: Environmental determinants of behavior.* Malabar, FL: Robert E. Krieger.

Museus, S. D. (2014). The culturally engaging campus environments (CECE) model: A new theory of college success among racially diverse student populations. In M. B. Palmer (Ed.), *Higher education: Handbook of theory and research* (pp. 189–227). New York: Springer.

Museus, S. D., & Jayakumar, U. M. (Eds.). (2012). *Creating campus cultures: Fostering success among racially diverse student populations.* New York: Routledge.

National Center for Education Statistics (2018). *The condition of education, 2018.* Washington, DC: Author.

Pascarella, E. T., & Terenzini, P. T. (1991). *How college affects students.* San Francisco: Jossey-Bass.

Pascarella, E. T. & Terenzini, P. T. (2005). *How college affects students (Vol. 2): A third decade of research.* San Francisco: Jossey-Bass.

Pérez, D., II, & Sáenz, V. B. (2017). Thriving Latino males in selective predominantly White institutions. *Journal of Hispanic Higher Education, 16*(2), 162–186.

Pope, R. L., & LePeau, L. (2012). The influence of institutional context. In V. Torres, J. Arminio, & R. L. Pope (Eds.), *Why aren't we there yet?: Taking personal responsi-bility for creating an inclusive campus* (pp. 103–130). Sterling, VA: Stylus.

Rendón, L. I., Jalomo, R. E., & Nora, A. (2000). Theoretical considerations in the study of minority student retention in higher education. In J. Braxton (Ed.), *Reworking the student departure puzzle* (pp. 127–156). Nashville, TN: Vanderbilt University Press.

Ropers-Huilman, R., Williamsen, K. M., & Hoffman, G. D. (2016). Afterword: Questioning the scripts of sexual misconduct. In S. C. Wooten & R. W. Mitchell (Eds.), *The crisis of campus sexual violence: Critical perspectives on prevention and response* (pp. 185–191). New York: Routledge.

Schreiner, L. A. (2010). The "thriving quotient": A new vision for student success. *About Campus, 15*(2), 2–10. doi:10.1002/abc.20016

Schuh, J. H., Biddix, J. P., Dean, L. A., & Kinzie, J. (2016). *Assessment in student affairs.* San Francisco: John Wiley & Sons.

Strange, C. C., & Banning, J. H. (2015). *Designing for learning: Creating campus environments for student success* (2nd ed.). San Francisco: Jossey-Bass.

Tinto, V. (1975). Dropout from higher education: A theoretical synthesis of research. *Review of Educational Research, 45,* 89–125.

Upcraft, M. L., & Schuh, J. H. (1996). *Assessment in student affairs.* San Francisco: Jossey-Bass.

Weigand, M., & LePeau, L. (2012). Different approaches to real issues. In V. Torres, J. Arminio, & R. L. Pope (Eds.), *Why aren't we there yet?: Taking personal responsibility for creating an inclusive campus* (pp. 145–184). Sterling, VA: Stylus.

Yosso, T. J. (2005). Whose culture has capital? A critical race theory discussion of community cultural wealth. *Race and Ethnicity in Education, 8(*1), 69–91.

Chapter 8

FUTURE DIRECTION

Cathy Akens and Zebulun Davenport

Higher education and student affairs organizations are experiencing dynamic and changing times. There are pressing challenges, such as changing demographics, decreasing funding of higher education, and external pressures to ensure students are completing degrees in four years. Increasingly, institutions are facing scrutiny by the public about whether higher education is worth it, and whether graduates leave college prepared for the challenges of the future. There are other campus climate issues that relate to student activism and First Amendment issues and student welfare. Higher education leaders, including those in student affairs, are often expected to be experts in dealing with issues that impact our campuses and our students, and yet this landscape is constantly shifting. Leaders must be equipped to determine how to best design environments for students within the context of these complicated issues. As previous chapters have made the case, for students to be successful, they must feel a sense of belonging on our campuses. Given the diversity of campus populations, there must be an emphasis on inclusion, so all students are able to find their place. Campus climate and culture matter more than ever.

This chapter broadly examines the future direction of higher education and student affairs and specifically provides insight into how anticipated changes and emerging issues will impact the direction of those who work on college campuses. This examination will explore how future higher education leaders can best prepare themselves now for the work they will do in shaping campus environments for years to come. It will further explore anticipated challenges and provide readers with some recommendations for use in practice.

Anticipating Change

As we consider the future direction of higher education and the role student affairs professionals play in shaping the environment for student success, we need to anticipate the future and begin to prepare ourselves for what students will need and not assume what we have done in the past will continue to be effective. For example, the use of technology and the world of reality shows have resulted in students entering our institutions with a set of social norms and communication patterns far different from what we have seen in prior years. Therefore, we must think about how such trends impact our work, and we must stay current with the changing needs of the students we serve now and in the future. Practitioners need to be engaged professionally by reading, researching, and engaging with students to understand their changing needs. Although students' needs and demands will constantly evolve, we will always need to meet students where they are and provide appropriate developmental opportunities that challenge their growth and learning, while also providing needed support to ensure their persistence. The systemic structures and models of program delivery we use today to meet student needs must also evolve. If we fail to adapt our approaches to addressing students' needs in the future, we will be ineffective in creating environments that help students succeed.

Whereas there are many trends and issues that have the potential to shape higher education and student environments, we have chosen to focus on six areas that we believe, from our experience as senior leaders in student affairs, most impact our current working environment and how we predict it will evolve in the future. Although entire publications have been written about each of these issues alone, we explore them briefly to provide a framework for thinking about the future. It is important for current and future professionals to understand these issues and think about how they might alter the experience of our students and future students. The six areas include (a) changing demographics, (b) funding of higher education, (c) the completion agenda, (d) accountability and assessment, (e) student activism, and (f) student welfare.

Changing Demographics

One of the issues of concern impacting the future of higher education has to do with who attends college. This was explored earlier in the book. The rapid growth in numbers of Hispanics, Asians, and multiracial Americans, along with the more moderate growth of African Americans/blacks and other non-white groups—the "browning" of America—is a real phenomenon that will have a direct impact on the campus environment in future years (Jones, 2017). Understanding the complexity that exists with serving the unique needs of racially diverse students must be a priority. The increase of students of color and other minoritized populations will require institutions to allocate additional resources directed toward serving their needs. More importantly, educating faculty, staff, and administrators will directly affect the environment and the experiences of these students. University personnel need to understand their students and the best way to create an environment that will foster their inclusion and growth.

Therefore, in student affairs, given our close work with students, it is our responsibility to stay current with students' needs and lead the way in educating our campus colleagues. It is also very important that faculty, staff, and administrators understand the importance of being culturally competent and intentionally inclusive, both inside and outside the classroom. Identifying teaching methods and pedagogies that encourage inclusivity will be crucial to engaging students in the future, particularly in classrooms. However, as noted previously, these practices and many others can also be utilized in the co-curricular environment. Previous chapters provided insight on this topic and examined why creating culturally inclusive learning environments is so important to student belonging and student success. Other demographic changes, such as the increase in adult learners, veterans, and online students, also changes the environment.

Adult Learners

The characteristics and needs of adult learners have also been explored in this book. Student affairs educators should consider the role they will play in supporting this population as it continues to grow on most campuses. Adult learners—usually considered students 25 years or older—represent a diverse population with varied needs, characteristics, and life experiences. Most of the student development theories that serve as a foundation for our work are rooted in the experience of more traditional students, such as those who are younger in age, dependent upon their parents, and engaged in the more traditional co-curricular opportunities on campus. Because of this, our approach to serving this population is at risk of falling short. We must consider the unique challenges and needs of adult students to ensure we design appropriate support systems with their distinct needs in mind. The Policy Institute of the National Association of Student Personnel Administrators (NASPA) published a brief as part of a series on critical issues in higher education. The brief, authored by Wesley (2018), outlined five things student affairs professionals should do to support adult learners.

1. "Identify promising opportunities and gaps in service" (p. 5). Student affairs educators should engage in self-assessment to determine how

policies, practices, and procedures impact the success of adult learn-ers. There are formal inventories that are designed to measure the campus climate for adult students. This type of data can then inform practice and allow professionals to design new and innovative ap-proaches to support the success of adult learners.

2. "Raise institutional awareness of the needs of adult learners" (p. 6). Student affairs educators should assume responsibility for familiariz-ing their institution with the profile and needs of adult learners so that institutional planners and leaders consider their needs as they reimag-ine policies, programs, and services for the future. Adult learners should be given opportunities to be visible on the campus, so that their stories remind the university of the diversity in life experiences and needs of its student population.

3. "Develop and maintain internal and external partnerships" (p. 8). Student affairs educators should seek ways to provide more integrat-ed services for future students and understand that our traditional siloed approach to providing one type of service in each different office may not be the most effective way to meet student needs. In-ternal partnerships with academic affairs, for example, could be devel-oped to assist adult learners in documenting their in-class and out-of-class learning in an integrated way. External partnerships with com-munity agencies could help leverage important resources for adult stu-dents with families, for example.

4. "Minimize perceived and real work-school-family conflicts" (p. 9). Student affairs educators should work to remove institutional barriers that create conflicts for students who have multiple responsibilities outside of their education. Adult learners with work or family respon-sibilities are at risk of not persisting if their school demands do not allow them to meet their other obligations. The author of the brief (Wesley, 2018) encouraged universities to ensure that difficult parts of attending college are associated with the learning process itself, and not with the other things students must do to remain enrolled.

5. Create accessible and relevant engagement pathways" (p. 11). Student affairs educators should provide adult learners with the opportunity to engage in relevant out-of-class experiences in a way that is convenient, and not necessarily always in person. Adult learners want to under-stand the value of their engagement, so they know whether it is worth an investment of their time. Adult learners should also be advised of family-friendly programs and any opportunities for engagement that do not require being on campus. Student affairs educators should be designing more online engagement opportunities for future students, especially the adult learners (Wesley, 2018).

Veterans

In 2009, approximately 500,000 student veterans received educational benefits. By the year 2013, over 1 million veterans received benefits. Although the total number of veterans in higher education is relatively small, this number is expected to grow as more service members return home from serving in conflicts. Most veterans attending colleges and universities are nontraditional students, meaning they are not entering straight from high school and are not dependent on their parents. Veterans are typically independent students, as defined by the FASFA (Free Application for Federal Student Aid), and they often have families. Only about 15 percent are between the ages of 18 and 23; the majority are between the ages of 24 and 40, and 62 percent of veterans and military service members are first generation students (The National Center for PTSD and Veterans Integration to Academic Leadership, 2014). This increase in veteran students should cause professionals to examine existing programs and services, consider how they are creating welcoming spaces, and more importantly, how they are educating campus constituents about this population. According to O'Herrin (2011), because of the diverse makeup of veteran students, there can be no "one size fits all" approach to serving their needs; however, this author provided several suggested practices that many institutions are employing that are assisting with their success:

1. Having a single point of contact for information and advice results in a consistent message and a familiar point of reference for student needs.
2. Creating an interdepartmental work group allows multiple departments to collaborate to address their needs comprehensively.
3. Creating partnerships with community and governmental organizations establishes a community-based approach maximizing resources to benefit veteran students.
4. Creating specialized orientations for all incoming veteran students ensures a thorough introduction to the university.
5. Establishing a veterans' resource center and veteran student groups improves the campus climate and educates faculty and staff about veteran-specific needs.
6. Creating a veteran-specific learning community provides students with a group of individuals who share common interests and experiences.
7. Streamlining disability and veteran services to accommodate any special needs these students may have (O'Herrin, 2011).

Online Students

According to the *2016–17 Integrated Postsecondary Education Data System (IPEDS) Methodology Report,* enrollment in online education continues to increase, even as overall enrollment in degree-granting postsecondary institutions is decreasing (Ginder, Kelly-Reid, & Mann, 2017). Fall enrollment trends from 2015 to 2016 indicate a 5.5 percent increase in the number of students enrolled in any distance education course. Nearly one in every three students will participate in online programming, according to this report. Unlike in the more recent past, online programming is now an expectation for many students as they consider colleges and universities.

The increase in online learning brings with it opportunities for student affairs professionals to begin exploring how to create programs and services to address the needs of students engaging in this learning environment. Crawley and Howe (2016) identified some challenges with online learning. The challenges included the lack of direct contact and interaction with instructors and students, inconsistent or poor contact and communication with instructors, and lack of student motivation. The results of the research would suggest that student affairs professionals need to engage online students in ways that connect them to our institutions. We have to think about how to deliver cyber services that help students learn and assist them in feeling a sense of belonging to the institution.

College students need resources to assist them in learning how to study, manage time effectively, and stay on course academically. These services are especially important for online learners due to the high level of self-direction and self-motivation necessary to succeed in the online learning environment (Crawley & Howe, 2016). The following questions remain unanswered:

- How will student affairs professionals identify students who need or want a more interpersonal approach to online support services?
- What approaches can these professionals take to make online student services more personal so they more closely resemble the human interaction of in-person services?
- How can these services be made readily available to online students who are learning around the clock?

Challenges and Opportunities

These demographic changes bring with them challenges and opportunities. There are opportunities to shift program delivery methods and reimagine our approach to engaging with different populations and determine how best to welcome and serve a new critical mass with different needs. However, to accommodate a different population of learners, there may need to be additional resources, trainings, and even a new approach to serving students. These changes will drive how we must view our work differently and recognize that the techniques we have used to impact student learning for today's students will be very different for future students. As we consider the changes in demographics, we have to focus on the impact these changes will have on the environment. Even as campuses are now becoming more diverse, there is still a tendency to serve the "majority" population. Whereas members of "other" populations exist on campuses and progress is being made, there is a long way to go. With this said, we would be remiss if we did not spend time considering what it means for campuses in the future. Funding from resources other than governmental agencies and tuition will have to be considered if we want to maintain the access mission that many colleges and universities desire to support.

Funding of Higher Education

In addition to the changing student demographics, we can anticipate that funding for higher education will also change the student experience and impact the campus environment. Higher education is receiving less money from both the federal and state government when compared to 10 years ago. According to Mitchell, Leachman and Masterson (2017), after the recession in 2007, states are spending on average $1,448, or 16 percent less per student now as compared to before 2007. They reported that 44 states spent less per student in 2017 than in 2008. Mitchell et al. suggested that these type of reductions in funding likely reduce quality of services, resources for students, and academic offerings for many colleges and universities. For example, Kacich (2017) reported that Eastern Illinois University eliminated 413 positions and mandated that all administrative and professional personnel take 18 furlough days. The Kansas Board of Regents cut approximately $900,000 in student scholarships across the state's public university system (Zeff, 2016). In May of 2016, the Kentucky Community and Technical College System cut 191 faculty positions and 315 staff posts, laying off 170 employees and eliminating 336 vacant positions (Blackford, 2016). These types of deep reductions mean that universities will need to do more with less or find alternative ways to fund their operations. In the absence of alternative funding, universities will have to reduce expenses, which often means cutting non-instructional services. These services often end up being those in student affairs, thus impacting the campus environment.

Decreased funding from governmental agencies also transfers more of the financial burden for obtaining postsecondary education to students. This means that college attendance will no longer be a right for individuals, but instead, a privilege reserved for those who can afford it. If only students who have the financial means to obtain an education attend college, then the demographic makeup will represent those individuals who come from middle and upper socioeconomic-status households, creating an "elitist" environment. This will essentially undo the last decade of efforts targeted toward the access mission, which aimed to reduce the barrier of cost for those wanting to pursue a college degree. Higher education leaders need to find ways to continue to increase access and affordability of college attendance.

The cost of attending college has been steadily increasing for the past two decades. The Department of Education reported that from 1993 to 2015 the average debt per undergraduate borrower went from an average of $10,000 to a projected $35,000. The report also suggested that the percentage of students borrowing money went from 40 percent to more than 70 percent (Sparshott, 2015).These are staggering statistics, considering that the greatest driver of social mobility is an advanced degree. Socioeconomic status will play a significant role in the makeup of students attending college in the future unless outside resources are identified to assist those who are less fortunate.

This critical issue of funding has the potential to impact the environment and makeup of student affairs as we know it. It is possible that divisions of student affairs will be smaller and operating with less. Now more than ever, divisions of student affairs are being subsumed into academic affairs and business affairs, and in some cases, totally dismantled. Whereas the alignment of student affairs with other divisions is critical to the overall completion of the educational mission of any college or university, it does not mean divisions of student affairs have to be subsumed or even dismantled to accomplish this outcome. As professionals, we must engage as thought leaders in critical conversations that impact the future of our campuses on many levels. Most importantly, we must show evidence of our contributions to the educational mission of higher education. College campuses encompass communities of educators, and we play a major part in such communities. Our programs and services must be designed with learning outcomes in mind. Effectively articulating and assessing the impact of our work on learning is key to maintaining financial support for the work we do.

Understanding the business side of our work is also crucial, yet too many professionals do not recognize the importance of this aspect of the profession. Oftentimes, educators shy away from budget management, proformas, cost analysis, and performance indicators. Because of a lack of knowledge, the revenue-generating areas of student affairs sometimes shift to other divisions. When this occurs, there can be a direct impact on the student experience, because many outside of student affairs do not know of the learning opportunities that exist in many of the auxiliary operations, such as residence halls or student centers. These areas might be managed solely as business function, with an emphasis on lowering costs and increasing revenues. In that situation, programmatic functions may be eliminated, and thus, the student experience and environment are impacted. As professionals knowledgeable about student development and student learning, we need to make certain all spaces are viewed as learning environments as well as revenue generators.

Completion Agenda

Another issue that will impact the future of the student affairs profession is often referred to as the *completion agenda,* which has to do with the push to get more people graduating with a college degree. This is particularly applicable to low-income and first-generation students who may lack the economic means and privilege other students have that allow them access to more opportunities and the social capital that is helpful to achieving success. The completion agenda is driven in part by reality that most new jobs in the future will require education beyond high school. It has also been well documented that having a college degree produces lifetime gains from an economic standpoint. Additionally, the soft skills employers seek often require education beyond high school. Competencies such as critical thinking, leadership, communication, and problem solving, are skills that are developed through the opportunities provided by higher education (Kruger, 2014). All these factors contribute to a need for institutions, including student affairs divisions, to focus on how they are helping the students who need the support the most, to succeed.

Much has been written about how universities can bolster their efforts to support the traditionally underserved populations on their campus. We highlighted several of these populations in this chapter. Student affairs educators must understand who the students are, on their own campus, who are most at risk of dropping out, and in turn, design strategies to frontload support that increases those students' chance of persisting to graduation. We cannot afford to design the environment for our majority population and expect that other students will adapt to that environment and thrive.

The *2018 National Freshman Motivation to Complete College Report* revealed that 97 percent of freshmen said they were "very committed to earing a college degree, no matter what gets in their way" (Ruffalo Noel Levitz, 2018, p. 2). Yet we know they face challenges to achieving their goal, and the challenges do get in the way. The report provided seven strategies universities can use to address the greatest needs and largest barriers related to student success, as follows:

1. Begin outreach before classes begin, so students start with strong academic and social engagement.
2. Identify each incoming student's noncognitive, motivational risks to completion and requests for assistance.
3. Use data to match campus services to the needs of specific populations.
4. Prioritize academic support services and student success interventions early in the first and second terms.
5. Engage students in timely conversations with advisors and student success professionals throughout the first year.
6. Initiate professional development conversations early by identifying where students are in their career planning process.
7. Develop first-and second-year programming with a focus on student engagement. (Ruffalo Noel Levitz, 2018, pp. 3-9)

Accountability and Assessment

Because of the decrease in higher education funding, together with the push for closing the achievement gap and improving graduation rates, student affairs divisions must be engaged in meaningful assessment in order to demonstrate the impact of their work. This issue will continue to impact the future of the profession. Assessment is a direct link between greater accountability and responsibility. Upcraft and Schuh (1996) referred to this notion by suggesting that nonacademic units will have to respond to funding pressures and internal and external expectations for accountability. Assessment is a way student affairs professionals can demonstrate the learning, worth, and quality of the programs and services emanating from our areas (Schuh, Upcraft, & Associates, 2001). The competency *assessment, evaluation, and research,* identified as one of the 10 professional competency areas for student affairs educators by the American College Personnel Association (ACPA) and National Association of Student Personnel Administrators (NASPA) (2015), includes essential knowledge, skills, and dispositions expected of all student affairs educators, regardless of functional area or specialization within the field. Because of the rising cost of education, decreasing funding from governmental agencies, increasing expectations for accountability and quality by accrediting bodies, and questions by parents and students about the worth of a college degree, we must be prepared to assess programs and services and share findings with invested audiences. It is important that student affairs professionals learn the value of assessment, evaluation, and research as well as understand the value of high-quality co-curricular programs, continuous improvement, and the need to validate learning outside of the classroom (Wise & Davenport, in press).

The increasing demand for accountability will impact how student affairs educators deliver programs and services in the future. Grounding our work in learning domains and providing evidence of learning will be critical to the existence of many of the departments traditionally located in student affairs divisions. Being able to connect learning in the co-curricular experience to the larger campus mission is a shift that student affairs professionals must be prepared to make. It is one thing to talk about *what* we do, and it is an entirely different matter to show *how* we contribute to learning and the educational mission of the university. Because of new accreditation requirements for learning in the co-curricular and program reviews, assessment and evaluation will become essential. Therefore, future educators must be able to identify desired learning outcomes, collect data, show evidence of impact to learning, and engage in process improvement. A failure to incorporate this into our work could negatively impact accreditation reviews and bring out additional scrutiny for divisions of student affairs.

Student Activism

Looking back in history, one understands that campus protests have always been a part of the fabric of higher education. Recent campus environments remind many of the 1960s, when there was a great deal of activity happening on campuses. Students are voicing their concerns with the political climate on their own campus by holding protests, marches, teach-ins, rallies, and sit-ins. Many of these efforts are high profile and have attracted a great deal of attention because of both traditional media and social media. These demonstrations, when we look at them in totality, seem far from isolated. There seems to be an upsurge in political activism happening on most campuses, with little indication that this activity will subside anytime soon.

Many student protests are in response to national issues but expressed through the lens of campus policies. According to Labanc, Melear, Fernandez, and Hutchens (2018), "At both public and private colleges and universities, students, faculty, and citizens beyond campus communities use higher education institutions—recognized as a marketplace of ideas—to voice opinions on countless issues through a variety of venues" (p. 8). Young Americans are *often characterized* as being politically apathetic, as indicated by voter turnout rates, but perhaps they see activism as a more effective means of creating change—particularly when the change they seek has little to do with formal politics.

Higher education administrators have long embraced the values of free speech and civil discourse. We seek to create environments where students will have opportunities to engage with others and feel comfortable talking about their values and beliefs and learn from the perspective of others. We know in doing so, students are developing skills that are essential to their development as citizens of a democratic society. Universities expose students to different perspectives through courses, speakers, art, film, and structured dialogues. Students on college campuses are exposed to thoughts that often differ from those they personally hold and those they were taught growing up. Universities embrace the idea that these opportunities foster greater learning. Students learn when they are exposed to multiple perspectives. Yet, developing civil discourse on campuses is becoming increasingly challenging. Although students—and society at large—will say they value free speech, they also often want to be shielded from anything that is offensive. Universities have the challenge of upholding their values, while creating safe, engaging environments where all students can feel valued and supported. Increasingly, this will be a primary challenge for future administrators.

Labanc et al. (2018) identified the top concerns that vice presidents for student affairs and other higher education administrators have in regard to this challenge. Public colleges and universities as well as private institutions must consider the legal commitments their institution has related to speech on campus. Additionally, public institutions are bound by the First Amendment to allow—and even support—all protected speech. Protected speech is broad, and concepts such as hate speech, speech zones, and harassment, complicate community members' understanding of why offensive speech is allowed on campus.

Finally, senior leaders are concerned about the costs incurred by having controversial speakers on campus. Due to legal obligations placed upon universities, it is now popular to *use* college campuses as the venues of choice for controversial speakers. Universities then face the financial implications of costs to maintain security for the speaker, space rental, crowd control, and other arrangements that may be made in the best interest of campus safety. Another cost, arguably the most concerning, is the impact on campus climate, campus culture, and student success. Students, especially those in underrepresented communities, are finding campuses "taken over" by external speakers and agendas. These speakers tend to have extreme agendas and use language that further marginalizes minoritized populations. They often use provocative language, which is frequently described as hate speech, to evoke negative responses. Students often ask their administration how they can allow such a speaker onto the campus. They see the presence of some speakers as compromising their safety and comfort on the campus.

In the consideration of campus environments, this last issue related to controversial speakers is the one to which higher education leaders need to be responsive, recognizing the impact on students and their sense of belonging at an institution. This becomes a delicate balance, especially for senior leaders who must balance the institution's legal obligation to protect free speech with advocating for student well-being.

Student Welfare

Student welfare is another issue that impacts how we think about our work in student affairs, both now and into the future. *Student welfare* is broadly understood as student well-being—the care we assume for the health and safety of our students. This is particularly the case in student affairs, where we often consider ourselves to be the stewards of care on the campus. We can predict that as campuses continue to become more diverse and serve a more diverse array of students, the complexity of issues to which we need to be able to respond will also grow. Today's students, for example, lead more complicated lives—many take classes online, have families, and work full time. Others, in growing numbers, have prior military experience or are transitioning back to school after a need to change careers. Universities can no longer operate under a philosophy that students will all adjust to the ways of the institution, a somewhat "sink or swim" mentality. Instead, we are called upon as professionals and educators to recognize that our students' well-being is interconnected with their academic success, and in fact institutions must customize support systems that will help our students "swim," providing them with what they need to be able to clear any obstacles they face and persist toward their goals. Higher education leaders must be able to adapt their practices and grow services that will address some common issues associated with student welfare, such as mental health, food and housing insecurity, and safety.

Mental health is one area related to student welfare that has received greater attention on campuses in recent years. Growing numbers of students come to college with previous history of mental health challenges, and more students than ever report taking psychiatric medications (The Steve Fund & JED Foundation, 2017). Research has also indicated that some students develop mental health challenges during college (Center for Collegiate Mental Health, 2016). Additional research has pointed to increased rates of depression, anxiety, self-injury, and suicide ideation (Center for Collegiate Mental Health, 2016). In fact, many mental health professionals and administrators would say we have a mental health crisis on college campuses. With no indication that this will change in the future, educators need to be aware of how quickly needs are outpacing existing infrastructures. In turn, they need to enact plans that equip institutions to serve students effectively. On many campuses, this has meant increasing staff in counseling centers, using alternative delivery of mental health support services, placing a greater emphasis on outreach and prevention, and forming new partnerships with community agencies. Whereas student mental health is an issue of concern on most campuses, research has indicated students of color are particularly impacted. Knowing our campus populations are becoming increasingly more diverse, this must be an issue future educators address. According to the Equity in Mental Health Framework (2017),

> While many college students arrive on campus feeling emotionally and aca-demically unprepared, demographic analysis has shown that first-year African American college students are more likely than their white peers to report feeling overwhelmed most or all of the time during their first term (51% vs. 40%). (The Steve Fund & JED Foundation, 2017, p. 3)

The Equity in Mental Health Framework: Recommendations for Colleges and Universities to Support the Emotional Well-Being and Mental Health of Students of Color (The Steve Fund & JED Foundation, 2017) includes recommendations designed to provide guidance to institutions in effectively developing, imple-menting, and refining on-campus programs or support for students of color. These recommendations are as follows:

1. "Identify and promote the mental health and well-being of students of color as a campus-wide priority" (p. 7). Institutions should center stu-dent well-being and mental health as part of their mission and recog-nize its impact on student success. Special attention should be given to serving the needs of a racially diverse student population.
2. "Engage students to provide guidance and feedback on matters of stu-dent mental health and emotional well-being" (p. 7). Institutions should regularly survey students, with attention to students of color, about their emotional well-being and sense of belonging on the cam-pus. This feedback should provide guidance for continuous feedback.
3. "Actively recruit, train and retain a diverse and culturally competent faculty and professional staff" (p. 8). Institutions should aspire to have a diverse faculty and staff, so students feel they have others who look like them and they can relate to on campus. Further, there should be investment made in training to ensure staff are culturally competent.
4. "Create opportunities to engage around national and international issues/events" (p. 8). The events happening, even when not directly af-fecting a campus, do affect how students are doing and feeling. There need to be opportunities for students to engage in discussion on cur-rent events. This can happen through university dialogues, classroom discussions, or other forums that foster student engagement.
5. "Create dedicated roles to support well-being and success of students of color" (p. 9). Institutions should hire top-level staff who oversee

diversity-related services, programs, and policies. Whereas it is the business of all educators to support students of color, there need to be advocates who champion these issues at the most senior level of the university.

6. "Support and promote accessible, safe communication with campus administration and an effective response system" (p. 9). Institutions should have processes by which any member of the university community can express concerns about the campus environment to key administrators. This feedback is essential to continuous improvement.

7. "Offer a range of supportive programs and services in varied formats" (p. 10). Institutions should provide a variety of culturally relevant program types that are intended to support the mental health of students of color.

Universities are also paying increasing attention to the issue of food and housing insecurity among students, and there is no reason to think this will not continue to be a need into the future. Palmer and Newland (2018) reported that in a recent survey assessing student needs,

> 36 percent of surveyed students at four-year institutions were food insecure in the 30 days preceding the survey compared to an estimated 42 percent of community college students. The Wisconsin Hope Lab found that housing insecurity affected 31 percent of four-year students and 46 percent of community college students. (p. 15)

We know hunger and homelessness negatively impact student learning and retention; students cannot learn if they are always hungry or worried about where they will live. Universities are opening food pantries or setting up programs with their meal plan provider that allow students to donate their unused meals to another student in need. Many schools have established programs to support homeless students. Campuses are also evaluating how they can better meet the emergency needs of students through emergency aid. For many low-income students, the small amount of money sometimes needed to get through a tough time can impact whether they persist and attain their degree. With a lack of savings and familial financial support, the cost of a text book or a car repair or an urgent need of a family member can derail students (Garmise, 2016). These interventions are important to the environment we provide for students. Student affairs professionals are often called upon to help students identify resources, often in communities where available resources are already in high demand.

Safety is another important aspect of student welfare and certainly shapes the campus environment and how students experience the university. For a number of years, there has been increased attention to how universities keep their campus communities safe, and in particular, how they plan for and respond to a crisis. Institutional stakeholders, including parents, community members, boards, and legislators, have an expectation that universities will protect their students. Although we can all think of examples of violent incidents on college campuses, students are more likely to be a victim of violent crime off campus as opposed to on campus (Cornell, 2008). Yet several laws, including the Clery Act and Title IX legislation, have been enacted to address safety issues on college campuses. University administrators are concerned about issues, such as alcohol and drugs, hazing, interpersonal violence, and other things that pose a threat to student safety. Universities have continued to invest resources in both the prevention and response to these issues. As campuses become increasingly diverse, student affairs educators also need to consider how students perceive their safety in the environment as related to their personal identities. Students need to have outlets to share their experiences with administrators who can impact campus climate and culture issues. This can come through surveys, town hall meetings, small group discussions, and the making available of methods for reporting concerns. Students need to be well advised of options they have for reporting incidents such as hate speech, interpersonal violence, hazing, bias, and harassment.

Student affairs educators need to be advocates for student welfare. Traditionally some on campus shied away from talking about student welfare, especially student mental health. Increasingly, universities are opening up this dialogue, and those in student affairs need to take the lead in helping others understand how an investment in student welfare is also an investment in student success.

Opportunities for Reimagining Student Affairs

Now more than ever, we can anticipate that the future for higher education leaders will be filled with challenges and opportunities to impact student success. This chapter has provided recommendations for practitioners that address some specific student populations or respond to issues we know impact the campus environment. Along with these suggestions, practitioners are encouraged to reimagine what student affairs can look like. Too often, leaders approach their work with little consideration for what could be done differently. Everyone is familiar with the "we've always done it in this way" mentality that permeates many organizations. When change does happen, it is often only in small pockets within an organization. We believe student affairs divisions have to essentially reimagine the way they do their work. For example, most divisions have been organized in relatively the same way for decades. We have functional departments that each serve a particular population or offer a specialized service or set of programs for students. On many campuses, those departments operate relatively autonomously of other areas within the division. Perhaps reimagining means taking a fresh look at all we do for students and asking questions, such as What are we trying to achieve? Are we achieving those outcomes? What outcomes are we not achieving? Are we organized to best meet our desired outcomes? Are we using our resources most efficiently? What are we doing that is not producing any desired outcomes? What services or programs are duplicated elsewhere on campus? Are we investing in the things that add the most value to the student experience? Are there partnerships we need to create?

A 2010 report issued by a task force appointed jointly by ACPA and NASPA, looked at the changing times of higher education and provided some implications for the future of student affairs work, which seem to still hold true as we anticipate how our work will continue to evolve. This report stated, "At no time in history has the incentive for real change been more powerful or the consequences for not changing more significant" (ACPA & NASPA, 2010, p. 7). The report provided several themes that capture the need to rethink student affairs work, which means (a) redefining roles and structure, (b) ensuring success for all students, (c) creating partnerships without borders, (d) making data-driven decisions, and (e) broadening the meaning of "the campus" (ACPA & NASPA, 2010). These themes or areas, many of which have been addressed in this chapter, are briefly summarized below.

Redefining Roles and Structures

Existing structures, such as university divisions and reporting lines, have little to do with students and often do not bring people together who are focused on student success efforts. "Providing leadership to meet the future effectively requires expanding the definition of student affairs work and focusing on ways that enable all who work with students to do so more effectively" (ACPA & NASPA, 2010, p. 8). This notion of eliminating institutional silos is not a new one, yet one that many campuses struggle to make happen. Student affairs leaders can take the lead on campus in engaging others around dialogue about students and how to best meet their needs on the campus.

Success for All Students

We are using retention and degree completion as our strongest indicators of educational progress, yet we face gaps in enrollment, achievement, and completion between "majority" students and those from underserved populations. We have to pay attention to student engagement and the quality of the learning environment to help all students succeed. Addressing this point, the 2010 report stated,

> Sixty years of research on college impact demonstrates that the most important factor in student success—more important than student characteristics—is student engagement, i.e., students' investment of time and effort in educationally purposeful activities. Institutions play a critical role in student engagement by creating environments, opportunities, and conditions facilitating—or exhibiting—student success. As the race, ethnicity, socioeconomic status, national origin, and age of college students change more dramatically than ever, we need a clear understanding of where our students are to create conditions for their success. (ACPA & NASPA, 2010, p. 9)

Student affairs leaders must focus their efforts on student success and be able to demonstrate they know who their students are, what they need to succeed, and that their work is having an impact on student success.

Partnerships Without Borders

In addition to removing internal barriers often caused by structure, universities must also seek external partnerships with community agencies, government entities, and private industries. An example of this is universities working with social service agencies to create services to support homeless students. We can no longer rely on internal resources alone to address the complex needs of our students. Student affairs leaders must be creative in engaging new partners who have greater expertise, resources and support to offer our students (ACPA & NASPA, 2010).

Data-Driven Decision Making for Accountability

There is increasing pressure that all aspects of higher education be able to demonstrate, through data, their effectiveness and efficiency. "The use of high-quality data to support decisions about policies, programs, and practices is increasingly expected. This climate of evidence-based accountability proves to be particularly challenging for student affairs" (ACPA & NASPA, 2010, p. 10). As has been stated, given the decrease in available funding at most institutions, student affairs leaders must be engaged in assessment that allows them to create an evidence-based culture and demonstrate the impact of their work on student success. Staff at all levels need to have access to development opportunities that teach them the skills to approach their work from this lens.

Broadening the Meaning of "The Campus"

As has already been discussed, with many campuses providing some type of distance education, traditional modes of delivery of services will not meet the needs of all students. Student affairs leaders should be prepared to reimagine how we deliver services and to understand the approaches that work in an online environment (ACPA & NASPA, 2010).

Role of Senior Leaders in Shaping Campus Environments and Professional Identity

Senior student affairs administrators will continue to play an important role in leading their divisions and ensuring institutions are best positioned to create inclusive and engaging environments for future students. They also play a key role in helping create environments that are conducive to staff developing their sense of professional identity as student affairs educators. A student affairs professional identity is shaped by one's beliefs, values, knowledge, and skills. We can think of our professional identity as that which shapes who we are as a professional and the ways in which we do our work.

As discussed in this chapter, understanding the differences between students who are currently attending colleges and those who will attend in the future will require leaders to focus on current and future trends, research, and the condition of the global society to prepare for the needs of our students. As we work to create welcoming and inclusive environments, senior leaders must continually assess their division's readiness and lead change where needed. Staff with many years of experience may have become accustomed to working with the "traditional" or more homogenous population on their campus and may not consider how their work will need to change. However, to be best prepared, it is incumbent upon the senior leadership to educate, train, and position their staff to address students' needs. Staff should understand the history and philosophy of our profession and how it has shaped the work we do with students today. Earlier chapters addressed this more completely, making the case that we must be responsive as campus population changes.

Although being nimble and reacting to change is good, it is better to prepare environments that anticipate students' needs and are ready to receive them upon their arrival. When addressing change, leaders should be visionary and expect their teams to engage in this process as well. One way to accomplish this is by evaluating the effectiveness of the programs offered from the division. Having a better understanding of the programs and services allows the service providers the opportunity to consider whether the programs are needed or if they can be delivered in new and different ways.

For example, it may be appropriate to add online services, design more family-friendly programs, alter the times current opportunities are available, or even eliminate programs all together. All of this requires informed staff who can engage in critical thinking and design the environment with intended outcomes in mind. This will require senior leadership to prioritize professional development so that staff can best be prepared to meet the changing needs of students. Senior leaders should ensure that an assessment is done to determine the competency levels of staff and the gaps where professional development is needed. The ACPA and NASPA (2015) professional competencies can serve as a good tool for this type of assessment. Even when financial resources are limited, the development of staff must be prioritized.

In addition, senior leaders need to insist that their division and the university are examining data related to climate and culture to determine other opportunities to assist students with feeling a sense of mattering on the campus. Whereas this text has examined a number of ways professionals can impact the environment, senior leaders in particular need to set expectations around staffing by ensuring that not only efforts are in place to recruit diverse staff members but also current staff have access to opportunities to develop competencies related to serving diverse populations. Leaders help shape student affairs educators' professional identity when they ensure they have access to opportunities that help them become more competent in key areas.

Senior leaders must also advocate for institutional practices that align with the needs of our future students. Student affairs senior leaders should be the individuals at the executive leadership level with the most direct knowledge about students and their university experiences. It should be the role of the senior leaders to share information about students and their needs and offer perspectives on how various decisions impact students' experiences and the campus climate and culture. This role of advocacy is critical to ensuring all students' needs are considered in the conversations that impact resource allocation, policy development, and future investments. To be effective, senior leaders should routinely use data to validate and support what they share about students, their needs, their experiences, and to help colleagues understand the connections between the environments they help shape and student success. This will require that senior student affairs leaders obtain relevant competencies to advance their learning and those whom they serve.

Conclusion

If there is one thing we can be certain about, the future of higher education and the work of student affairs is changing. Professionals need to anticipate what is on the horizon and begin to prepare for what students will need. Student success is impacted largely by the environment students experience at college. Rather than expecting that all students adapt to the environments we have traditionally offered on campuses, we have a responsibility, as scholars and practitioners, to design environments that are engaging and inclusive, and allow all students to succeed. Every student who comes through our doors deserves that opportunity.

Reflection Questions

1. What are ways to gauge students' perceptions about campus environments?
2. How can universities be most responsive to increasingly diverse populations?
3. How can you prepare to be able to best serve future student populations?
4. What will student affairs divisions need to do to be responsive to increasingly diverse student populations?
5. What opportunities might exist to partner with outside agencies or seek external funding to help create more inclusive and responsive environments for students?
6. How might current staffing models evolve over time to better serve the students of the future?
7. How can universities best foster the inclusion and success of nontraditional students?
8. What institutional partnerships should student affairs divisions consider to best impact student success?
9. What are ways senior leaders can use their position to advocate for a more inclusive campus environment?

References

American College Personnel Association (ACPA)–College Student Educators Internationals & National Association of Student Personnel Administrators (NASPA)–Student Affairs Administrators in Higher Education. (2015). *Professional competency areas for student affairs educators.* Retrieved from https://www.naspa.org/images/uploads/main/ACPA_NASPA_Professional_Competencies_FINAL.pdf

ACPA College Student Educators Internationals & NASPA Student Affairs Administrators in Higher Education. (2010). *Envisioning the future of student affairs: Final report of the task force on the future of student affairs.* Retrieved from https://www.naspa.org/images/uploads/main/Task_Force_Student_Affairs_2010_Report.pdf

Blackford, L. (2016, May 18). KCTCS cuts 500 faculty, staff positions. *Lexington Herald-Leader.* Retrieved from http://www.kentucky.com/news/local/education/article78360412.html

Center for Collegiate Mental Health. (2016, January). *2015 annual report* (Publication No. STA 15-108). University Park, PA: Penn State University.

Cornell, D. (2008).Threat assessment in college settings. *Change: The Magazine of Higher Learning, 42*(1, winter), 8–15. doi:10.1080/00091380903448997

Crawley, A., & Howe, A. (2016). Supporting online students. In G. McClellan, J. Stringer, & Associates (Eds.), *The handbook of student affairs administration* (4th ed., pp. 343–364). San Francisco: Jossey-Bass.

Garmise, S. (2016). Implementing an emergency aid plan. *Leadership Exchange, 14*(2, summer), 15–16.

Ginder, S. A., Kelly-Reid, J. E., & Mann, F. B. (2017). *2016–17 Integrated postsecondary education data system (IPEDS) methodology report* (NCES 2017-078). U.S. Department of Education. National Center for Education Statistics. Washington, DC. Retrieved from http://nces.ed.gov/pubsearch

Jones, F. (2017, May 23). The millennial movement: The browning of America. Retrieved from http://www.theoklahomaeagle.net/home/2017/05/23/the-millennial-movement-the-browning-of-america/

Kacich, T. (2017, March 8). Higher-ed leaders: More state cuts would be devastating. *News-Gazette.* Retrieved from http://www.news-gazette.com/news/local/2017-03-08/higher-ed-leaders-more-state-cuts-would-be-devastating.html

Kruger, K. (2014). A critical imperative. *Leadership Exchange, 11*(4), 4.

Labanc, B. H., Melear, K. B., Fernandez, F., & Hutchens, N. H. (2018). Freedom of speech at what cost? VPSAs grapple with impact on student success and campus climate. *Leadership Exchange, 16*(1), 8–13.

Mitchell, M., Leachman, M., & Masterson, K. (2017, August). *A lost decade of higher education funding: State cuts have driven up tuition and reduced quality.* Washington, DC: Center on Budget and Policy Priorities.

National Center for PTSD and Veterans Integration to Academic Leadership. (2014). *Who are today's student veterans?* Retrieved from https://www.mentalhealth.va.gov/studentveteran/aboutus.asp

O'Herrin, E. (2011). Enhancing veteran success in higher education. *Peer Review, 13*(1, winter).

Palmer, A., & Newland, A. (2018). Creating conditions for learning: Meeting basic student needs is precursor to academic success. *Leadership Exchange, 16*(2), 14–19.

Ruffalo Noel Levitz. (2018). *2018 National freshman motivation to complete college report.* Greenwood Village, CO: Noel-Levitz, Inc. Retrieved from https://www.ruffalonl.com/completion2018

Schuh, J. H., Upcraft, M. L., & Associates. (2001). *Assessment in student affairs: An application manual.* San Francisco: Jossey-Bass.

Sparshott, J. (2015, May 8). Congratulations, class of 2015: You're the most indebted ever (for now). *The Wall Street Journal.* Retrieved from https://blogs.wsj.com/economics/2015/05/08/congratulations-class-of-2015-youre-the-most-indebted-ever-for-now/

The Steve Fund & JED Foundation. (2017). *Equity in Mental Health Framework: Recommendations for colleges and universities to support the emotional well-being and mental health of students of color.* Retrieved from https://equityinmentalhealth .org/wp-content/uploads/2017/11/Bibliography-Equity-in-Mental-Health -Framework-ver-2.0.pdf

Upcraft, L. M., & Schuh, J. H. (1996). *Assessment in student affairs; A guide for practitioners.* San Francisco: Jossey-Bass.

Wesley, A. (2018). *Five things student affairs professionals can do to support adult learners.* (NASPA Research and Policy Institute brief). Washington, DC: NASPA–Student Affairs Administrators in Higher Education.

Wise, V. L., & Davenport, Z. R. (in press). *Student affairs assessment, evaluation, and research: A guidebook for graduate students and new professionals.*

Zeff, S. (2016, May 18). Kansas higher education takes a bigger than expected cut: Tuition could go higher. KCUR Radio. Retrieved from http://kcur.org/post /kansas-higher-education-takes-bigger-expected-cut-tuition-could-go-higher #stream/0)

Chapter 9

CASE STUDIES FOR APPLYING
THEORY TO PRACTICE

Delma Ramos

Case Studies as Teaching Tools

The use of case studies as a teaching tool and analytical method of instruction began at Harvard Law School back in the 1800s (Gue, 1977). Over time, this approach has been popularized across disciplines, including education (Campoy, 2004), management (Ambrosini, Bowman, & Collier, 2010; Romm & Mahler, 1991), nursing (Popil, 2011), physiology (Casotti, Beneski, & Knabb, 2013), and operations research (Penn, Currie, Hoad, & O'Brien, 2016). A case study offers students a vivid description of a practical problem, with the goal of identifying solutions collaboratively (Campoy, 2004). The narrative presented in case studies offers participants a vicarious experience through which they can indirectly engage and expand their learning and awareness, leading to the co-construction of new knowledge on important matters (Stake, 2000). Furthermore, case studies present an opportunity to apply theory to practice that can support students in the development of an analytical framework for thinking critically about pressing issues in student affairs.

Using case studies in teaching can support instruction in the following ways: (a) promote discussion of real-life scenarios that encourage all students in the room to contribute their perspectives, (b) allow for inquiry of diverging views, and (c) foster the collaborative development of solutions through decision making (Argyris, 1980; Dowd & Davidhizar, 1999). Additionally, case studies empower students to solve problems in a controlled environment where the decisions made will not directly impact an actual person (Campoy, 2004; Vaccaro, McCoy, Champagne, & Siegel, 2013). However promising, the practice of using case studies in teaching also presents some challenges. In early work on the topic, Argyris (1980) argued that the intended objectives in this practice are not accomplished when the instructor dominates the conversation and prevents participants from contributing and when fewer cases related to students' current job or area of interest are discussed. This chapter contains case studies designed to investigate current issues in student affairs settings that involve a variety of contexts and stakeholders.

A Note on Case Study Analysis

An important component of engaging case studies as a teaching tool is making decisions informed by careful consideration of the case and its context. To these ends, it is important to offer students guidance on how to approach the analysis of case studies. Although scholarship on decision making using case studies in student affairs is limited, Vaccaro and colleagues proposed a decision-making framework (DMF) for student affairs professionals (Vaccaro et al., 2013). The DMF consists of four sequential decision-making phases, which are supplemented with tasks and questions and considerations to aid in the analysis and decision making of case studies. The four phases of the DMF include (a) identifying the problem, (b) conducting a scan of possible solutions, (c) implementation, and (d) assessment of agreed-upon decisions/solutions. In more detail, *identification of the problem* requires an initial appraisal of the case, definition of the concerns presented, and thoughtful determination of desired outcomes. In the same vein, *scanning for possible solutions* requires consideration of precedent related to the issues at hand and examination of other solutions. This phase also calls for careful analysis of the potential impacts and implications of solutions, along with choosing one course of action. The last two phases, *implementation* and *assessment,* call for moving forward with the selected course of action and assessing its success, along with reflections on the impact and learning that emerged from the process (Vaccaro et al., 2013).

Informed by the work of Vaccaro et al. (2013), what follows are considerations for analyzing the case studies presented in this chapter. First, read the case carefully and engage in identification of all the key elements and stakeholders. Define the issue(s) at hand, the urgency of the concern(s), and the various points of view presented. At this time, also consider your role in the situation, additional information that can inform your decision about next steps, the authority you possess to address the case, and the people that need to get involved, moving forward. Furthermore, consider desired outcomes: what you want to change and the potential impact this change will have on stakeholders and the larger campus community.

Second, considering the context of the institution, contemplate potential resources available to help you work through the case, propose options to address the situation(s), and define obstacles that can impede your progress.

Choose one approach to address each concern and determine stakeholders that will benefit from implementing this approach and those that might be impacted negatively. Third, considering the approach you chose to address the different concerns presented in the case, define and prioritize specific tasks to accomplish your desired outcomes. Also keep in mind alternative courses of action, should you need to make changes to your chosen approaches. Finally, use the reflection questions included at the end of each case, in combination with the analysis considerations outlined above, to support your decision-making process.

Cases

The following 10 cases are presented below: (a) Notions of Equality at Rock Valley University, (b) Inclusion in Orientation Programs, (c) Creating a Place to Call Home on Campus, (d) Challenges to Student Success, (e) The Experiences of Students with Children, (f) Invisibility in Inclusion, (g) Rethinking Teaching Pedagogies and Practices, (h) Religion and Spirituality on Campus, (i) Policies That Promote Affirming College Environments, and (j) Controversial Speakers on Campus at Public Universities. In addition to the considerations provided above, use each case as a point from which to explore pressing issues in student affairs by engaging and applying the theory and literature presented in each chapter of this volume.

Case 1
Title: Notions of Equality at Rock Valley University
Institutional Context

Rock Valley University (RVU) is a regional predominantly White institution serving the west region of the state. Most students attending the institution come from local communities. The student population encompasses 20 percent Latino/Hispanic, 15 percent African American/black, 10 percent Asian American, 50 percent White, 0.5 percent Asian Pacific Islander, 1 percent Native American/American Indian, and 3.5 percent students from other racial/ethnic backgrounds. The institution prides itself on supporting all students equally. Recently, the Division of Student Affairs created a position for Director of Affinity Groups within the purview of the Director of Student Success Initiatives.

Key Stakeholders

Key stakeholders in this case include affinity group student leaders, the Latinx Student Association (LSA) president, the Director of Affinity Groups, and the Director of Student Success Initiatives.

Scenario

You are the Director of Affinity Groups at RVU. Your job includes overseeing all undergraduate affinity groups at your institution, providing guidance, leadership, and support. During your first meeting of the fall semester with affinity group leaders, you engage students in a discussion about what they would like to accomplish this fall. During this discussion, it is evident that some groups are eager to share their semester plans, whereas others remain quiet during the conversation. The most vocal leaders include those in the Presbyterian Student Association, the Global Health Student Group, the Muslim Student Association, and Black Students United. (You are eager to hear from the LSA, but despite your efforts to get them excited about the semester and their goals, they share little. You decide to follow up with the LSA president the next day.

You schedule a meeting with the LSA president. The LSA president quickly responds, and you meet in your office later that day. During this meeting, you prompt the LSA president to tell you more about their semester goals. As you try to engage the student in conversation, the LSA president seems hesitant to share. Then, you point out that you were surprised by how little they shared during the initial meeting and were concerned about their response and wanted to learn more about what is going on. The LSA president discloses that they did not feel comfortable sharing during the meeting because they feel unsupported by your office, despite the fact that the proportion of Latinx students on your campus continues to increase.

The student shares that they do not feel supported by your office because the only communication they receive is a request to meet twice a semester, with little to no additional outreach. These comments concern you, and you bring up areas where you believe the president of LSA could have improved contact and communication with you.

Following your meeting, you go to your supervisor, the Director of Student Success Initiatives, to discuss the feedback you received from the student. Your supervisor tells you that some students just do not want to be helped.

Guiding Questions for Faculty, Staff, Practitioners

1. As Director of Affinity Groups, what is your role in maintaining proactive outreach to all student groups?
2. How do you design meetings so that students feel supported and are willing to share their goals and concerns? Discuss what your conversation with these students would include.
3. What would you do differently during your one-on-one exchange with the LSA president?

4. How would you respond to your supervisor's comment that "some students just do not want to be helped"?
5. If you were in your supervisor's position, how would you address this situation?
6. How would you express the urgency of rethinking the role of your office in serving the evolving demographics in the student body?
7. In your role as Director of Affinity Groups, how can you support strategic efforts for student success, specifically knowing the changing demographics of your campus?

Case 2
Title: Inclusion in Orientation Programs
Institutional Context

Flagship University (FL) is a medium size institution with an enrollment of 27,000 students. In the past few years, the university has seen an increase in enrollment of students who come from first-generation (to college) and lower socioeconomic backgrounds, many of whom are students of color who come from families whose primary language spoken is not English.

Key Stakeholders

The key stakeholders in this case include the Director of Orientation Programs, Office of Parents and Families, full-time personnel and graduate assistants working in the Office of Orientation Programs, and students and families served by orientation programs.

Scenario

You are the Director of Orientation Programs at FU, where you earned your master's degree in student affairs. In your role as director of orientation, you are in charge of overseeing the direction of the office and supervising the personnel who plan and deliver orientation programming to new students and their families. Over the past few years, your institution has experienced an increase in enrollment from students who come from first-generation and lower socioeconomic backgrounds, who often are students of color. You oversee a team of five full-time staff and two graduate assistants, most of whom do not have a degree in higher education. Though everyone on your team is committed to doing an excellent job, their limited content expertise in student affairs limits their understanding of how to make orientation programming more inclusive.

During your biweekly check-in, your team shares attendance numbers from the orientation sessions that took place this past summer. In reviewing the figures, you notice that although sessions were well attended, there were low numbers of lower socioeconomic status and first-generation students and families. When you attempt to demonstrate the importance of examining attendance figures closely and in relation to the changes in enrollment your campus has seen, only one staff member seems to understand your perspective. The rest of the team members rationalize attendance trends by asserting that the people who attend orientation are those who are truly invested in the success of their children in college, and those who are not present simply do not care. One full-time staff member also mentions that they have tried marketing orientation more actively by calling all families of incoming students and inviting them to attend, but that strategy did not seem to work for the groups who did not attend.

You decide to schedule a follow-up meeting to examine the structure of orientation programming and how your team is reaching students and their families. During this meeting, you realize that orientation sessions are only offered during weekdays between 9am and 5pm. You also learn that the fee for attending orientation sessions is now $90 per student and $70 for each family member in attendance. These fees help pay for the cost of orientation. You also learn that orientation sessions and marketing materials are only offered in English. You know that some changes need to be made to make orientation programming more inclusive for students and families your office serves. You and your team need to develop a plan moving forward.

Guiding Questions for Faculty, Staff, Practitioners

1. In what ways does the current orientation programming restrict attendance?
2. Who is being included and who is being excluded from participation in orientation programing and how so?
3. In your role as director of this office, how can you help your team understand issues of inclusion and equity in orientation programs?
4. What is your response to the perspectives presented by your team that "people who attend orientation are those who are truly invested in the success of their children in college and those who are not present simply do not care?"
5. How do you communicate to your team that change is necessary to develop more inclusive programming?
6. What would a more inclusive orientation program look like?

Case 3
Title: Creating a Place to Call Home on Campus
Institutional Context

Lake Community College (LCC) is a small two-year institution located in the Midwest. Its enrollment is 3,000 students. The college is known as the institution of choice for the local community; however, it struggles to attract and retain racially minoritized students. This challenge prompted leaders to establish the Diversity Office three years ago.

Key Stakeholders

Key stakeholders in this case include the Program Coordinator of the Diversity Office, students served by the Diversity Office, and the Director of Enrollment Management.

Scenario

You are a program coordinator at LCC and are responsible for overseeing the Diversity Office, which was established only three years ago. The mission of the Diversity Office is to promote learning, celebrate cultures, and support student success. These goals are to be accomplished with limited financial, structural, and human resources. You are the one person supporting diverse students and diversity efforts at your institution, and you report to the Director of Enrollment Management. The Diversity Office serves 60 students who have made your office their home on campus. Many of these students embody other identities, including single mothers, LGBTQ+ students, and students with varying levels of ability.

A large component of your job is to advocate for students, bringing to light the structural barriers within the college that hinder their success and sense of belonging. Being aware of the limited support for historically underserved students at your college, you take it upon yourself to make your office a place students can call home. When you first started in your role 3 years ago, not many resources were provided to establish your office.

During the first year in your role, you engaged in fundraising and secured donations to set up the office. You were also able to secure two work-study students who help with outreach and programing. Despite the success of the Diversity Office, the support from the institution has not increased.

Furthermore, the college as a whole is currently at risk of losing accreditation. There was a community town hall meeting held last week, attended by staff and members of the accrediting board, where your supervisor, the Director of Enrollment Management, highlighted the excellent work of the Diversity Office and took credit for its success. Your supervisor highlighted the efforts of the Diversity Office in attracting and retaining diverse students at the college. You felt disappointed to hear your supervisor take credit for your and your students' efforts, knowing that there has been a lack of institutional commitment to diversity initiatives.

Guiding Questions for Faculty, Staff, Practitioners

1. Reflect on what has taken place in this situation.
2. How can student affairs practitioners who are working in highly politicized campus environments advocate for student support?
3. How can institutions of higher education mobilize their commitment to diversity into action?
4. What factors contribute to the invisibility of diversity on campus, and what is their impact on student development and sense of belonging?
5. In this case, the responsibility for marginalized student access and success was placed on one office, one person, and on the students themselves. What does this dynamic say about institutional commitment to increasing access and success of these students?
6. What can institutions with limited resources do to foster a culture of inclusion on campus?
7. Considering the organizational hierarchy of student affairs and campus administration, how can staff at the lower levels of the structure vocally and actively advocate for students without jeopardizing their role and the existence of entities, such as the Diversity Office at LCC?

Case 4
Title: Challenges to Student Success
Institutional Context

Mountain College (MC) is one of the larger institutions in the state, with over 25,000 students. The institution is well known for supporting first-generation students through programs, including TRiO and several cultural centers that support students of color.

Key Stakeholders

The key stakeholders in this case include Luna, a student in her second year at your institution; her TRiO counselor; and the CASA coordinator.

Scenario

Luna is a first-generation student of color who comes from a family who struggles financially. Luna enrolled at MC last year as a freshman. Prior to her arrival on campus, Luna's sister, who graduated from MC the year before, brought her to campus to show her places where she would be safe and connect her with people whom she could trust. Luna's summer visit to campus culminated with her deciding to apply to become a TRiO student and be actively engaged with CASA, the Latinx office on campus. Later in the summer, she received acceptance into the TRiO program. She also started receiving monthly newsletters from CASA and was in close communication with you, her TRiO counselor, and Sonia, the CASA coordinator.

Luna's first-year in college was challenging. It was difficult financially, because as a first-year student, she was required to live in the residence halls, which cost more than tuition at MC. She was far from home, and it was difficult for her or her family to travel to see one another. Luna also struggled to find her way on such a large campus, especially realizing that her older sister was right in her perspective that there were only a few offices on campus committed to supporting students from diverse backgrounds. Despite all of the challenges, Luna passed all her first-year courses and began to feel more comfortable navigating the MC campus. She moved out of the residence halls at the end of the year and spent the summer with family.

Luna returned to MC this past August, excited to begin her second year in college. Although Luna had overcome attrition, which many students experience between their first and second years of college, challenges remained. Luna is currently living in an apartment off campus, which she is renting with her friend. Though Luna is no longer living on campus and paying high fees for residence halls and dining, she is still responsible for her living expenses off campus. Her financial aid is just enough to cover tuition and fees and nothing else.

Luna came to see you, her TRiO counselor, today. She is desperate and overwhelmed because she has not been able to find employment, and her rent and utilities are due in two weeks. Luna has been looking for a job since the summer. She was interviewed by three places on campus but received no offers. She also applied to fast food restaurants and retail stores but had no success. Luna's sister was able to help her purchase textbooks and has been sending her money for food, but she is not able to support Luna further financially. Luna has even tried volunteering at some of the offices on campus, hoping that some opportunities will open, but it is the end of September and Luna has yet to secure something. Your job as TRiO counselor is to support students' personal development and retention to degree completion. However, beyond the services offered by TRiO, which include one-on-one mentoring and a variety of workshops, the program has very limited funds to support other student needs. You are concerned that Luna's current situation will create even more challenges for her that represent real threats to her ability to stay in college.

Guiding Questions for Faculty, Staff, Practitioners

1. As the TRiO counselor, how do you respond to Luna's sharing her struggles with you?
2. What additional difficulties is Luna likely to experience as a result of her financial struggles?
3. How can you advocate for Luna in this situation?
4. What does Luna's story tell us about barriers to student success?
5. How can institutions, faculty, and staff become more attuned to factors that threaten student success?
6. How can TRiO programs strengthen assistance for needs that require support beyond traditional TRiO services?
7. What structures can higher education institutions create to support students with similar struggles as Luna's?
8. How do you collaborate with leadership, faculty, and other staff to support students like Luna?

Case 5
Title: The Experiences of Students With Children
Institutional Context

Local University (LU) is the preferred university in your city for transfer students. With affordable programs and strong access initiatives in place, the institution attracts large numbers of diverse students, including students with children. However, the institution falls short when it comes to student retention and completion.

Key Stakeholders

The key stakeholders in this case include the Dean of the School of Psychology, Julie (student), Department Chair, Dr. Smith, and the larger population of students with children.

Scenario

You are the Dean of the School of Psychology at LU. As the Dean of the school, you care about student needs and are intentional about staying in touch with the students. You hold office hours each week and encourage students to visit you. This week you received three student visits, but one of them was especially memorable. You cannot stop thinking about what Julie shared with you this morning, and you ponder how to address the situation.

Julie is a single mother who transferred to LU from the local community college. As the mother of two young boys, Julie works hard to manage school, work, and other family responsibilities. During her meeting with you, Julie shared that she recently met with her academic advisor, Dr. Smith, to select courses for the spring semester. During this meeting, Julie told Dr. Smith about her struggles as a single mother and about her frustration with the school not offering courses that work for students with children or students who work full time. Upon sharing her concerns with her academic advisor, Julie received a rather unexpected response. Dr. Smith told Julie that she should have known better before becoming a mother and that it would be hard for her to go to college. Dr. Smith also told Julie that it might be better for her to consider taking a break from college, since it seems like this is not a good time for her to be in school. Although Julie's struggles to remain in school are many, she is excelling academically. Julie left her meeting with Dr. Smith feeling defeated, unsupported, and questioning whether Dr. Smith was right and maybe she should stop pursuing her bachelor's degree.

As the leader of the School of Psychology, you feel the need to discuss Julie's interaction with Dr. Smith with her department chair. As you share the experience Julie had with Dr. Smith and ask the department chair for their thoughts, the department chair responds that what Dr. Smith told Julie is a common sentiment shared by academics in the field and that Dr. Smith was just trying to help the student. The department chair advises you to let the incident go because there are far more pressing issues at the school than calling out faculty for what they believe in.

That was not the response you were expecting from the department chair. You have always believed that academia is not welcoming to people who do not fit the traditional student mold (single, 18–24 years old, childless, etc.), but as the Dean of this school, you believe what Dr. Smith told Julie is problematic and threatens the retention and persistence of students with similar backgrounds. You also start to look into services and support for student parents, but you are unable to find any.

Guiding Questions for Faculty, Staff, Practitioners

1. What are the issues at stake in this case and who is impacted by them?
2. You are the Dean of the school, but the department chair does not seem to understand the urgency of this concern. How do you challenge the chair's acceptance of the status quo?
3. How do you address Dr. Smith's interaction with Julie?
4. How do you help Julie process this interaction and give her hope that she can be successful?
5. How can you help senior leadership understand the need to provide more services for students with children?

6. What can you do to change the narrative and challenge traditional perceptions of who can be in college and what attributes are necessary for success?

Case 6
Title: Invisibility in Inclusion
Institutional Context

Regional University (RU) is a four-year private institution committed to the enrichment of its community. In recent years, the region has seen increases in residents who are immigrants and refugees. Nonetheless, these population changes are not reflected in the composition of the student body at RU.

Key Stakeholders

Key stakeholders in this case include the Director of Student Access, a team of program coordinators, and the students participating in the college academy.

Scenario

Your job as Director of Student Access includes the development of initiatives to increase enrollment of diverse students in your school. Currently, your institution's student population is primarily white, which has lower enrollment than other student groups, including students from marginalized communities. Although the area where your institution is located has seen an increase in the population of refugees and immigrant families, your institution has not seen growth in enrollment of these groups.

You consult with your team about how you can provide better outreach to these communities, and staff propose you develop a week-long college academy that would invite high school students in their junior and senior year to spend an entire week at your institution. The goals of this program are (a) for participants to become immersed in the different aspects of being a first-year college student, including attending classes, staying in the residence halls, attending affinity group meetings, and engaging in a variety of student life events; (b) for participants to become familiar with the process of applying to and enrolling in college; and (c) for the program to have the effect of demystifying the idea of attending college, by showing students that college is within their reach. To be eligible to participate in this program, students must be in their junior or senior year of high school, be from immigrant or refugee families, and have at least a 3.5 cumulative high school GPA.

Upon deciding on the eligibility and goals of your week-long college academy, you task a smaller group of program coordinators within your department with the development of the curriculum for the program. Although none of the staff in your department is affiliated with the populations your college academy will include, you choose people who you think have the best intentions to support underrepresented students. The small group tasked with curriculum development met for one month before they shared their plan with you.

Your staff propose that student participants in the academy attend college classes and stay in the residence halls. They also suggest the offering of the following workshops: (a) financing college (b) securing part-time employment, (c) getting involved on campus, (d) developing healthy roommate relationships, (e) learning how to integrate fully into the college experience, and (f) learning study skills and achieving academic success. Upon reviewing the sessions your team proposed, you notice that although useful, their plan is not particularly designed to cater to the unique populations you are interested in supporting.

Guiding Questions for Faculty, Staff, Practitioners

1. What are your initial thoughts on the program goals, eligibility and curriculum?
2. As noted, your staff has no experience working with your populations of interest. What is the impact of this on program development and structure?
3. What are the implications of including a 3.5 cumulative high school GPA as part of the eligibility requirements?
4. What is your assessment of the sessions the team proposed? Do these seem inclusive of the populations you want to support?
5. What additional sessions can be offered to address the unique needs of the populations you want to reach?
6. It is evident from the proposed academy components that families have not been included in the program. What implications can this have in the success of the college academy?
7. How can the academy be developed to be more inclusive of families?
8. There is a session in the curriculum that frames college transition as full integration into the college environment. What is problematic about this session? How might this session perpetuate normative notions of the college experience?
9. What experts on campus do you recommend to get involved in the development of the college academy?

Case 7
Title: Rethinking Teaching Pedagogies and Practices
Institutional Context

Northern State University (NSU) is a four-year teaching-focused institution. This year, the university launched a faculty recruitment initiative to attract and recruit faculty of color to serve its diverse student body. Student demographics indicate that students of color, enrolled across all degree programs, account for 30 percent; however, only 2 percent of its faculty are persons of color.

Key Stakeholders

The key stakeholders in this case include diverse graduate students in a higher education course and an assistant professor of higher education, who is also a person of color.

Scenario

You are an assistant professor in the field of higher education, and this is your first semester teaching courses at your institution. Your training, which was primarily in the traditional and positivist traditions, has a large influence on your pedagogical approach to teaching and the ways you engage with students. Your biweekly lessons usually include a short review of content covered in the previous class, a quiz on the assigned reading, and a PowerPoint lecture. At the end of each lesson, you allow five minutes for students to ask questions.

After Week four, you started to notice a decrease in student attendance to your class and a drop in student performance on the quizzes. You also notice students in class seemed disengaged (often on their computers and phones) and uninterested in the class content. By Week six, you decide to conduct a class evaluation to request student input about how the class is going.

The course evaluation survey was anonymous, but some students opted to disclose their identities as part of their responses. There are two key pieces of feedback that stood out to you. The first comment came from a student of color who feels their experience is not represented within class readings and content. This student also feels isolated in class because they are one of only two students of color in your class. The student added that they were excited to finally have a professor of color but that you seem too out of reach for them. The other comment came from a student with a learning style that does not align with your teaching practices and whose academic performance in your class is poor. Other students provided feedback that your lectures are long and difficult to understand. Students do like the quizzes and wonder if you can develop other ways to measure their growth and learning in the class. Another student expressed concern that not being able to ask questions until the end of class makes it difficult to follow along during lectures.

You consider how you can alter your approach to be responsive to the students' feedback. You have always approached teaching the same way your professors did. Their pedagogical perspectives and teaching practices worked well for you and allowed you to learn and succeed in courses, so it is difficult for you to understand why your students are not thriving with the same methods. You are also uncomfortable with the idea that some students find you unapproachable.

Guiding Questions for Faculty, Staff, Practitioners

1. Who in the classroom is included and who is excluded, with the use of these traditional pedagogical approaches and teaching practices?
2. How can this professor make class content more relevant and reflective of the experiences of the students in their classroom?
3. How can the professor incorporate more student interaction in the class, aside from the five minutes students have to ask questions every class?
4. What types of activities or structures can be used to cater to diverse learning styles?
5. Propose a new structure for this faculty member's biweekly classes.

Case 8
Title: Religion and Spirituality on Campus
Institutional Context

Minority Serving University (MSU) is a medium-sized, minority serving institution on the West Coast. The university boasts a multitude of programs and services for students from diverse backgrounds. Although MSU is not a religiously affiliated institution, a large number of students participate in religiously affiliated organizations.

Key Stakeholders

Key stakeholders in this case are the Director of the Intercultural Center at MSU and Rose, a sophomore currently enrolled at MSU.

Scenario

You are the Director of the Intercultural Center at MSU. Though your main responsibilities include overseeing the daily operations of the center and supervising program coordinators who provide support to various student populations, your constant contact with students who come into the center has allowed you to develop strong connections with many of them. This morning while you were conversing with a group of students at the center, you were approached by Rose. Rose identifies as Pacific Islander and is currently a sophomore at MSU. You met Rose when she first started her education at MSU, and among other things, you learned that she was raised Catholic.

Today, Rose came to you with two concerns. First, she is overwhelmed by her peers who expect her to continue to be a practicing Catholic. Although she was raised Catholic, since Rose graduated high school and started college, she became very critical of the teachings of the Catholic church and has decided that she no longer wishes to be Catholic. Her other concern is that she has embarked on a self-exploration journey of her spirituality but has not found any support on campus for students engaging in this quest. It appears that your campus is dominated by three larger religiously affiliated student groups: Catholic, Protestant, and Muslim, and no obvious support is provided for students who do not wish to engage in organized religion.

When you engage her in conversation, Rose explains that she is frustrated with her Catholic peers, because she does not believe people should be tied to a religious group. Furthermore, Rose thinks much of what she was taught as a Catholic is in direct contradiction with what she is learning at school. Being a biology major, Rose often finds specific aspects of Catholic teachings that do not make sense, and in an effort to counter her peer's pressure to engage actively in Catholicism, she spends much time explaining discrepancies between Catholicism and science. Nonetheless, her arguments go largely ignored. At the time of your conversation with Rose, you were not sure how to respond, other than encouraging her to continue to remain firm in her perspectives. Rose left your office, but you are now thinking of potential resources that can support her and students in similar situations at MSU.

Guiding Questions for Faculty, Staff, Practitioners

1. What are your reactions to the case?
2. The Director of the Intercultural Center advised Rose to stay firm in her perceptions in the face of peer pressure. What do you think about this advice?

3. How can leaders, such as the Director of the Intercultural Center, become attuned to student populations and concerns that are invisible on their campuses?
4. How can you identify resources for students who do not want to be affiliated with a religious group?
5. What role can faculty play in supporting students' spiritual development?
6. How can the classroom become a space to nurture this aspect of student development?

Case 9
Title: Policies That Promote Affirming College Environments
Institutional Context

Maroon Bells College (MBC) is a small liberal arts college in the Midwest. It is one of the oldest liberal arts colleges in the nation and prides itself on its progressive efforts that promote more inclusive and affirming college environments. One of these efforts is the establishment of a preferred-name policy for students. This policy allows students to select a preferred name to be used in most college business.

Key Stakeholders

Key stakeholders in this case include Director of the LGBTQ+ Advocacy Center; David, a student member of the LGBTQ+ student organization; LGBTQ+ student leaders; and a financial aid counselor.

Scenario

You currently serve as the Director of the LGBTQ+ Advocacy Center. Your responsibilities include overseeing programmatic efforts for the LGBTQ+ community and advising the LGBTQ+ student organization. You also advocate for the needs of LGBTQ+ students within the broader campus community.

At your last LGBTQ+ student organization meeting, one of the group leaders brought to your attention a concern that was raised by one of their members. The concern was brought forward by David, a student whose legal first name is Jennifer but prefers to be addressed as David, which is the name he believes aligns with his gender identity. David experienced an incident at the Office of Financial Aid, where a financial aid counselor refused to address David by his preferred name and instead referred to him as Jennifer. David explained to the financial aid counselor that he preferred to be called David, despite the fact that Jennifer is his given legal first name.

David also told the counselor that MBC has a preferred name policy in place, which states that students may choose a preferred name other than their legal first name to be used during most college business, except on legal documents, such as transcripts, diplomas, and financial aid documentation.

The financial aid counselor seemed surprised that such a policy existed at MBC and continued to refer to David as Jennifer. She also told David that calling him David was simply too confusing, because his name on his financial aid records was Jennifer, not David. David left the financial aid office feeling defeated and humiliated. It was his understanding that staff and faculty at MBC must abide by the preferred name policy once a student selects a preferred name.

Upon hearing of this incident, you tell the LGBTQ+ student leaders that you will investigate this case, and you ask them to have David set a time to meet with you. Later that day, you review MBC's preferred name policy and discover the college does not have a process in place to address complaints related to the preferred name policy.

Guiding Questions for Faculty, Staff, Practitioners

1. What are your initial reactions to this case?
2. In your role as Director of the LGBTQ+ Advocacy Center, how would you respond to student leaders sharing this concern with you?
3. What next steps would you take in addressing this issue?
4. What would you do if you learned that a majority of MBC faculty and staff are unaware of the preferred name policy?
5. How can faculty support David in the classroom?

Case 10
Title: Controversial Speakers on Campus at Public Universities
Institutional Context

University of the East (UE) is a large public research university located in the eastern region of the country. The university is actively engaged in the pursuit of a more inclusive campus. The university pays close attention to the national landscape and how the national climate impacts students at UE.

Key Stakeholders

Key stakeholders in this scenario include the Director of the Office of Diversity and Inclusion and students, faculty, and staff in attendance at a meeting.

Scenario

You are the Director of the Office of Diversity and Inclusion (ODI) at UE. Your job is to manage an office that serves as a primary resource for diverse students on the UE campus. Your office serves various student populations, including students of color and LGBTQ+ students. The current national political climate is not too favorable for some of the groups your office serves; students at your institution feel the impact of this and are concerned about campus climate as well. In response to these concerns, you create a series of town-hall style meetings around topics that impact the communities of your students. These meetings are held at the ODI, which offers a welcoming space for students to share their experiences and voice their concerns.

Last night's meeting was to discuss the current national climate around gender. Your goal was for students and other campus stakeholders to come together to talk about the national gender climate, how the current climate impacts different groups on campus, and how students and other campus stakeholders can support each other. The meeting was attended by 30 people, including students, faculty, and staff. The meeting began with introductions, asking each person present to share their name, pronouns, and department or major. After introductions, you asked people to share why they attended the meeting. The room was quiet for the first few minutes until one of the students in attendance said, "I am here because I want to know why my campus allows speakers that promote ideologies that hurt people." The student went on to say that in the past year, UE has had two controversial speakers on campus, specifically speakers who embrace and promote conservative ideologies. Another student commented, "Yes, why does an institution like UE, which says they care for all students, allow those people on university grounds?" The comment was followed by another student who said, "I don't understand why, if the university is talking to us about campus climate, they also bring people here who fuel hostility?" The room went silent again after the last comment. You explain to the students that UE is a public university and must allow for divergent views to be present. Your comment was welcomed with more silence. This time you did not know what else to say, so you allowed for a few minutes of silence before you redirected the conversation to strategies on campus that support LGBTQ+ students. The meeting did not seem to accomplish the intended goals.

You have a meeting with your supervisor this morning and plan to discuss what took place at the meeting last night. You want to understand how to best address student concerns regarding controversial speakers. Personally, you feel conflicted because you understand where students are coming from with their concerns about the university sending mixed messaging. On one hand, the institution promotes efforts to create a more inclusive campus environment, but on the other hand, it also allows for the presence of speakers with ideologies that are counter to inclusion efforts.

Guiding Questions for Faculty, Staff, Practitioners

1. What is your reaction to this situation?
2. How would you address the student concerns about the university allowing controversial speakers on campus?
3. What are the implications of the presence of controversial speakers on campus, especially when the national climate for certain groups is hostile?
4. What role, if any, should offices like ODI play in the planning and delivery of programming that engages controversial topics and speakers?
5. How can universities develop spaces that allow for the presence of opposing ideas on-campus?

Conclusion

Case studies have been used as teaching tools to foster analytical thinking and problem-solving skills for over a century. They allow students the opportunity to work through day-to-day challenges arising within the diverse functionality areas of student affairs in a controlled environment. This chapter presented cases that offer real-life examples inspired by today's colleges and students. Through the cases presented in this chapter, readers were encouraged to critically assess different institutional contexts, leadership roles, and diverging perceptions to determine a course of action in addressing the issues presented. It is my hope that the cases in this chapter spark conversation about pressing issues in higher education and empower current and future leaders to reconsider current practices and perspectives that do not align with serving the constantly evolving demographic landscape and the sociopolitical context of today's higher education, its students, and their environments.

References

Ambrosini, V., Bowman, C., & Collier, N. (2010). Using teaching case studies for management research. *Strategic Organization, 8*(3), 206–229.

Argyris, C. (1980). Some limitations of the case method: Experiences in a management development program. *Academy of Management Review, 5*(2), 291–298.

Campoy, R. W. (2004). *Case study analysis in the classroom: Becoming a reflective teacher.* Thousand Oaks, CA: Sage.

Casotti, G., Beneski, J. T., & Knabb, M. T. (2013). Teaching physiology online: Successful use of case studies in a graduate course. *Advances in Physiology Education, 37*(1), 65–69.

Dowd, S. B., & Davidhizar, R. (1999). Using case studies to teach clinical problem-solving. *Nurse Educator, 24*(5), 42–46.

Gue, L. R. (1977). *An introduction to educational administration in Canada.* Ryerson, Toronto, Canada: McGraw-Hill.

Penn, M. L., Currie, C. S. M., Hoad, K. A., & O'Brien, F. A. (2016). The use of case studies in OR teaching. *Higher Education Pedagogies, 1*(1), 16–25.

Popil, I. (2011). Promotion of critical thinking by using case studies as teaching method. *Nurse Education Today, 31*(2), 204–207.

Romm, T., & Mahler, S. (1991). The case study challenge—a new approach to an old method. *Management Education and Development, 22*(4), 292–301.

Stake, R. (2000). Case studies. In N. K. Denzin & Y. S. Lincoln (Eds.), *Handbook of qualitative research* (2nd ed., pp. 435–454). Thousand Oaks, CA: Sage.

Vaccaro, A., McCoy, B., Champagne, D., & Siegel, M. (2013). *Decisions matter: Using a decision-making framework with contemporary student affairs case studies.* Washington, DC: NASPA.

INDEX

ABOUT THE EDITORS

Cathy Akens is the Vice Chancellor for Student Affairs at University of North Carolina at Greensboro. In this role, she provides leadership for staff who oversee a wide array of programs and services that focus on impacting student success and learning through the co-curricular experience. Dr. Akens previously served as Associate Vice President for Student Affairs and Dean of Students, Assistant Vice President, and Director of Residential Life at Florida International University. She held other positions in residential life early in her career at Bowling Green State University. Dr. Akens has been engaged in professional service, scholarship and graduate teaching throughout her career. Her areas of interest include crisis management, student success, student development, and campus environments. She earned a bachelor's degree in communication from the University of Toledo and a master's degree in college and university administration from Michigan State University. Her doctorate in higher education is from Florida International University.

Raquel Wright-Mair is Assistant Professor of Higher Education at Rowan University. She conducts research that is grounded in social justice and focuses on issues of access, equity and inclusion in higher education. Dr. Wright-Mair's research agenda seeks to transform and advocate for the creation of more equitable and inclusive campus environments for underrepresented populations, specifically racially minoritized faculty. Through her research, she explores the experiences of racially minoritized populations on college campuses and examines ways in which institutions can create more supportive environments for these populations. Dr. Wright-Mair is also an affiliate faculty member at the National Institute for Transformation and Equity (NITE), where she conducts research focused on institutional transformation. In her role, she collaborates with institutions of higher education nationally to transform educational policies and practices to cultivate more inclusive campus environments for racially minoritized populations. Dr. Wright-Mair has produced several conference presentations and publications focused on diversity and equity initiatives and is active in several national education associations.

Joseph Martin Stevenson is the former Provost at Jackson Sate and Mississippi State Universities. He has also served as a Provost for Golden Gate University, Chicago School of Professional Psychology, York College of CUNY, and as a Visiting Provost in Residence for the National Association for Equal Opportunity in Higher Education. As a Kellogg Leadership Fellow, he served in the Office of the President at Howard University, and as a Senior Fellow for the Institute of Higher Education at the University of Georgia. He is a graduate of the Institute of Educational Management at Harvard, International Business Education Institute at Yale, and he has lectured a for senior leadership programs at Stanford and University of California at Berkeley. Joseph presently teaches ethics, creative leadership and social justice for the University of Virgin Islands, Union Institute University, and serves as a Visiting Scholar of Higher Education at Miles College in Alabama. He is the author and coauthor of many books, publications and presentations. He is an advocate of liberal arts, research literacy, backward design, and "crisscrossing relationship-building" between and among student affairs, diversity affairs, and academic affairs.